HISTORIOGRAPHY
and
IMAGINATION

EIGHT ESSAYS
ON ROMAN CULTURE

EXETER STUDIES IN HISTORY
General Editors: Jonathan Barry *and* Tim Rees

Other paperbacks in this series include:

Roman Political Life, 90BC–AD69 (1985)
edited by T.P. Wiseman

The Administration of the Roman Empire, 241BC–AD193 (1988)
edited by David Braund

Roman Public Buildings (1989)
edited by I.M. Barton

Satire and Society in Ancient Rome (1989)
edited by Susan H. Braund

Flavius Josephus: Death of an Emperor (1991)
edited with an introduction and commentary
by T.P. Wiseman

Roman Domestic Buildings (1994)
edited by I.M. Barton

Exeter Studies in History No. 33

HISTORIOGRAPHY *and* IMAGINATION

EIGHT ESSAYS ON ROMAN CULTURE

T.P. WISEMAN

UNIVERSITY
of
EXETER
PRESS

First published in 1994 by
University of Exeter Press
Reed Hall, Streatham Drive
Exeter, Devon EX4 4QR
UK

© T.P. Wiseman 1994

British Library Cataloguing in Publication Data
A catalogue record of this book is available
from the British Library

ISBN 0 85989 422 3

Typeset in 10/12pt Sabon
by Colin Bakké Typesetting, Exeter
Printed and bound in Great Britain
by Short Run Press Ltd, Exeter

In memoriam
MWF   EDR

CONTENTS

Introduction ix
1. The Origins of Roman Historiography   1
2. Roman Legend and Oral Tradition 23
3. Monuments and the Roman Annalists 37
4. Lucretius, Catiline and the Survival of Prophecy 49
5. Satyrs in Rome? 68
6. The Necessary Lesson 86
7. Who Was Crassicius Pansa? 90
8. *Conspicui postes tectaque digna deo* 98

Abbreviations 117
Notes 119
Index 163

Illustrations

Figure i.	Acroterion from Forum Bovarium temple	9
Figure ii.	The Ficoroni Cista	15
Figure iii.	Roman didrachm showing Victoria	43
Figure iv.	Antefix from temple of Castor	72
Figure v.	Bronze mirror from Bolsena	75
Figure vi.	Antefix from Satricum temple	77
Figure vii.	The Palatine and its neighbourhood	103
Figure viii.	The Augustan complex on the Palatine	105

Introduction

History mattered to the Romans. Cicero called it the light of truth, and declared that to know only one's own time is to be for ever a child. For Livy, it was the guide to moral conduct; for Tacitus, the key to understanding the nature of power.[1] It is one of the great moments in Virgil's epic when Aeneas, at the end of book VIII, takes up the shield that is emblazoned with the history of Rome from Romulus to Augustus Caesar:

> These figures, on the shield divinely wrought,
> By Vulcan laboured, and by Venus brought,
> With joy and wonder filled the hero's thought.
> Unknown the names, he yet admires the grace;
> And bears aloft the fame and fortune of his race.

And yet, for more than a third of its history Rome had no history.

The first Roman historians were Q. Fabius Pictor and his lesser-known contemporary L. Cincius Alimentus, writing probably in the last decade of the third century BC. By that time Rome had been in existence for four or five hundred years, depending on how you define the starting-point. How did the Romans think about their past before they had historians to interpret it for them? How did the historians themselves deal with the long centuries of pre-history (and pre-literacy)? And how, with such source-material, can we moderns construct a credible picture of early Rome?

Fabius and Cincius wrote in Greek, at a time when Rome had just established permanent control over the Greek cities of south Italy and Sicily, and was about to embark on the conquest of Greece itself. 'In less than fifty-three years,' wrote Polybius of the period from 220 to 167 BC, 'the

HISTORIOGRAPHY AND IMAGINATION

Romans succeeded in bringing under their rule almost the whole of the inhabited world, an achievement which is without parallel in human history'[2]—and by 'the inhabited world' he meant above all the Hellenized world, the world of civilization.

The reciprocal impact of Greek civilization is a fundamental theme in the history of Rome. Horace offers the classic formulation:[3] 'captive Greece took captive her savage conqueror, and brought the arts to uncivilized Latium.' That clash of cultures has stimulated some of the best work on Roman history in recent years. Two brilliant collections of essays by Erich Gruen have explored the phenomenon in the second century BC,[4] and the studies of (for example) Mary Beard on Cicero, Francis Cairns on Tibullus and Andrew Wallace-Hadrill on honorific monuments[5] have illuminated with subtlety and finesse the significance of Greek culture for the first-century world of the late Republic and the early years of Augustus.

For the first century BC, we have excellent contemporary literary sources; for the second, we have some contemporary texts (the plays of Plautus and Terence) and information from later authors who used good authorities lost to us. But the further back we go, the harder it is to get a clear idea of what Rome was like—and the Hellenization of Roman culture provides a good example of the problem.

If we take Horace literally (and there is no reason to suppose he didn't mean it), the arts of Greece were unknown in Rome before the period of imperial conquest. Writing about 15 BC in the capital of a world empire, Horace may well have believed that. But it is very far from the truth, as the first four illustrations in this book are enough to show. The random survival of artefacts, in terracotta, bronze and silver, offers us fragmentary glimpses of the visual world of Rome in each of the four centuries of her pre-imperial history—roughly 530 BC (p. 9), 490 BC (p. 72), 320 BC (p. 15) and 260 BC (p. 43). The very fact that approximate stylistic dating is possible shows that Rome as a city-state was part of the Greek cultural world, familiar with the idioms, and no doubt the practitioners, of Greek art in its archaic, classical and Hellenistic phases. The 'sturdy old farmers' of Horace's picture of early Rome were not quite as rustic as he patronizingly imagined.[6]

Horace was discussing the origin and development of Roman drama, and it is the question of Roman drama that reveals most eloquently the limitations of our surviving evidence, even for the best-documented period of Roman history, the Ciceronian age. In his book on politics in the ancient world, Sir Moses Finley had this to say about ideology:[7]

INTRODUCTION

> With respect to political reflection and discussion, the difference between Greeks and Romans was about as wide as it is possible to be. ... [The Romans] lacked any public, generally shared communal mode either for representing political conflict or for putting their politics to the philosophical question. None of the vehicles for political reflection that we enumerated in fifth-century Athens existed in Roman society. Roman dramatists, notably, were men of low social status who rarely dared jibe at important figures and never discussed fundamental questions of political institutions or obligations.

True, there is no Roman equivalent of Sophocles' *Antigone* or Aristophanes' *Acharnians* (cited by Finley for fifth-century Athens), but that does not mean there was no politically significant drama at Rome.

For an example of city-state political ideology, in a milieu which any Athenian would have recognised, let us look at an episode of July 57 BC, related at second hand by Cicero.[8] A distinguished member of the Roman élite is in exile, for putting citizens to death without trial as consul six years earlier. The tribune whose law banished him has had the exile's house demolished, and a shrine of Liberty dedicated on the site; he is now out of office, but still enjoying much popular support. The *ludi Apollinares* are on: a substantial proportion of the urban population, in holiday mood, is crowded into the Circus Flaminius piazza, at one end of which, in front of the temple of Apollo, a large temporary theatre is packed with citizens waiting for the shows to begin. Applause or derisive whistles greet the better-known senators and equestrians as they take their places in the privileged seats.[9] One of the plays chosen for performance this year is Accius' *Brutus*, a Roman tragedy (*fabula praetexta*) about L. Iunius Brutus, who brought about the expulsion of the despotic Tarquinius Superbus and the setting up of the Republic. The play begins, to the accompaniment of shouts and cheers at what seem to be significant lines. One of the characters refers to Tarquin's predecessor, good king Servius Tullius, who had introduced the census system on which the first Roman popular assembly was based. 'Tullius, who established liberty for the people ...' Cries of *encore* from the front seats; Tullius was also the family name of their friend the exile. (Those at the back, we may guess, associated him with Tarquin.[10]) A month or so later, the centuriate assembly did in fact pass a bill for his recall.

The exile, of course, was Cicero himself. It is only because his own political survival was so directly involved that he mentioned the scene at all; normally, popular events like the dramatic festivals did not interest him. So although his surviving works provide an unparalleled picture of political life in his time, it is one which omits a major element in the life of most Roman citizens—and which caused even so sharp an intellect as Sir Moses Finley's to draw a quite fallacious conclusion about the realities of Roman politics.

If a great historian can get it so wrong about a period where our information is (relatively speaking) so good, it might seem that the rest of us have no chance at all of making sense of early Rome, about which so little is known.

All we have, to understand the past, is evidence and argument—what survives, and what we make of what survives. Literary evidence is the most revealing, contemporary evidence is the most reliable; and when the contemporary evidence is not literary, and the literary evidence is not contemporary, then argument about how to use what survives is a large part of the investigator's duty. The first five essays in this book are examples of that sort of argument—attempts to make later literary texts, with a little help from archaeology, reveal something about an earlier world.

Discussions of methodology are always tedious. Let me cite just two comments from distinguished Hellenists which seem to me to be relevant. First, the late Lionel Pearson, recalling the advice he was given when setting out as a young man to investigate the origins of Greek historiography and the lost works of Hecataeus of Miletus: 'Read Herodotus,' he was told, 'and ask yourself, what does this presuppose?' Second, Martin West in his book on the Orphic poems: 'I know that for some readers any speculation is "mere" speculation, and its denunciation an automatic victory for scholarship.'[11] What is at issue here is *imagination*.

Every statement about the past is, necessarily, a hypothesis. To be of any value it must be based on evidence and argument. If a hypothesis seems unchallengeable, and the evidence for it overwhelming, we call it a fact. Thus we can say, without misuse of language, that we *know* Caesar was assassinated on 15 March 44 BC: it is a hypothesis, but in practice it is hard to imagine what kind of evidence or argument could invalidate it. We extend our understanding of the past by forming new hypotheses and testing them by appeal to evidence and argument. Those that survive the process take their place in an epistemological spectrum that runs from remote possibility, through various degrees of probability, to 'fact'.

INTRODUCTION

Forming a hypothesis, making an inference from evidence, is in its small way a creative act. A few years ago, a reviewer commented on 'the very great element of fantasy' in a book of mine. He liked much of the book, but on certain points he could only regret that I had not 'restrained my imagination'.[12] What he meant, I think, is that some of the hypotheses I offered seemed probable to him, and others not. But all of them were dependent on imagination. 'Fantasy' is as pejorative a term as 'mere speculation'; but imagination, controlled by evidence and argument, is the first necessity if our understanding of the past is ever to be improved.

In the first two essays, 'The Origins of Roman Historiography' and 'Roman Legend and Oral Tradition', I consider the possible social contexts for story-telling, historical and otherwise—some of the ways in which the Romans may have created and transmitted a view of their city and its past. I emphasize the early and continuing influence of Greek culture, and the likelihood of drama as an important medium of communication. Historiography, once introduced, had its own ways of recreating and reinterpreting the Roman past, not least, as 'Monuments and the Roman Annalists' tries to show, by the exploitation of visual representations. The next two items, working back from Lucretius and Horace respectively, draw attention to neglected aspects of Roman culture—ecstatic prophecy and satyric drama—which may illuminate both early Rome itself and the ways in which its thought-world could still be present in the sophisticated first-century culture of our literary sources.

The last three essays are concerned with late-republican and early-imperial Rome, for which we do have contemporary literary evidence. But it is never enough; our information is still haphazard and inadequate. Cicero's works, for instance, are voluminous and on some matters wonderfully informative; but as I try to show in 'The Necessary Lesson', even about Cicero, and even about his political career and writings, widely different interpretations are possible. Similarly, we are comparatively well informed about the triumviral and early Augustan periods, but the investigation of one minor figure ('Who Was Crassicius Pansa?') can still lead us into a very unfamiliar world—and it is one in which Greek culture and the theatre are once again central to the enquiry. The last piece in the collection is an attempt to 'read the city' by imagining the visual impact of the great houses of the late-republican élite, and the Augustan complex on the Palatine that developed into the imperial palace. Since much of the argument turns on the topography of the Roman foundation legend and its exploitation in Virgil's *Aeneid*, it is again (or still) the creation and interpretation of the Roman past with which we are concerned.

All but one of these essays have been published before: 'Roman Legend and Oral Tradition', *Journal of Roman Studies* 79 (1989) 129–37; 'Monuments and the Roman Annalists', in *Past Perspectives: Studies in Greek and Roman Historical Writing* (ed. I.S. Moxon, J.D. Smart and A.J. Woodman, Cambridge 1986) 87–101; 'Lucretius, Catiline and the Survival of Prophecy', *Ostraka* 1.2 (1992) 7–18; 'Satyrs in Rome? The Background to Horace's *Ars Poetica*', *Journal of Roman Studies* 78 (1988) 1–13; 'The Necessary Lesson', *Times Literary Supplement* (15–21 June 1990) 647–8; 'Who Was Crassicius Pansa?', *Transactions of the American Philological Association* 115 (1985) 187–96; '*Conspicui postes tectaque digna deo*: the Public Image of Aristocratic and Imperial Houses in the Late Republic and Early Empire', in *L'Urbs: espace urbain et histoire* (Collection de l'École française de Rome 98, Rome 1987) 395–413. I am very grateful to the editors and publishers concerned for permission to reprint. I have done no rewriting beyond adding translations where necessary, cutting out one or two repetitions, and providing notes for items 2 and 6. Additions to the notes are included in square brackets.

'The Origins of Roman Historiography' was a public lecture given in October 1993 at Wolfson College, Oxford, in memory of Sir Ronald Syme; I am very grateful to the College for the invitation, and for its generous hospitality. Sir Ronald died full of years and well-deserved honours; but Roman history in Oxford was distinguished also by two scholars whose work was cut short by untimely death, Martin Frederiksen (1930–1980) and Elizabeth Rawson (1934–1988). This book is a modest offering to their memory.

1

The Origins of Roman Historiography

The 1993 Ronald Syme Lecture.

I

The twelfth chapter of Ronald Syme's *Tacitus* is entitled 'History at Rome'. It begins, with characteristic elegance, as follows:[1]

> History at Rome took a long time to emerge from humble and documentary origins. The old chroniclers might set down the facts in order, they had no art to exploit and transcend them. Enough for an annalist that he told no untruths, and brevity was the highest praise. Now the fundamental laws of history, as all men know and concede, are veracity and honesty. But history calls for style and composition. It is not enough to record the events, they must be interpreted and judged, with movement and eloquence in keeping. The orator will supply what is needed.
>
> Such were the opinions given utterance by Cicero in the dialogue entitled *De Oratore* ...

At that point, in a footnote, Syme adds a laconic phrase: 'Not the whole story.' It is the purpose of this lecture to endorse that reservation, and expand it. I hope to show that, despite what Cicero says, the supposed documentary origin of Roman historiography is not only not the *whole* story; it is not the story at all.

The argument in Book II of Cicero's dialogue begins with a discussion between Q. Catulus (consul 102 BC) and M. Antonius (consul 99 BC), on the scope of the orator's competence. The dramatic date is 91 BC. Antonius maintains that the orator's competence is practically universal—not only political and forensic oratory, but ethical persuasion, praise, blame, consolation and so on. Also history, 'the witness of crises, the illumination of reality, the life of memory, the mentor of life, the messenger of antiquity'; whose voice but the orator's could entrust *that* to immortality?[2] History is the mentor of life, *magistra vitae*, and takes its place naturally within the orator's ethical responsibilities as a means of moral education.

The traditional rhetorical handbooks were quite inadequate on this matter. They had a crude division of oratory into political, forensic and epideictic, of which the last category consisted essentially of panegyric and its converse, censure (*psogos*). The theme Cicero makes Antonius develop at this point is much broader and more humane; for him, the rhetorician's third category should be understood as the whole range of moral exhortation, and in that context he comes back naturally to history.[3]

'What kind of an orator, how great a speaker, do you think should write history?' asks Antonius, and Catulus replies: 'Very great indeed, if you're talking about Greek historiography, but not if you're talking about ours, which doesn't need an orator at all. The sole criterion is not to be a liar.' At which point Antonius is made to deliver the brief sketch of the origins of Roman historiography which was paraphrased by Syme. 'You mustn't be too hard on our historians,' he begins:[4]

> After all, in the beginning the Greeks too wrote just like Cato, Pictor and Piso. For historiography was simply an aggregate of the annals [*annalium confectio*]. Indeed, it was with this in mind [*cuius rei ... causa*], and also to preserve some kind of public record, that each high priest from the beginning of Roman history down to the pontificate of P. Mucius entrusted all the events of each year to literary form, transposed them on to a whiteboard, and displayed the board at his official residence in the interests of public information. The *Annales Maximi* are still so called even today, and it was this kind of writing which many historians followed: they transmitted, without any elaboration, only plain notices of dates, persons, places and events. So, just as the Greeks had their Pherecydes, Hellanicus, Acusilas, etc., we had their equivalents in Cato, Pictor and Piso, who did not possess the subjects required to produce elaborate discourse [*quibus rebus ornetur oratio*], which have been imported here only recently. Provided their reports were intelligible, they thought brevity was the sole criterion of praise.

It is important to remember that Cicero is speaking through the mouth of M. Antonius—that is, one master-orator impersonating another. And he has a case to make, that history is part of the universal range of the orator's competence. We need not expect the neutral exposition of objective data, but the marshalling of arguments to prove a point. It suits his case to present a schematic picture of Roman historiography developing in the same way as Greek historiography 350 years earlier: first the artless chroniclers, then the true historians who can deploy *eloquentia, ornatio* and *dicendi artificium*. For Greece, the turning point came with Herodotus; at Rome, Antonius is made to say, the moment is only now approaching. Coelius Antipater has tried his best, but isn't good enough: as for the rest, they merely 'set down the facts in order'.[5]

It is helpful to Cicero's argument to make out that the second-century Roman historians were as dry and succinct as the pontiffs' chronicle. But there are both internal and external reasons to resist this premiss. First, notice that even Cicero doesn't say that *all* Roman historians imitated the pontiffs' chronicle, only that many did. Who were the others? What did *they* do? Those are questions we are not encouraged to dwell on. Second, we happen to know that two, at least, of the very authors Cicero names did *not* imitate the pontifical chronicle anyway. Cato, at the beginning of book IV of the *Origines*, explicitly distanced himself from it: he would not write what could be found on the board of the *pontifex maximus*, how often corn was dear, how often the light of the sun or moon had been obscured in an eclipse.[6] As for Fabius Pictor, Dionysius tells us that he narrated the events of his own time in detail, because he was well informed about them; it was only 'the early events after the foundation' that he dealt with summarily.[7]

For the third historian named by Cicero, the question is a little more complicated. L. Calpurnius Piso Frugi was censor in 120 BC, and since he is regularly cited as *Piso censorius* it is a reasonable inference that his historical work was written soon after that date.[8] Dionysius, who does not normally cite the titles of his sources' works, three times specifies 'Piso in his *Yearly Records*'—*en tais eniausiois pragmateiais*, or *en tais eniausiois anagraphais*. Some years ago I suggested that Piso may have been the first 'annalist' in the true sense, the first historian to exploit the reconstruction of the consular and triumphal *fasti* by including an entry for every year.[9]

If so, many of his entries were probably as jejune as those of the pontifical chronicle, and it may well have been with him in mind that

Sempronius Asellio made his famous attack on *annales*, not long before the dramatic date of the *De oratore* dialogue:[10]

> Between those who have desired to leave us annals, and those who have tried to write the history of the Roman people, there was this essential difference. The books of annals merely made known what happened and in what year it happened, which is like writing a diary, which the Greeks call *ephēmeris*. For my part, I realize that it is not enough to make known what has been done, but that we should also show with what purpose and for what reason things were done... For annals cannot in any way make men more eager to defend their country, or more reluctant to do wrong. Furthermore, to write over and over again in whose consulship a war was begun and ended, and who in consequence entered the city in triumph, and in that book not to state what happened in the course of the war, what decrees the state made during that time, or what law or bill was passed, and with what motives these things were done—that is to tell stories to children, not to write history.

So it may well be that Cicero was right to attribute to the nineties BC a sense of the inadequacy of annalistic chronicles and a feeling that it was high time for something better. But that certainly does not mean that the rest of his account is acceptable, or that such chronicles were all the Romans had produced up to that time. If I am right about Piso, that question had only arisen comparatively recently.

It is nearly sixty years since Matthias Gelzer, in his article 'Der Anfang römischer Geschichtsschreibung', argued for a clear distinction between *Annalistik* on the one hand and 'senatorial historiography from Fabius Pictor to Cato' on the other.[11] It is more that twenty years since Elizabeth Rawson demonstrated that Roman historians hardly used the *Annales maximi* at all, even where you would expect it, for the recording of prodigies or for the explication of chronological questions.[12] For a long time now it has not been enough to say, as Hermann Peter said in 1914, that the origins of Roman historiography are to be sought in the annals of the *pontifex maximus*.[13] If we want to understand how Roman historiography began, we must simply abandon Cicero's misleadingly schematic argument and look instead at what survives of the first Roman historian.

The material is there. Indeed, we are extraordinarily fortunate, in that an important episode from the early part of Fabius Pictor's history—nothing less than the first half of the foundation story itself—is reproduced at length and independently by two surviving authors: Dionysius of Halicarnassus in his *Roman Antiquities*, and Plutarch in his *Life of Romulus*.[14] I suspect that some modern historians find it slightly beneath their intellectual dignity to pay serious attention to Romulus and Remus. But this episode is not just a myth. It is a political tale of betrayal and revenge: how Amulius cheated his brother of the throne of Alba, and was eventually deposed and killed by the long-lost grandsons of the rightful king.

The narrative is very tightly plotted (particularly the final scene of the overthrow of Amulius), and it is full of dramatic confrontations that result in recognition and reversal in the best Aristotelian tradition.[15] We even have some evidence for its reception. Plutarch tells us that some readers were suspicious of the story, as being *dramatikon kai plasmatōdes*, 'theatrical and similar to fiction'. Plutarch himself had no such worries: if it *was* a play, it was one composed by the Demiurge, the creator of the world. After all, the greatness of Rome was evidence enough for divine marvels at its origin.[16]

It is worth repeating that what we have here is a major episode from (presumably) the first book of the first-ever history of Rome. And if it is characterized by dramatic and quasi-fictional narrative, that seems to me to be a fact of no small importance for the origins of Roman historiography. To put it crudely, I should like to propose, in place of the 'history from documents' idea, which I believe to be untenable, an alternative model of 'history from dramatic fiction'. That is quite a fashionable polarity, now that the old positivist certainties of documentary history are under attack from theorists who would like to abolish the entire distinction between history and fiction, veridical and non-veridical discourse. However, it is not (far from it) because I am persuaded by the theorists that I urge the dramatic-fiction model for the origins of Roman historiography. It is because I believe, in the old empirical way, that that is what the evidence suggests.

But before we look at that evidence, let us first reverse our point of view entirely, and attack the problem from the other end. What was archaic Rome like? How did the Romans of the seventh, sixth, fifth, fourth, third centuries BC make sense of their city, and visualize its past?

It is obvious that any answers we try to give to those questions will be very largely conjectural. Contemporary evidence is desperately inadequate, where it exists at all, and the view of early Rome offered by our later literary sources is systematically anachronistic, and therefore unusable. But the situation is not beyond hope. The archaeological evidence for early Rome is immeasurably more substantial, and more illuminating, than it was half a century ago, and rational inferences may, with due caution, be made from it.

At this point I turn again to Sir Ronald Syme. He never dealt with early Rome, but he knew what was necessary to make sense of periods for which the surviving evidence is haphazard and enigmatic: 'conjecture cannot be avoided, otherwise the history is not worth writing.' That comes from the preface to *Tacitus*. In a public lecture 26 years later, Syme spelled out what he meant with ruthless irony:[17]

> The dearth of reliable evidence encourages constructive fiction—or, as sober historians style the process, 'rational conjecture'. When other practitioners take that path, it becomes 'idle or barren speculation'.

II

Let us begin with Andrea Carandini's recent discovery of the eighth-century BC defences on the northern slope of the Palatine,[18] which has excited predictably exaggerated claims for the historicity of the foundation story: 'fait totalement nouveau: aujourd'hui, la fondation de Rome est perceptible archéologiquement.'[19] What is actually perceptible is the fortification of Palatium—if that is what the village on the Palatine was called—at some date not far from 730 BC. That is exciting enough, for it takes us to the second generation of the Euboeans of Pithekoussai, 'the first western Greeks', merchant venturers who brought, via the Aegean, something of the culture and technology of the ancient near-eastern civilizations to the central Mediterranean, and to western Italy in particular.[20]

The Palatine village controlled the lowest crossing-place on the Tiber, arguably the most important route junction in central Italy. It is inconceivable that the Euboeans were unaware of it. At just this moment, according to David Ridgway,[21] the pottery evidence from Quattro Fontanili allows us to infer

> the presence in the eighth century not only of imported Euboean pottery but also of at least one imported Euboean potter in Southern Etruria, based either at Veii or within striking distance, capable of preparing and using the local clay and of teaching others to do the same . . . In human terms, it is surely possible that when

some Euboeans felt that the time was ripe to put down roots at Pithekoussai, others—including potters—had already established themselves (perhaps by intermarriage) in the native communities of the mainland.

If that happened at Veii, it could have happened twelve miles south. At any rate, we can be sure that something of the cultural baggage the Euboeans brought with them had affected the *Weltanschauung* of the builders of the Palatine wall.

Another item from the same archaeological horizon is a Rhodian *kotyle* buried in the tomb of a ten-year-old boy at Pithekoussai about 720. It has an inscription alluding to the cup of Nestor described in *Iliad* XI 632–7. I quote Ridgway again:[22]

> The verses seem to offer a playful challenge to the cup of wise old Nestor, the Homeric king of sandy Pylos:
>> Nestor had a fine drinking cup, but anyone who drinks from *this* cup will soon be struck with desire for fair-crowned Aphrodite . . .
>
> [The inscription] affords a rare glimpse of the kind of usually invisible cultural cargo that the first Western Greeks brought to Italy, and eventually to ourselves. It is worth noting that the cheerful tone of the verses is highly inappropriate to their funerary context, and particularly so to the last resting place of a small boy. They are more redolent of the adult drinking parties, all male, known as *symposia*: and interestingly enough, the grave that contained the Nestor kotyle also yielded a set of pottery kraters for mixing wine . . .

The *symposion* was where the collective memory of the group was rehearsed and celebrated.[23] The custom was evidently taken over by the native aristocracies of central Italy in the eighth and seventh centuries BC; the best evidence comes from Ficana, just eleven miles down-river from the now-expanding Palatine community.[24] That community was now, in the seventh century, the 'Septimontium': Palatium, Velia, Fagutal, Cermalus, Caelius, Oppius, Cispius.[25] Its cemetery on the Esquiline received about 640 BC a Greek called Kleiklos, who had scratched his name on a Corinthian vase that was buried with him.[26] One would very much like to know what tales he told, and what tales he heard from his fellow-drinkers, at the *symposia* in this fast-developing Latin town.

So far, I have deliberately avoided using the name 'Rome'. I see no reason to doubt that it meant, from the beginning, *rhōmē*, strength; and my guess is that it was the name given to the *polis* that was created in the late seventh century by the draining and development of the valley between the Palatine and the Capitol, and by the establishment there of an *agora* for a citizenry that had now added the Quirinal and Viminal hills to the territory of the Septimontium. Strength—that is, power and resources—must certainly have been needed for the huge engineering works involved in the remodelling of the Forum valley,[27] and it is likely enough that the new city was developed, and then ruled, by a succession of powerful *tyrannoi* whose memory survives, how garbled we cannot tell, in the traditional story of the dynasty of the Tarquins.

The cliché-phrase 'la grande Roma dei Tarquinii' reflects a historical reality: sixth-century Rome was, in its local context, a great power. A late source alleges that Rome made an alliance with the Phocaeans of Asia Minor, at the time of their foundation of Massilia; the alliance itself is perfectly credible, given the prominence of Ionian Greeks in the sixth century at the coastal station of Gravisca, not far from Rome, and it is also credible that it should have been reported and remembered, since with the Phocaeans in the West we have come within the memory-range of Greek historiography.[28]

Around the four regions of the sixth-century city were distributed the twenty-seven 'chapels of the Argives' (*Argeorum sacraria*). These *Argeioi* were supposedly chieftains of Argos who had accompanied Herakles on his travels through Italy with the cattle of Geryon.[29] That aetiology may look late and literary, but we now know that the story of Herakles and the cattle in the Forum Bovarium was already current in Rome in the sixth century. The terracotta *akroterion* of a temple built about 530 BC in the Forum Bovarium itself, just a stone's throw from the Ara Maxima, the ancient altar of the deified hero, shows Herakles being presented to the gods of Olympus by Pallas Athene [fig. i].[30]

This was a city with a history of its own, and a place in the international story-world of Greek mythology. Where, how, and in what contexts did the Romans tell the stories that defined their city and celebrated its achievements? No doubt the custom of the *symposion* continued, though perhaps controlled, if not monopolized, by the ruler at the expense of other aristocrats. (One likely subject for celebratory song may have been the coming of the ruler's ancestor, Demaratus, from Corinth.)[31] Elsewhere in the Greek world, however, other forms of communal story-telling had become established. One thinks of Thespis

THE ORIGINS OF ROMAN HISTORIOGRAPHY

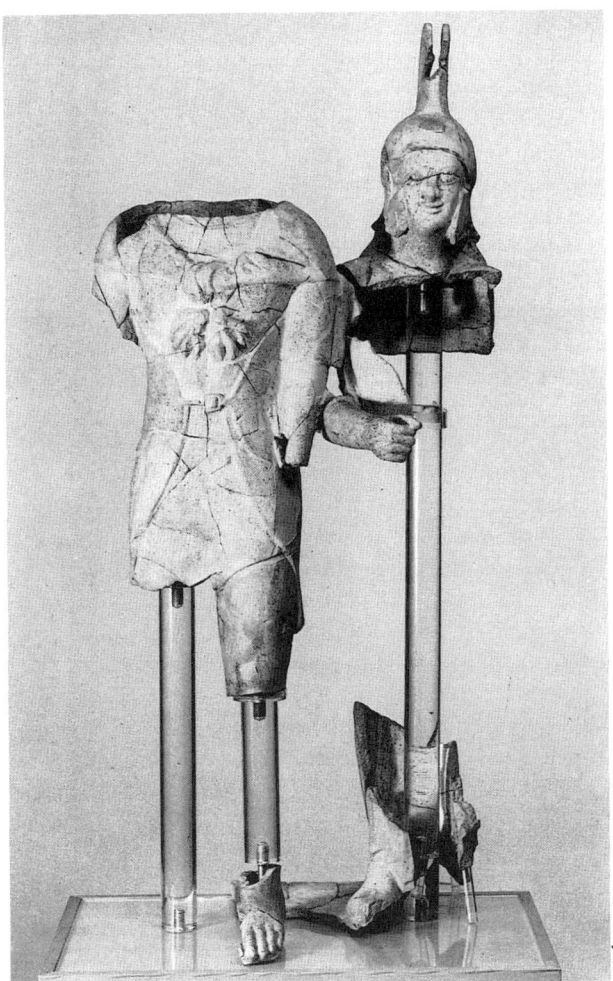

Figure i

Acroterion of Herakles and Athene from a temple in the Forum Bovarium, c.530 BC (Rome, Antiquario comunale). The Forum Bovarium was named after the cattle (*boves*) of Geryon, brought by Herakles from the far West as the tenth of his twelve Labours; the nearby Ara Maxima was supposedly dedicated by Herakles himself on that occasion after his apotheosis had been prophesied; the shrine of the prophetess, Carmenta, was also close by. The story of the tenth Labour was told at length by the sixth-century Sicilian poet Stesichorus in his *Geryoneis*. [Photo by courtesy of the Archivio Fotografico of the Capitoline Museums, Rome.]

at Athens, of the 'tragic choruses' that recounted the deeds of the hero Adrastus at Sikyon, of the philosophical comedian Epicharmus at Syracuse.[32] Plutarch knew a passage of Epicharmus which said that Pythagoras was a citizen of Rome; that was probably the work of a fourth-century BC pseudo-Epicharmus, but it may still serve to remind us that Rome was no stranger to Greek culture.[33]

It is in this context that we must consider the *ludi Romani*. They were in honour of Iuppiter Optimus Maximus, whose huge Tuscan temple on the Capitol was one of the great achievements of sixth-century Rome. Traditionally attributed to Tarquinius Priscus,[34] the games may well be seen as an aspect of the power and confidence of that time. They consisted primarily of chariot-racing, but one cannot imagine the events being limited to that alone. We have Fabius Pictor's description of the *ludi Romani* of his time, the details of which have been convincingly combined with Etruscan vase-painting of the sixth and fifth centuries BC to produce a tentative reconstruction of a festival that featured actors, dancers and performers of all kinds.[35] Not only that, but the very vocabulary of Roman drama seems to derive from Etruscan versions of Greek—*scaena* from *skēnē*, *persona* from *prosōpon*, *ludius* from *aulōdos*, *histrio* from *histōr*—in deformations reminiscent of the versions of Greek proper names that are found on Etruscan mirrors. Indeed, it is likely that those garbled names are themselves the result of oral transmission and mispronunciation in plays or performances.[36] The implication is that the performing arts came to Rome not directly from the Greek world but through Etruscan mediation, and that in turn implies that they were introduced during the period of greatest Etruscan influence on Rome, namely the sixth or early fifth century BC.

Of course, all this is very uncertain. But even on *a priori* grounds, I think we may reasonably assume that the Romans used the 'Roman games' for celebrating their civic identity, and their own and their forefathers' *res gestae*. Even more so, of course, after the expulsion of the *tyrannoi*, the establishment of the first speakers' platform in the Comitium,[37] and eventually, by about the mid-fifth century, the achievement of a written law-code on Athenian lines.

Those were great days; but in the later fifth century Rome became impoverished, evidently torn by internal strife and harried by constant pressure from unfriendly neighbours. For the effect of this 'dark age' on Rome's conception of her own past, I know of no better statement than two paragraphs written by Tim Cornell in 1980. I have quoted the passage elsewhere, but if we want to make sense of the great stories of

Roman legend, from Tanaquil and the eagle to the death of Verginia, it cannot be repeated too often:[38]

> The century down to the Twelve Tables has yielded many archaeological finds. Monuments, buildings and other tangible relics belonging to this period are frequently mentioned in literary sources, which also refer to important public documents. Moreover the literary tradition on this period is rich in lively and romantic stories. The succeeding century, however, is represented by very little archaeological material, and the literary evidence, which mentions hardly any monumental buildings or documents, is a dismal and monotonous catalogue of dry annual notices.
>
> The conclusion is clear enough. Rome arrived at a peak of power and prosperity towards the end of the sixth century but subsequently underwent a recession; however, a strong and vivid memory of the age of greatness was preserved throughout the period of decline and subsequent recovery. We can well imagine that the Romans of the fourth and third centuries were impressed by the imposing archaic buildings which surrounded them, and by the monuments and ancient inscriptions which survived from a remote and half-forgotten epoch.

It might seem paradoxical to invoke a strong and vivid memory of a half-forgotten epoch; but we are not concerned here with the genuine memory of real events as they actually happened. It is now abundantly clear, despite the wishful thinking of scholars, that accurate oral transmission of the historical past is possible only for one generation at the most. 'There is no such thing as an oral tradition stable over a long period of time.'[39] Some part of the events, mixed with much that never happened, becomes a story, to be told and retold, adjusted and elaborated, shaped by the narrator's art.

The tale of Troy provides a good analogy: on the one hand, we can be reasonably certain that some sort of historical reality lies behind it; on the other hand, we cannot possibly reconstruct what really happened. More important for our purposes is what was done with the story. Here is a recent description of the *Iliad* as oral epic activated in performance:[40]

> The epic performance can be considered as the *re-enactment* of an event that is crucial enough to be foundational for the collective experience of the community. More than that, the re-enactment of the epic story is a reactivation, a re-creation of the epic past in the

here and now of the performance shared by the performer and his audience. The reactivation of the epic in performance creates a strong overarching sense of involvement in which the entire community participates ...

This emphasis on public performance and community participation is important. The Romans had no Homer; in using the Greek 'dark age' as an analogy for the Roman one, it has to be admitted that there is no sign in the Roman tradition of narrative poetry as the story-telling mode. But the bard's epic song was not the only way of re-enacting the collective experience of the community.

I am a great admirer of Macaulay's *Lays of Ancient Rome*; his historical insight seems to me quite brilliant, but I think he was misled by Cato's report of the songs that used to be sung at banquets. That was probably a reference to the survival of the archaic *symposion*,[41] which I imagine must have been a peripheral phenomenon by the late fifth and fourth centuries BC. Rather than ballads, perhaps we should think of dramatic performances, both at the *ludi Romani* and no doubt also at the *ludi plebeii*, which were clearly set up in rivalry.[42] We have already inferred the possibility of Etruscan-style performing arts in early Rome, from the terminology of Roman drama. We can now add a metrical argument, since Helmut Rix has inferred, from the 'brevis brevians' rule of iambic prosody, the existence at Rome of a pre-literary genre 'not far removed from the dialogues of comedy and tragedy', as far back as the late fifth century BC.[43] We know from later theatrical history that both the *Atellana* and the mime developed from a non-literary to a literary form;[44] it does not seem wholly absurd to imagine that the same might be true of the *praetexta*, and that pre-literary performances on Roman historical themes developed by the third century into a formal genre of written drama.

I suspect it is not wholly fortuitous that the rape of Lucretia became an opera, and Coriolanus a Shakespearean tragedy. Even in the form we have them, absorbed into continuous historical prose, the great stories fall naturally into dramatic scenes. Macaulay imagined the story of Verginia being recited in the Forum by a 'popular poet' just after the re-election of Licinius and Sextius as tribunes in 375 BC. It's a good context, but I doubt the *mise-en-scène*. Rather, perhaps, a piece of agitprop for the militant audience at the Plebeian Games.

When the power-sharing compromise was finally achieved (367 BC is the traditional date), we are told that the 'great games'—the *ludi*

Romani—were reorganised under the control of the curule aediles.[45] Three years later, when the plebeian hero Licinius Stolo was consul, *ludi scaenici* are said to have been introduced from Etruria. Livy attaches to the latter notice his famous digression on the development of Roman drama, almost certainly taken from Varro's *De scaenicis originibus*, or from the tenth book of his *Antiquitates divinae*.[46] If so, then it is the result of the best antiquarian research available in the first century BC; but how much did even Varro know about conditions in the fourth century?

It is important to remember that nothing is so fleeting and evanescent as the performer's moment on the stage. Styles and fashions change year by year, decade by decade. Without play-texts or descriptions in contemporary authors, the development of drama simply cannot be documented. Livy's digression is a scholarly reconstruction created three centuries after the event; there is very little chance that it transmits anything usable about the realities of Roman drama in 364 BC. Even the assertion that the stage performances were a novelty is probably no more than an inference: no doubt an annalistic notice from that year was the earliest piece of evidence Varro could find.[47] On the other hand, the very fact of an annalistic notice reveals that stage performances at the Roman games were something that *mattered* in those years of fragile compromise.

That is how I would interpret Tim Cornell's 'strong and vivid memory of the age of greatness'; I think the strength and vividness came from patriotism and political passion mediated through performances at the communal festivals of the Roman people. By the 360s BC the 'dark age' was all but over; the second half of the fourth century BC saw more conflict, internal and external, but also the beginning of that extraordinary burst of energy and achievement which ended with the Romans in control of all Italy south of the Apennines.

Once again Rome was a significant element in the panhellenic world: Aristotle knew of her as a city founded by Achaeans scattered by storm as they returned from Troy.[48] But her position was ambiguous. On the one hand, as the opponent of the enemies of the Greeks (Gauls, Etruscans, Samnites), she could even count as a Greek city herself, as in Heraclides of Pontus and later in Callimachus; on the other hand, she was a threat to the Greek cities, and must therefore count as barbarian, as in Aristoxenus of Tarentum. The ambivalence was well expressed by Demetrius the Besieger in about 295: complaining about the pirates of Antium, he referred reproachfully to Rome's kinship with the Greeks and the temple of the Dioscuri in her *agora*.[49] So it came about that, in just this period, the Aeneas legend evolved as the ultimate origin of the Romans: not Greek, but nearly, and with a distinguished ancestry in Hellenic legend.[50]

How did it evolve? How, for that matter, did the Romulus story take shape? It is absurd to think that the Romans depended on Greek authors for their ideas about their own past. We have no evidence, but on *a priori* grounds the Roman festivals are the obvious place to imagine the Roman community's self-image being created. Oliver Taplin has now revealed the lively state of drama in south Italy in the fourth century BC; he emphasizes Athenian influence, but the Sicilian tradition from Epicharmus to Rhinthon must also have been important throughout the fifth and fourth centuries.[51] When we consider the range of borrowings from the Greek world made by the Romans in the late fourth century—from senatorial *cognomina* to the artistic craftsmanship of the Ficoroni *cista*[52] [fig. ii]—it becomes implausible to imagine that they remained blind and deaf to the possibilities of drama as a means of articulating their civic identity.

One of the borrowings, then or a little later, was the circular Comitium, remodelled in the likeness of an *ekklesiasterion*.[53] In a Greek city, the place where the citizens assembled was also where they honoured their gods with dance and drama. The *agora* was used as a theatre, and when purpose-built theatres were introduced, they were used for political assemblies as well.[54] In fact, the distinction is anachronistic: dance and drama, judgement and deliberation, all were equally political, the business of the *politai*. The same was surely true of Rome in the fourth century. Why else should C. Maenius, as censor in 318, have built balconies for spectators on the shops along the Forum piazza?[55]

It has often been observed that much information about early Rome was preserved by later antiquarian authors but systematically ignored by the historians; one thinks, for instance, of Mastarna the Etruscan, or the *praetor maximus*.[56] Emilio Gabba, in an important recent discussion, explains the phenomenon as a deliberate process of selection, in the late fourth and early third centuries, which created the 'historical corpus' of material inherited by the historians.[57] In general terms, that is surely right. But I think we must go further, and ask who did the selecting, and why, and how. You can't select material for a genre that doesn't yet exist, and Professor Gabba's formulation ('l'annalistica . . . e prima d'essa la tradizione che ne fu alla base') still leaves open the

Figure ii

The Ficoroni Cista (Rome, Villa Giulia): a cylindrical bronze chest, c.320 BC. It bears the inscription: 'Dindia Macolnia gave [me] to her daughter; Novios Plautios made me at Rome.' Handle: Dionysus and satyrs. Decoration on the side: Argonauts; Amykos tied to a tree after his defeat by Polydeukes (p. 73 below). [Photo by courtesy of the German Archaeological Institute at Rome.]

question of what preceded historiography. How are we to translate his hypothesis into concrete terms?

Jürgen von Ungern-Sternberg has recently argued that control of the Roman past was always in the hands of the *pontifices*, amended only by the rival traditions of competing aristocratic families. Similarly, Dieter Timpe insists that the history of the *populus Romanus* was simply the *res gestae* of the élite, whose 'social authority' controlled what was and what was not remembered.[58] That idea, it seems to me, is no more than a half-truth. The Roman People had its own *res gestae*, and its own means of celebrating them. I would prefer to suppose that the selection of themes was, in part at least, the work of successive producers of patriotic and partisan drama at the *ludi scaenici*.

I have argued elsewhere that even for the late Republic, where the literary sources are fullest, our knowledge of what actually went on at the *ludi scaenici* is hopelessly inadequate.[59] For the early and middle Republic, it is non-existent. *A priori* argument is all we have, and the absence of contemporary sources means that the argument from silence has no value. The traditional assumption has been that Roman drama began with Livius Andronicus in 240 BC, or possibly in 238 in connection with the newly-founded *ludi Florales*.[60] But what Andronicus brought from Tarentum was *literary* drama, plays with texts, the formal genres of comedy and tragedy in the Attic manner. His were the earliest texts available to the late-republican antiquarians; but it does not thereby follow that there had never before been plays with Greek mythological and Roman historical content performed at Rome.

What I think Andronicus, and then Naevius, did was to turn into literature what had previously been produced for the people without benefit of text. And with Andronicus and Naevius we have reached at last what Erich Gruen has well described as 'the cultural convergence of Hellas and Rome'[61]—the generation of Fabius Pictor and the beginning of Roman historiography.

III

Enough of constructive fiction, rational conjecture, idle or barren speculation. It is high time to return to the safe ground, the texts of classical literature. They too can be revealing, if we know what to look for.

Here is Pausanias, for instance, commenting in the second century AD on the belief that Theseus founded the Athenian democracy:[62]

> There are many false beliefs current among the mass of mankind, since they are ignorant of historical science and consider trustworthy whatever they have heard from childhood in choruses and tragedies.

And here is Plutarch, also on Theseus:[63]

> As for the terrible fate of Phaedra and Hippolytus, there is no contradiction between the versions of the historians and the tragic poets, and so we must suppose that it happened as all the tragedians represent it.

Belief in the historicity of drama was evidently not restricted to the ignorant multitude. As for Rome, it is clear from St Augustine's reading of Varro that in the late Republic it was assumed that a person's knowledge of what we would call mythology was expected to come from the stage.[64] Not only mythology, of course: in a casual comment, Cicero names the stage—along with parents, nurses, teachers, poets and public opinion—among the sources of our opinions on all matters.[65] Books were expensive and cumbersome; only the wealthy had slave *lectores*; for the great majority of the population, what was known about the doings of gods and men must have been very largely what was seen on the stage at the festivals of the Roman people.

That included, of course, the history of Rome. From Naevius' *Clastidium* to the pseudo-Senecan *Octavia* three centuries later, there is no shortage of evidence for plays with Roman themes, even (or especially) contemporary ones. Some, like Accius' *Brutus*, were tragedies; in other cases, like the play on Q. Claudia referred to by Ovid, we have no idea what form they took.[66] Later, we know there were stage performances glorifying the emperor, which both Augustus and Trajan took care to control.[67] Pliny says that Trajan preferred to be praised 'in serious poems and the eternal glory of *annales*', which suggests that the performances he disapproved of were themselves, in the broadest sense, historical.

The texts of the historians themselves are also helpful. I have mentioned already the way the great legends of regal and and early-republican Rome seem to fall into dramatic scenes. Livy has a revealing comment about one of them, the story of Ser. Tullius and his wicked daughter: 'the Roman royal house *too* [the house of Tarquin, like the house of Atreus] has provided an example of a crime fit for tragedy.'[68] He is more explicit in the narrative of the fall of Veii in book V, where he includes a *fabula* about the Roman sappers tunnelling their way into the city. The king of Veii was sacrificing; the *haruspex* announced that victory would attend whoever offered the entrails of the victim; the Romans heard, burst out of the tunnel, snatched the entrails and brought them to Camillus. 'This story,' says Livy, 'is not worth affirming or refuting; it is appropriate not to belief but to the vain display of the stage, which delights in marvels.'[69]

Sometimes, however, Livy may have taken Plutarch's line, and accepted dramatists' versions as historical. He reports without hesitation ('satis convenit') that when the 306 Fabii perished at the Cremera, there was only one boy left to keep the *gens* alive. Dionysius will have none of that. 'This is a false report,' he asserts; 'for it is not possible that all the Fabii who went out to the fortress were unmarried and childless.' And he knows from where such false reports arise: 'such situations resemble myths and fictions of the stage.'[70] But Dionysius too is inconsistent. He relates in detail, with conscious *akribeia*, the fight between the Horatii and the Curiatii in Tullus Hostilius' war with Alba; but in the very introductory sentence where he takes credit for his accuracy, he observes that the events were like reversals of fortune in the theatre.[71]

I am not, of course, suggesting that Livy or Dionysius took such episodes directly from dramatic sources; but I do suggest that much of the traditional material on early Rome which they found in their second- and first-century BC predecessors had been processed for the stage long before it ever appeared in the pages of any historian.

The final set of texts I want to use is a short selection from Hellenistic historiography. After all, Fabius Pictor was a Hellenistic historian. The Greek historians of the third and second centuries BC were used to performing in theatres, and before large audiences who wished to be entertained as well as instructed.[72] One of the best known was Duris of Samos, whom Fabius may well have used for the great war of 295 between Rome and the Gallic–Etruscan–Samnite coalition. Besides his historical works, Duris wrote treatises on tragedy and tragic poets, and in a famous polemic against his historical predecessors he set out clearly the common ground, as he saw it, of historiography and drama:[73]

> Ephorus and Theopompus fell far short of the events. They achieved no *mimesis* or pleasure in their presentation, but were concerned only with writing.

What sort of *mimesis* and pleasure did Duris have in mind? Polybius tells us, in his own polemic against Phylarchus' melodramatic account of the Macedonians' capture of Mantinea:

> [Phylarchus] introduces graphic scenes of women clinging to one another, tearing their hair and baring their breasts, and in addition he describes the tears and lamentations of men and women accompanied by their children and aged parents as they are led away into captivity. Phylarchus reproduces this kind of effect again and again in his history, striving on each occasion to recreate the horrors before our eyes.

In doing this Phylarchus has failed to distinguish between history and tragedy. 'The tragic poet seeks to thrill and charm his audience', but according to Polybius the historian has no business to do so.[74] Duris too would have fallen under Polybius' disapproval. His account of the Athenians' capture of Samos dwelt on the brutal torture inflicted by Pericles on the Samian captains; Plutarch, observing that there is no hint of this in Thucydides, Ephorus or Aristotle, comments that Duris has 'turned the events into a tragedy'.[75]

It is important to remember that Polybius represents a minority view—and even he was quite prepared, where necessary, to speak of historical events as a spectacle to be presented to his audience.[76] History as drama was a natural way of thinking, for both Greeks and Romans. In Plutarch's essay on the fame of the Athenians, he likens historians to actors on the stage, 'exhibiting the deeds of generals and kings, and merging themselves with their characters.' *Mimesis* is the aim, 'the vivid representation of emotions and characters', as exemplified by Thucydides.[77]

That, surely, is the view of historiography Fabius Pictor inherited from his Greek models. And it lasted long in the senatorial historiography of Rome. When Cicero wrote to L. Lucceius in 55 BC—one senator to another, discussing contemporary political history—he took it for granted as the criterion of historiographical quality:[78]

> The monotonous regularity of the *Annales* has as much effect on us as if we were reading through official calendars; but the unpredictable and fluctuating circumstances surrounding a great figure induce admiration, anticipation, delight, misery, hope and fear. And if they have a memorable outcome, the reader feels a warm glow of pleasure.

> So I'll be all the more gratified if you do decide to separate the drama (so to speak) of my experiences from the on-going narrative in which you deal with the continuous history of events. You'll find that it has its various 'acts' and numerous examples of dramatic reversal.

Contemporary history presented as vivid drama—that, if Gavin Townsend's reconstruction is sound, is how I think we may also describe Cluvius Rufus' history of the period from Caligula to Vitellius.[79] I suspect that Cluvius Rufus was the last in the sequence Fabius Pictor began, of Hellenized senators writing Roman history according to the canons of Greek historiography.

The common ground of history and drama, which I have been trying to reconstruct in almost every period of Roman history we can imagine, is really just another aspect of the common ground of drama and public life. Rome was a theatre, her politicians thought of themselves as performers on a stage—'in contione, id est in scaena', as Cicero put it.[80] Even more, perhaps, under the emperors than in the Republic. Certainly no-one was more aware of the theatricality of dynastic politics that Tacitus, as Tony Woodman has recently shown with reference to the narrative of the Piso conspiracy.[81] That was what made Tacitus valuable for later ages: 'here,' wrote Justus Lipsius in 1581, 'are kings and monarchs and, as it were, the theatre of our life today.'[82]

Mention of Tacitus reminds us of the great scholar whose memory we are honouring. At the end of his treatment of the style of the *Annals*, Syme reflected on the attraction of dramatic poetry to Roman senators under the principate:[83]

> Did not the tragedy of the Caesars embody a sequence of dramatic themes, with ambition, power, and crime recalling the House of Atreus? The attitude disclosed in the *Annals* might have found expression and renown with a *Sejanus* or an *Agrippina*.

But it was too late for that:

> Epic and drama were finished, and so was political eloquence. They could be perpetuated only if transfused into another medium. If history was that medium, it demanded the talents of writer, dramatist and poet. It would have to be narrated with splendour and dignity and power.

That paragraph appeared in 1958. Four years later, in a lecture to the British Academy, Syme returned to the theme, and applied it to Thucydides:[84]

> Diagnosis and narration are conducted with supreme literary power. The ancients (and who shall hold them superseded?) assumed that history is close to poetry and drama. Thucydides' theme is in itself a tragedy, by the facts—the ruin of an empire.

Twenty years later again, in the James Boyce Memorial Lecture from which I have already quoted, Syme extended the idea to his new subject of 'fictional history':[85]

> Historians in antiquity learned from epic and from tragedy. In the more recent time, prose fiction has become the dominant genre. Gibbon confessed that he owed not a little to the reading of novels, and one might wonder about Macaulay or Mommsen. Indeed, history, so it has been contended, needs to be as convincing as fiction.

It is no surprise to see, in that footnote where he added 'not the whole story' to the documentary origin of Roman history, a reference to Hellenistic historiography. Alas, he chose not to elaborate it.[86]

The argument I have developed here is a threefold one. Firstly, the theory that Roman historiography began by imitating the bare chronicles of the *pontifex maximus* rests on wholly inadequate evidence. Of course Roman historians did seek out and exploit documentary sources,[87] but it was not the existence of such sources that gave rise to historiography in the first place. Secondly, in so far as we can gain any notion of archaic Rome uncorrupted by the anachronistic literary tradition, it suggests a community open from the beginning to influences from the Greek as well as the Etruscan world; it is possible, with proper caution, to imagine the Romans creating their own identity, and celebrating their own past, first in the *symposion* and then in the performances at the public festivals. Thirdly, the notion that historiography grew out of such celebratory performances receives support from various items, not always given sufficient attention, in our surviving texts. For most people, drama was one of the main sources of information about the past; for historians, it was obvious that much of their material was dramatic in origin; and for the Hellenized literary world in which Fabius Pictor wrote, history and drama were inextricable.

I have no idea what Sir Ronald Syme would have said about the origins of Roman historiography if he had chosen to expand that elliptical footnote. I can only hope that his reaction to the hypothesis I have offered today might have been in the phrase he once remembered from his reading of Proust:[88]

> As Albertine somewhere declared, 'c'est la bonne solution, la solution élégante.'

2

Roman Legend and Oral Tradition

Review of: J.N. Bremmer and N.M. Horsfall, *Roman Myth and Mythography* (Bulletin of the Institute of Classical Studies, Supplement LII), London 1987.

I

Did the Romans have any mythology? Not according to Georg Wissowa or Kurt Latte: 'for these unspeculative and unimaginative people . . . no myth-creating imagination winds its tendrils round the gods.' What passed for myths were merely late aetiology and borrowings from Greek poets.[1] But that idea was sharply rejected by the 'Frankfurt School' of Walter Otto, in a series of monographs designed to show, in the words of Carl Koch, that 'there exist on Roman soil sure signs of a non-literary mythology untouched by the influence of Greek poetry. The signs are divided equally among the archaic Roman, the Etruscan, and the Greek components of the historical Roman religion.'[2]

Since then, major new discoveries—the Dioscuri at Lavinium, Astarte at Pyrgi—and continuing research in comparative religion have made Wissowa's position progressively harder to sustain. In 1924, H.J. Rose picked out Acca Larentia and Mater Matuta to illustrate his contention that '"Roman mythology" is almost altogether Greek . . . It may be that the Italians told no tales of their gods whatsoever.' Compare that with Filippo Coarelli's recent analyses of those very stories, in his books on the Roman Forum and the Forum Bovarium.[3] It is a different world— and one with its own dangers of over-exuberant interpretation.

Since there has not been much work in English on this important subject, Bremmer and Horsfall's collection of essays is particularly welcome. The authors 'do not aim to speak with one voice' (vii), and certainly two distinct personalities emerge. H. is interested in texts, B. in ritual; H. has a dense and allusive style that demands close reading, B. is more expansive and colloquial. But that makes for variety, not incoherence, and the book does indeed have a thematic unity.

It begins with a general essay by H. on 'myth and mythography at Rome',[4] at much of which Wissowa might have nodded in agreement. H. defines its purpose as follows (2):

> Two central questions above all have been neglected [in previous accounts]: first, how the Romans themselves regarded what was or might pass for a myth; and secondly, how the stories were transmitted and transmuted. This discussion is intended as a first step towards remedying that neglect.

By the end of the chapter the reader has learned a lot, but is very little nearer to an answer to either question. It is worth asking why.

Part of the problem is H.'s style. Allusive and sometimes elliptical, it does not always make for clarity of exposition. For instance, a paragraph on the effect of Greek culture in driving out all but a few indigenous narratives turns without explanation into a warning not to distinguish too clearly between *fabula* and *historia* (5): 'Livy lays down no firm periodisation in terms of chronology and credibility. Etruscan art even juxtaposes the mythological Cacus with the historical Vibenna.' We may dispute the first statement ('ante conditam condendamve urbem'?);[5] we may wonder what the force of 'even' is in the second; but above all, we want to know the connection with what has gone before.

One frequent stylistic trait may be defined as the grudging admission. H. has a thesis to argue, that most Roman myth is 'secondary'—that is, the work of Hellenized antiquarians rather than ancient stories rooted in their society. Evidence or argument that tends the other way is usually mentioned in a concessive clause, or otherwise dismissively. For example (4): 'The name Erulus [Virg. *Aen.* VIII 563] is interesting, but clearly need not in origin have belonged to an authentic figure of primitive Praenestine myth.' One could equally argue that his name, with no known aetiological significance, does not look like a late invention. Or again, where H. is attacking Arrigoni on Camilla (9): 'A case for sceptical analysis remains. Metabus, whom Virgil makes Camilla's father, may have no long-standing connections with the town of Privernum, and therefore may not himself constitute a tiny fragment of ancient Volscian legend, or myth.' Of course; but on the other hand, he may.

When H. allows himself to make the positive argument, it is concealed in multiple negatives (7): 'But it should not be thought either that there were not writers who toured central Italy in pursuit of information on the ground, or that there were not at least a few local myths to be uncovered.' That way of putting it does not encourage the reader to dwell on the implications of those possible local traditions. Nor does H. dwell on them himself, as he passes on to a very reductive analysis of the Italian catalogue in the *Aeneid*, concluding (9, my italics): 'So, *aside from* some minute but suggestive scraps, the thirteen leaders have yielded up *precisely* one native myth [i.e. Caeculus].' It would have been just as easy to emphasize the 'suggestiveness' of Virbius, Oebalus and Metabus and come to a substantially higher total. 'Precision', of course, is unobtainable by either procedure.[6]

So careful readers, when they follow H.'s argument, may come to distrust it. But that is not the only source of disquiet. H.'s conception of the subject depends on a very clear dichotomy. As he says on the first page:

> Very few students of Roman myth have paused to draw a distinction between:
>
> (i) those very few Roman and Italian myths whose evidently great antiquity, predating both regular contact with Greek literature and the spread of literacy in its application to the preservation of narrative, is indicated both by their form and by copious Indo-European (and indeed non-Indo-European) parallels (Romulus, Cacus, Caeculus), and which have survived all the vicissitudes of accretion and transmission; and
>
> (ii) those, which I shall call 'secondary myth', that are the products of antiquarian industry, literary activity, a desire for impressive antecedents, a good nose for suggestive analogies and for what might pass as a credibly antique story, a talent for creating a seductive but illusory patina of hoarily ancient authenticity, and, lastly, wide reading. The poets of classical Greece create or retell myth for society at large; Roman men of letters construct secondary myth for *recitationes*.

This distinction is surely over-schematic.

H. seems to have taken two extreme cases—the ancient story surviving in its primordial form, and the wholly artificial creation of a sophisticated litterateur—as if there were nothing in between, and then used them as categories into one or other of which *all* stories must fall.

He refers more than once (6, 100) to Callimachus' 'I sing nothing that is unattested', and knows that oral stories would count as attestations. But the corollary of that is that 'secondary' myth may easily contain elements of 'primary'—a possibility that fatally undermines his conclusion (11):

> A technique which can distinguish the fundamental difference between Caeculus and Camilla, which can, that is, isolate 'secondary myth', is essential if we are to make any progress in our understanding of Italian mythology, yet the same range of texts transmit the two stories and make no differentiation between them.

Is there really such a fundamental difference? Are not both stories, as we have them, likely to be an amalgam of old and new?

In his definition of the first type of myths, H. refers forward to the following passage on Greek literature and the spread of literacy (5):[7]

> There was now [after about 240 BC] a growing literate public, and Roman armies were bringing back scraps of Greek stories, language and mores from the south. Two and a half centuries earlier, the Roman purchasers of black-figure and red-figure vases, if they could read (unlikely), were clearly Greekless, and even if there were itinerant polyglot storytellers, their skills have left no trace. Before Livius Andronicus, no vehicle existed whereby Greek myth could attract or retain the attention of a population monoglot and not long literate.

Here I think he has begged two serious questions—about the degree of Greek influence on archaic Rome, and about the necessity of literate transmission. Perhaps a little progress can be made on each of these.

II

It is in Italy that Greek literature is first attested, in the eighth century BC:[8]

> [...] Nestor's cup, good to drink from.
> Whoever drinks from this, shall him straightway
> Desire for fair-crown'd Aphrodite seize.

The owner (and inscriber?) of the cup was one of the Euboeans whose settlement on Ischia had been established in order to exploit the iron workings of Elba, two days' sail to the north. One convenient anchorage, about half-way, was provided by the outflow of cis-Apennine Italy's largest river. The Tiber was navigable upstream at least as far as the crossing-place by the island, from where the 'salt way' led off northeastwards into the mountains of the interior. There was a village, perhaps more than one, controlling the crossing-place. What it was like at this date we can hardly say (no doubt already bounded by the ritual course of the skin-clad Luperci), but there is no reason to suppose that it was unknown territory to the merchant venturers of Pithekoussai—or for that matter to those from any other part of the Mediterranean.[9]

Two or three generations after 'Nestor's cup', *a priori* likelihood gives way to actual evidence for Greeks at Rome. Some time about 640 BC, one Kleiklos scratched his name on a Corinthian vase that was later buried in one of the tombs of the Esquiline cemetery. His name meant 'he who is famed for his fame', and he was a contemporary of the 'bastard noble' Aristonothos who painted a mixing-bowl for his patrons in neighbouring Etruscan Caere with a sea-battle on one side and the blinding of Polyphemus on the other.[10] It was about this time that 'Larth Telikles' was evidently bottling *lekythoi* of olive oil for the Etruscan market; 'Rutile Hipukrates' is a good parallel for his Greco-Etruscan name.[11] Even earlier are the 'princely tombs' of Praeneste with their astonishing wealth of 'orientalizing' luxury goods; similar tombs at Cerveteri and Vetulonia in Etruria and Pontecagnano in Campania show that the wealth and wide horizons characteristic of the early seventh century were not restricted to 'Latium vetus'—where the Castel di Decima cemetery demonstrates the impact of both on a broader social spectrum.[12]

Our next archaeological 'snapshot', two or three generations later again, is of the Greek settlement that flourished at Gravisca, one of the ports of Tarquinia. The dialect of the dedications—to Hera, the goddess of Samos, among others—suggests a high proportion of Ionians.[13] One of the dedications, a Sardinian bronze boat, is paralleled by a stray find at Porto, at the mouth of the Tiber;[14] and high-level contact between Tarquinia itself and Rome is demonstrated by the beautiful ivory lion, also of the first half of the sixth century, dedicated at the S. Omobono sanctuary by the Tarquinian Araz Silqetanas Spurianas.[15] The Forum valley was now drained, no longer a barrier between villages but the common ground of a synoecized community which was decorating its 'public buildings' with terracotta reliefs; one of the earliest fragments surviving from the Regia shows a Minotaur.[16]

Greek influence is seen in other ways too. At the 'great altar' of Hercules, which faced the S. Omobono sanctuary across the Forum Bovarium, the cult was performed *Graeco ritu*; so it was at the Saturnus temple on the slope of the Capitol; the *xoanon* of Diana on the Aventine was a replica of the one the Phocaeans had brought from Ephesus to their first western colony, Massilia; and at the nearby temple of Ceres, Liber and Libera, the ritual was entrusted to priestesses from Phocaean Velia or Cumaean Naples.[17]

The Ceres temple brings us down to the early fifth century, the approximate date of two magnificent works of archaic art. First, the marble relief of Orestes killing Aegisthus, found at the sanctuary of Diana at Nemi—clear evidence of the identification of Diana Aricina with Artemis Tauropolos, and the associated legend of the flight of Orestes to Aricia.[18] Second, the terracotta group of Tydeus and Melanippus from temple A at Pyrgi, which was probably the temple of Leucothea sacked by Dionysius in 384;[19] Leucothea was the metamorphosed Ino, sister of Semele, which no doubt accounts for the Theban subject. Geographically between the two, and rather earlier than either, is the splendid terracotta akroterion from the S. Omobono temple in Rome, of Athene introducing Herakles to Olympus [fig. i].[20]

All this, before Herodotus was born.

As the archaeological record gets fuller, it becomes ever more clear that for about two and a half centuries—from the origins (essentially) to the first pinnacle of her power—Rome had been in more or less close contact with people whose minds were full of Homer and Hesiod, the *Nostoi*, the *Telegoneia*, and the works of mythological innovators like Eudemus of Corinth and Asius of Samos.[21] The beginning of the whole process was the arrival in Italy of Euboeans in the 'orientalizing' period—the very people, that is, who are now convincingly credited with the 'innovation and transformation ... that brought the epic to its astonishing acme in the eighth and seventh centuries'.[22] It is hardly too much to say that Rome and Greek mythology grew up together.

By contrast, the age of 'classical' Greek literature—the great Athenian century from Aeschylus to Plato—coincides with a period of obscurity and comparative poverty at Rome. By the time the recovery came, followed by the period of spectacular expansion that saw the conquest of cis-Apennine Italy, Alexander and his successors had changed the nature of the Greek world. That is, Rome can be described as 'Hellenized' in the archaic and Hellenistic periods of Greek culture, for which our literary evidence is most fragmentary, and not in the classical period, about which we know most.

Tim Cornell (quoted at p. 11 above) makes an excellent point about the difference between 500 BC and 350 BC at Rome. We can see this; but as Cornell goes on to point out, Polybius, Cicero and Livy were quite unaware of it. For them, Rome's history was one of gradual but uniform progress. They knew nothing of the fifth- to fourth-century 'dark age' that followed the heroic age of the great Roman legends. As Cornell rightly remarks, the parallel with Greece is striking.[23]

Livy compares the house of Tarquin to the house of Atreus (I 46.3)—and he is more right than he knows. Like the tale of Troy, like King Arthur for that matter, his 'lively and romantic story' had passed through centuries of story-telling in a different world before emerging into literature. (It seems to me quite likely that Tarquin the Proud is about as much like the real ruler of late sixth-century Rome as Dietrich of Bern in the *Nibelungenlied* is like Theoderic; however, our concern here is not with what *we* think of as history.)

We have fragments of Naevius and Ennius, Fabius and Cincius, Cato's *Origines* and Polybius' *archaiologia*; but the overwhelming majority of our information about the Romans' view of their own past comes from the second half of the first century BC and the first and second centuries AD—from the *De republica* to the *Parallel Lives*. Our various authors apply very different criteria of acceptability—Cicero's notion of *to eikos* (what is probable) was very far from Plutarch's—but none of them could even have formulated the question we want to ask about each of the stories they transmit. Was it created by a poet or historian of the Hellenistic age? (If so, from what?) Or was it already being told when Sostratos of Aegina was plying the coasts of Latium and Etruria,[24] and the priest of Diana in the Arician wood guarded the bones of Orestes? Or does it go back even further, to the time when Greek prospectors first hauled their ships up the Tiber? And above all—since oral tradition omits or transforms what is not useful for the present time—what happened to it in the 'dark age'?

III

The new journal *Oral Tradition* has begun an annotated bibliography of all work published in this rapidly expanding interdisciplinary field. Of the 313 items in the first two instalments, not one is concerned with

Rome. That is all the more striking when one considers that the present explosion of research in the subject is very largely due to Milman Parry's work on Homeric epic, and its systematic exploitation by Eric Havelock to explain the development of Greek culture.[25] Now that we know how close early Rome was to that development, certainly in the sixth century BC and in all probability in the seventh as well, the omission appears almost scandalous.[26]

H. is aware of the need to take oral tradition seriously, but his phraseology suggests a certain discomfort (10):

> The stories of Romulus or, more interestingly, Caeculus, to look no further, demonstrate the possibility that narrative can—at least in Latin—survive, whether in priestly formulae, in incised texts, in song or in folk-memory. One might almost be tempted to wonder whether the paucity of myths is not itself a reflection of the limitations of form and language in archaic literature overall, and, did one wish to persevere in peculiarly fruitless speculation, in particular to the *carmina convivalia* [songs sung at banquets].

The footnote attached to the last phrase (n. 75) claims that '*carmina* aside, no other pre-literary vehicle for myth is known'.[27] Let us see whether that is likely to be true.

The first thing we must do is to watch our language. In the last paragraph of the previous section, I found it natural to use 'it' (i.e. 'the story') as the subject of the sentence, as if the story had an existence of its own. Justifiable metaphor, no doubt; but metaphor can give the wrong impression. Similarly, historians sometimes speak of a 'body of information' being preserved or transmitted. That would be an appropriate phrase only for a literate society which kept its information in archives. When we talk about 'a kernel of truth', we know we are being metaphorical. But when we say 'handed down by oral tradition', we are in the grip of cliché—the metaphor is so innocuous, the abstraction so familiar, that we think we have said something that has a meaning.

In a society which cannot, or does not, write its stories down, all there is is what one person says, or sings, to another, or to a group of others. That is (to return to the abstractions of our literate world), transmission presupposes a social context. The difficult thing is to imagine what it could have been.

'Could the Orientalizing tombs in Campania, Latium and Etruria be an early example of permeation by Hellenic usage (whether really understood or not)?' Ridgway's guess was immediately confirmed by the publication of a 'banquet service'—the mixing-bowls and drinking-cups for a *symposion*—from a seventh-century house at Ficana, eleven miles from Rome on the road to the Tiber mouth. As Annette Rathje puts it, 'we have identified the *aristoi* at Ficana'.[28]

To understand the *symposion* from the inside, as it were, one turns to early Greek elegy,[29] and in particular to one of those Ionian Greeks who came to the Tyrrhenian coast of Italy in the sixth century, Xenophanes of Colophon:

> Praise him who drinks and gives a noble lesson
> From his memory, or of virtue speaks.
> 'Tis wrong to speak of Titans' wars, or Giants',
> Or of Centaurs'—fancies of old time—,
> Of bitter quarrels in which lies no profit;
> Honour to the gods is ever good.

Similarly strong views about symposiac conversation were expressed by Anacreon:

> I don't like him who when the bowl is brimming
> Talks as he drinks of strife and tearful war.

But normally, one imagines, the noble lesson was drawn from precisely such martial subject-matter, whether the heroism was contemporary—

> Pour wine for Cedon, servant, nor forget him,
> If it is right to drink to gallant men—

or, more often, remembered in old men's tales of the fighters of the past:

> Not his such puny strength and flinching temper,
> So my elders told me: him they saw
> Routing the serried ranks of Lydian horsemen
> In the plain of Hermus with his spear . . .

This recycling of the *klea andrōn* (famous deeds of men) also served for the instruction of the young; the values of the society were inculcated by oral narrative. Sit next to a man of good sense, says Theognis to his young friend, and learn from him.[30]

Was the conversation very different, in whatever language it was conducted, at a *symposion* in seventh-century Ficana? There is no reason to think so—nor even to doubt the essential continuity, at least so far as the talk was concerned, between the aristocratic *symposion* and the dinners the elder Cato enjoyed, where there was 'much praise of honourable and worthy citizens.'[31]

It is possible that Plutarch got that item from the passage in the *Origines* where Cato looked back with nostalgia to the ancient custom, obsolete in his own day, of praising famous men in songs sung by the guests at banquets. Varro reports the *laudes maiorum* as sung by boys, either unaccompanied or to the pipe. That is reminiscent of Theognis on the fame of Cyrnus—

> To clear-voiced pipes fair youths in due decorum
> Shall sing your praise, a sweet and lovely song—

where *neoi andres eukosmōs* is very close to Varro's *pueri modesti*. As Momigliano rightly insisted, both Cato's and Varro's versions of the ancient Roman custom are perfectly intelligible in either Greek or Etruscan terms.[32]

Another type of praise-singing in early Rome was the dirge, or *nenia*, which a woman singer hired for the purpose sang at the house of the dead man, praising his valiant deeds. This too we know from Varro: in the *De lingua Latina* he cites Aristotle's *Nomima barbarika* on the custom, and in the *De vita populi Romani* he says it went out of fashion at the time of 'the Punic war'.[33]

So far, our search for 'oral tradition' has been restricted to aristocratic society; popular story-telling is not so easy to identify. Eric Havelock acutely draws attention to Heraclitus:

> What is the intelligence or wit of them? To the bards of the peoples they attend, and make the conversation of the crowd their instructor, not knowing that the many are inferior and the few are superior.

As he points out, the second sentence indicates 'the epic recital being given in a city square as a regular civic performance'. Even Demodocus in Phaeacia is 'honoured by the people', as his name implies, and does not sing only for the palace. Moreover, Havelock insists on the plural 'peoples' (*demoi*): 'the minstrel is presumed to be moving from city to city.'[34]

We cannot simply transpose this to archaic Italy. It may be applicable to the Greek colonies themselves, but hardly to their non-Greek-speaking neighbours. For early Rome, we are reduced to *a priori* argument about humbler performers. 'Assem para et accipe auream fabulam':[35] we know of the professional story-teller from literary sources,[36] but he certainly predates the world of literacy. The '*circulator* in the Forum' was an itinerant,[37] travelling from village to village and town to town like Autolycus in *The Winter's Tale*; his equivalent in archaic Rome would have picked up material from all over Latium and south Etruria, with some of his best tales no doubt coming from the more Hellenized harbour towns.

The *circulatores* represent the culture of the unprivileged.[38] But their material found its way into every stratum of society, through the tales told to children by their nurses. Though *fabulae aniles* (old women's tales) were treated with contempt by serious-minded persons, they must have filled the young minds of much of the *populus Romanus*. When Cicero enumerates the sources of *opiniones*, his first two categories are parents and nurse.[39]

We should probably not draw too clear a distinction between story-telling and drama. Here is Suetonius on Augustus' dinner-table entertainers: 'He used to bring in entertainers and actors and even street-corner performers from the Circus, and frequently story-tellers too.'[40] Between the 'legitimate' actors and the story-tellers come the performers from the Circus Maximus, whom I think we should imagine as strolling players. Comparative evidence may suggest that their performance could be described as either narrative or drama.

After the First World War, Walter Starkie was wandering through Italy as a vagabond musician. In Palermo he teamed up with a story-teller called Michele, whose performance he describes as follows:[42]

> The lanky Michele then started to tell his story, a traditional one, like the subjects I had seen painted on the carts, for it was all about Rinaldo, Orlando, Clarice, and Bradamante, but it was not the story-telling to which I was accustomed. Rather it was a species of mono-drama in which Michele spoke and made all the gestures of a whole company of actors.
>
> He told the complicated story of the Paladins' enterprises, their battles against the Saracens, and as he became launched into the throes of the drama he intoned his voice like a priest. He moved his body up and down. He stepped forward and backwards as if he was dancing in honour of some ritual. He stamped upon the ground and

at times raised his voice into a hoarse shriek. When the battle scenes reached their height he overwhelmed the audience with a torrent of adjectives, describing the flashing of the swords and the resounding blows on the armour, the horses rolling on the plain, the heap of bleeding corpses and the cries of triumph of the Christians.

The behaviour of the rustic audience was at times as surprising as that of the rhapsodist. At moments they hung upon his words, at other moments they gave shouts of approval when the favourite Christian Paladin destroyed his enemy. Occasionally they would burst into harsh roars of laughter when the story-teller gave some humorous twist to the events. Occasionally, also, they would curse under their breath and roar their disapproval when a traitor escaped punishment for his misdeeds.

It is scenes like that that we should bear in mind when we try to reconstruct the circumstances of 'oral tradition'.

Unlike the *symposion* and the funeral praise-singer, the story-teller (in all his guises) continued long into the literate world of late-republican and imperial Rome. So when Ovid says a story comes to him by word of mouth, we should take it seriously. Tales from such sources were as much grist to his mill as were the creations of his literary predecessors.

IV

It is well known that orally transmitted stories change over time to suit the changing social context in which they are told. In the literary tradition too, as H. shows particularly well, there were many motives for embroidery and invention. So creativity of one sort or another, conscious or otherwise, was at work on the Roman stories throughout their history. All we can do is to analyse the episodes and variants known to us, and use whatever we know to try to see what date, context and purpose can most plausibly be assigned to each. And that is what B. and H. do very well.

After the introductory essay, we have an excellent account of the development of the Aeneas legend, 'corrected, expanded and updated' from H.'s contribution to the *Enciclopedia Virgiliana*. Then follows B. on Romulus and Remus, reading each episode of the story against comparative material from other societies—though the twins' respective deaths remain 'very much an enigma'. B. again, with a textual appendix by H., discusses Caeculus and the foundation of Praeneste, arguing for the incorporation of Roman elements in the story. Then comes a revised version of H.'s 1981 article on Manlius and the geese, explaining how and when the fall of the Capitol was transformed into the heroic story of a hair's-breadth escape. B. offers a convincing functional analysis of the Nonae Capratinae festival, entitled 'myth and ritual', though there is not much in it about myth. H., returning to Corythus after fifteen years,[43] deploys some new and subtle arguments to defend his identification of Dardanus' home with Tarquinia (despite Silius), and his attribution of the story of 'Tuscan Dardanus' to the *Etruscologia* of the first century BC. Finally, B. once more applies his expertise in comparative mythology, this time to account for Cybele's 'hesitation' at the Tiber mouth in 204 BC.

As one expects from such good scholars, these studies are erudite and judicious, offering little scope for the critic to carp about details. The only significant omission this reviewer noticed was the important discussion by Fritzi Jurgeit of *Cistenfüsse* from Praeneste which show a child suckled by a lioness.[44] If Jurgeit is right to identify him as Caeculus, then the parallels between the Praenestine and the Roman foundation stories are even closer than B. thinks. There may be some supporting evidence: Coarelli argues independently that an Augustan fountain decorated with reliefs of animals suckling their young was erected in Praeneste at the place where the infant Caeculus was found by girls going to the well.[45]

Jurgeit dates the *Cistenfüsse* to the late fifth century BC. That may still allow the possibility that the Praenestine foundation legend was borrowed from the Roman one. But B.'s argument from the 'vagueness' of the Caeculus story as opposed to 'the colourful Roman account' (57) seems inadequate to justify conclusions about their respective priority. As he rightly says, 'the omission of circumstantial details may be a natural result of the processes of summarizing and transmission which underlie our texts'. I see no way of guessing which story influenced the other.

On the Nonae Capratinae (83), B. refers without comment to the existence of a play on the subject;[46] similarly on Cybele (105), he mentions—but only mentions—that Ovid's story comes from a play.[47] That brings us back to the question of transmission. B. is primarily interested in the *origins* of the stories; but even so, the reader of a book on Roman myth and mythology may reasonably expect some attention to be paid to the natural meeting-point of myth and ritual in the dramatic performances of the Roman festivals.

H. regards it as significant that 'only one mime-title proves relevant, the *Anna Perenna* of Laberius' (2), ignoring the same playwright's *Caeculi* and *Gemelli*. Such titles, with Novius' Atellana *Picus* and the Qunita Claudia play referred to by Ovid, are surely enough to show that the theatrical festivals are indeed likely to be relevant to the transmission of the Roman stories.[48]

Even for the second and first centuries BC, we are pitifully ill-informed about what went on at the dramatic festivals of Rome. We happen to hear from Cicero of quasi-historical dialogues between poets and philosophers; over a century earlier, Plautus reveals that the *scurra*— both story-teller and stand-up comic—starred in public performances as well as entertaining his patrons' dinner parties.[49] When our knowledge of even the 'literate' stage is so haphazard, how are we to imagine the *ludi Romani* of the fifth and fourth centuries BC?

One thing we may be sure of: Rome knew drama before Livius Andronicus introduced Greek plays in Latin. There is no shortage of visual evidence for the performing arts in sixth- and fifth-century Etruria, and Livy's account of the Etruscan origin of Roman drama may well reflect reality, even if the precise date (364 BC) and the schematic development are no more than late-republican reconstruction. O. Szemerényi makes a strong case for deriving *scaena*, *persona*, *ludius* and *histrio* from Etruscan versions of Greek terms for stage, mask, piper and actor, which would imply a Hellenized-Etruscan form of drama at Rome long before Livius Andronicus.[50]

It is surely inconceivable that the 'Roman games' did not celebrate in some form the Romans' conception of their own origins and achievements. As an analogy, we may compare the 'ancestral' *ludi scaenici* at Patavium, supposedly inaugurated by Antenor himself, and the annual celebration at the same city of the repulse of Cleonymus in 302.[51]

Remember Cicero's comment on the sources of *opiniones*, cited above in the context of nurses' stories. His full list is 'parent, nurse, teacher, poet, *the stage*'—and for the formation of opinion it is surely immaterial whether or not the dramatic performance had a written text.

3

Monuments and the Roman Annalists

I

In book VI of Apuleius' *Metamorphoses*, the girl kidnapped by robbers—who has just listened to the old woman telling the Cupid and Psyche story—makes a desperate attempt to escape by leaping on to the back of the ass and galloping off. Unaware that Lucius can understand her words, she rehearses aloud the rewards she will give him if he brings her to safety. Among these *honores* will be a sort of triumphal procession before cheering crowds, and a *dignitas gloriosa* which she defines as follows:[1]

> I shall preserve the memory of my present fortune and the divine providence in a permanent record, and dedicate a painted picture of this escape in the *atrium* of my house. It will be looked at, and heard in stories, and perpetuated by the pens of learned authors—the simple history of 'The Princess who fled Captivity on Ass-back'.

This little episode seems to me to offer a useful model for our understanding of the annalists of the second and first centuries BC, and for the place of historiography in the value system of the Roman Republic. First comes the *res gesta*, the exploit worthy of record;[2] then the rewards for achievement, *honores* and the triumph;[3] then the *monumentum* to preserve the memory of the deed;[4] then the celebration of it by storytellers and learned historians, for the unlettered multitude and the literate élite respectively.

The role of the professional story-teller and the proximity of history-writing to fiction and the novel are important subjects which are now at last receiving proper attention,[5] but the point I want to explore here is a different one—the relation to both *fabulator* and historian alike of the *monumentum* which provided them with their material. It is clear from the train of thought in Apuleius that the primary record of the exploit would be the painting, logically prior to the *fabulae* and the *historia*.[5a] They would be interpretations of it, and not necessarily accurate interpretations either. The girl was not, after all, a princess. Her family was rich, and of high aristocracy in the locality—*domi nobilis*, certainly, but not royal.[6] The learned author's history of the *virgo regia* would evidently be based on a misinterpretation of the pictorial record, the *monumentum*.

Monuments formed an important part of the early Roman historians' material, from the so-called tomb of Romulus in the *comitium* to the *tabulae triumphales* of victorious second-century proconsuls.[7] For the regal and early-republican periods, of course, we may suspect that they were used as foundations for whatever aetiological stories they could be made to fit. The monument under the black paving-stones in the *comitium* is itself a good example: the tomb of Romulus (though not if you believed that Romulus miraculously disappeared at the *palus Capreae*); or the tomb of Faustulus, killed in the faction-fight between the supporters of Remus and Romulus; or the tomb of Hostus Hostilius, killed in the battle against the Sabines.[8] Similarly, there was a monument under white paving-stones somewhere near the Circus which was known as the Pyre of the Nine Tribunes: nine patrician ex-consuls, killed as *tribuni militum* in battle against the Volsci; or nine tribunes of the *plebs* burnt alive by their colleague P. Mucius for complicity in Sp. Cassius' attempted *coup d'état*; or nine bold tribunes 'delivered to the flames' by the populace at the secret instigation of the patricians.[9]

We cannot simply assume that accurate knowledge of the true nature of such monuments survived till the beginning of the Roman historiographical tradition—and the same may be said of such other 'documents' of early history as the tombs of the Horatii, the *tigillum sororium*, the statues of Horatius Cocles and Cloelia (or Valeria), the Column of Minucius and the *busta Gallica*.[10] The stories that accounted for them were part of the 'expansion of the past' (to borrow Badian's expressive phrase)—the elaboration into satisfying detailed 'history' of the meagre record of Rome's early past that was available to Fabius Pictor and Cincius Alimentus at the end of the third century.[11]

For events after about the time of the Samnite wars, however, the situation is different. In general, more reliable information was available, since what happened was within the memory of the fathers and grandfathers of men Fabius and Cincius could have talked to. And, in particular, the *monumenta* of the period were of a kind with which the first historians were wholly familiar. It is precisely in the generation around

300 BC—that heroic age of Roman conquest and expansion—that we see reliably manifested for the first time the familiar self-glorifying ethos of the Roman republican ruling class: in 312, with Ap. Claudius, the first road and aqueduct to be named after their originator; in 293, with Sp. Carvilius, the first self-portrait statue dedicated by a *triumphator*; in 272, with L. Papirius Cursor, the first known pictorial representation of a triumph; and so on.[12] Fabius, Cincius and their senatorial successors understood that ethos at first hand. Indeed, their own works were a part of it—*monumenta litterarum* designed, like other *monumenta*, to preserve *res gestae* from oblivion.[13]

But Fabius, Cincius and their senatorial successors are one thing; first-century, non-senatorial historians like Quadrigarius, Antias and Livy himself are quite another. *They* could quite easily make mistakes in the interpretation of monuments from the middle Republic. For instance, the existence of a statue of Africanus on the façade of the tomb of the Scipiones gave rise to the false tradition that he was buried there, and not at Liternum.[14] Inscriptions below honorific *imagines* were notoriously unreliable, as Livy complained; and we know from Cicero's correspondence that any historian who relied on the *tituli* of Q. Metellus Scipio's statues of his ancestors on the Capitol would by misled by the aristocratic dedicator's own ignorance of his family history.[15] On top of honest errors of that sort is the suspicion that the later annalists continued to use for third- and even second-century history the technique that enabled them to fill the wide open spaces of the early Republic,[16] with the result that third-century monuments which Fabius and Cincius would have understood correctly could be interpreted as 'evidence' for the late-republican historian's own irresponsible inventions.

It is against that background that I want to consider two unhistorical episodes from that important and ill-documented decade, the 260s BC. In one case the historian's invention was based, like the 'Princess on Assback', on a misinterpreted monument; in the other, it was only made possible by the disappearance of the monument that proved it false.

II

Suetonius opens his *Tiberius* with examples (three each) of the good and bad deeds of the emperor's Claudian ancestors.[17] The *egregia merita* are: first, Ap. Caecus' speech against making peace with Pyrrhus; second, Ap. Caudex's command of the first Roman army to cross to

Sicily; and third, C. Nero's defeat of Hasdrubal at the Metaurus. The *sequius admissa* begin with Appius the Decemvir's attempt to make Verginia his slave, and conclude with P. Claudius Pulcher's treatment of the sacred chickens; between those two, however, comes a very mysterious item:

> Claudius †Drusus† statua sibi diademata ad Appi Forum posita Italiam per clientelas occupare temptavit.
>
> Caecus, *Mommsen*; Crassus, *Hirschfeld*; Rusus, *Fruin (potius* Russus, *Ihm)*.
>
> Claudius Drusus[?] set up a diademed statue of himself at Forum Appi, and attempted to take possession of Italy through his clients.

Both lists are in chronological order, so 'Claudius Drusus' must antedate the consulship of P. Claudius Pulcher in 249. Mommsen's suggestion is surely ruled out by the presence of Caecus in the list of good Claudii, while that of Hirschfeld is hard to reconcile with the placing of the statue at Forum Appi: the 'forum' presupposes the road on which it was founded (Via Appia, 312 BC), while the *cognomen* Crassus is only attested for Claudii of the fifth century and the first half of the fourth.[18] The Fruin/Ihm solution is clearly preferable: 'Russus' as the *cognomen* of Ap. Claudius (*cos.* 268), already attested by the 'Chronographer of AD 354', was confirmed in 1925 by the discovery of the relevant part of the Augustan consular *fasti*,[19] and the corruption to Drusus—a name which appears frequently in the *Tiberius*—is a particularly easy one to explain.

Ap. Claudius Russus was Appius Caecus' eldest son, consul in 268 with P. Sempronius Sophus. Both men celebrated triumphs over the Picentes (attested in the *fasti triumphales*), but Claudius died soon after—probably right at the end of the year, since no suffect was elected.[20] The defeat of the Picentes was practically the final stage in the Roman conquest of cis-Apennine Italy.[21] It is true that the Sallentini in the far south-east remained (they were dealt with the following year), but it must have been tempting for the consuls of 268 to claim the credit of having brought all of Italy under Roman control.

One of them at least evidently did so. Sempronius vowed the temple of Tellus during his campaign, and presumably built it *ex manubiis* after his triumph. In it, there was a map of Italy painted on the wall.[22] The known parallels—Ti. Gracchus' map of Sardinia in the Mater Matuta temple, and the plan of Carthage exhibited in the *forum Romanum* by L. Mancinus—strongly suggest that the map was not mere decoration, but meant as visual evidence of the founder's *gloria*.[23]

Claudius Russus died before he could create a similar *monumentum*, but his statue was set up where his father's memory lived on most strongly: Appius' *forum* on Appius' road. It is reasonable to suppose that he was portrayed in triumphal costume, and as certain as can be that the inscription on the base made the most of his achievements. We may compare the *elogium* of T. Annius on the base of the statue set up at Forum Anni on *his* road, or that of Sempronius Tuditanus below his statue at Aquileia, presumably copied from the *tabula triumphalis* dedicated on the Capitol;[24] the tombs of Scipio Barbatus and his son show that a third-century version could be just as boastful as these second-century ones. It was only ten years since old Appius' speech of defiance to Pyrrhus' envoy; the Claudii had plenty to be proud about, and might well have emphasized the completion of the conquest of Italy by Russus' triumph, just as his colleague evidently did on the walls of the temple of Tellus. Did some such phrase as *tota Italia occupata* occur on the statue-base of Claudius Russus?

According to Suetonius, the statue was *diademata*. The *diadema*, a white head-band tied at the back, was the symbol of kingship in the Hellenistic world ever since Alexander took it over along with the rest of the apparatus of the Persian monarchy.[25] Most conspicuous, and clearly visible on the coins of all the rulers of the Successor kingdoms, were the two ends behind the knot, that hung, or floated like streamers, over the neck and shoulders of the king.[26]

By the time of the late Republic, the *diadema* was retrospectively attributed to the kings of Rome, but there is no evidence—or likelihood—that this idea predates the second century BC.[27] Similarly, Dionysius I of Syracuse is credited with a *diadema* only in the context of the posturings of Hieronymus in 215 BC; a century earlier the worst that could be said of him was that he wore a golden *stephanos*.[28] So I am sure Weinstock was wrong to take Suetonius' report literally.[29] Even if one could believe in an early-third-century attempt at *regnum*, the symbol of that aspiration would not be a *diadema*. Whatever Claudius Russus' statue was crowned with, it wasn't that.

Crowns and wreaths could signify many things in the early and middle Republic,[30] but in the case of Claudius Russus there is no need to look further than the symbols of the triumph. It was precisely in this period, as we should expect, that the ceremony and trappings of the triumph took on their classic form, as the glorification of the *triumphator* to an all but superhuman level.[31] Prominent among those trappings were the laurel-wreath worn by the *triumphator*, and the gold-leafed *corona Etrusca* held above his head by the slave whose duty it was to repeat the apotropaic formula 'hominem te esse memento' ('remember that you are human').[32] It would be reasonable to expect that Russus was portrayed wearing one or other of these.

Any wreath or garland could be made more honorific by the addition of *lemnisci*, coloured ribbons binding the leaves or flowers.[33] In particular, they were attached to the victor's laurel-wreath, hanging from it like streamers: the coins of the Roman Republic show many examples of the laurel-wreath, usually in the hands of Victory, with the two *lemnisci* fluttering below.[34] (The *corona Etrusca* was decorated in the same way, though for that the 'ribbons' were of gold leaf.)[35] The earliest representation we have is almost contemporary with Russus' statue, and an illustration of precisely the ideological value-system that caused it to be set up. At some date between 265 and 242 BC the Romans minted silver didrachms with a superb reverse design of Victory attaching a wreath to a palm-branch [fig. iii]; the goddess is hanging the wreath by its *lemnisci*, two long ribbons which would be floating out behind the wearer's neck and shoulders if the wreath were on a *triumphator*'s head.[36]

We do not know what Russus' statue was made of (presumably bronze or terracotta); nor what condition it was in when it was seen by the historian Suetonius used; nor how high it stood on its base, and how visible were the details of its headgear. But it is a natural and obvious conjecture that the unknown historian misinterpreted the ribbons of a triumphal crown or laurel-wreath as the ends of a *diadema*. The colour is important: a *diadema* was white, and *lemnisci* were brightly coloured (or gold).[37] If the statue was painted clay, the colours might well have faded away after two hundred years or so. If it was bronze, or if its crown at least was metal, there would be no way of distinguishing the type of ribbon intended.

But surely anyone could tell the difference between a wreath of laurels (or a crown of gilded leaves) and a plain headband? Perhaps it was not as simple as that. At the Lupercalia in 44 BC, the *diadema* Antony offered Caesar was not just a plain headband, but 'a diadem twined in a wreath of laurel'.[38] Evidently you could have something that looked like an innocent laurel-wreath but incorporated a diadem, presumably in the form of white binding ribbons. A few days earlier, Caesar's statue

Figure iii
Roman silver didrachm, mid-third century BC. The goddess of Victory (Greek Nike, Roman Victoria) attaches a laurel-wreath to a palm-branch by its ribbons (*lemnisci*). The temple of Victory on the Palatine (p. 105 below) was dedicated in 294 BC. [Photo by courtesy of the British Museum.]

had been crowned with a 'corona laurea *candida fascia* praeligata'; the tribunes Marullus and Flavus had no objection to the laurel-wreath itself, but demanded the removal of the white binding and imprisoned the man who had put it there.[39] People evidently looked with care at these symbolic objects, interpreting the significance of every detail. And that no doubt applied as much to Pompey in the fifties as to Caesar in the forties; then too honorific crowns and quasi-diadems were among the signs that might indicate a coming *regnum*.[40]

My guess is that at some time in the fifties or forties BC, when such matters were much on people's minds, the old triumphal statue of Ap. Claudius Russus was misinterpreted—wilfully, I imagine—by a historian anxious to find one more episode in the brutal and arrogant story of the patrician Claudii. The abuse of *clientela* was a commonplace in that story;[41] with the help, perhaps, of an ambiguous phrase in the *elogium* beneath the statue, all he had to do was see the ends of a *diadema* in the *lemnisci* of Russus' wreath or crown, and he could produce the dramatic episode of which Suetonius' sentence is the one surviving echo.

I think it is likely that the whole tradition of *superbia Claudiana* was created by a historian writing at precisely that period.[42] Whether or not that is accepted, I hope at least to have shown that the *statua diademata* at Forum Appi is not a historical but a historiographical phenomenon. Like the girl in the story of the escape on ass-back, Russus is given royal rank through the misreading of his *monumentum*.

III

In 264 BC, the consuls were Ap. Claudius C.f. Caudex and M. Fulvius Q.f. Flaccus. Claudius was famous in Roman history for being the first to lead a Roman army overseas, in the opening campaign of the First Punic War.[43] Fulvius continued the war against the 'slaves' of Volsinii after the previous Roman commander's death from wounds; he besieged the city and took it, bringing back 2,000 bronze statues in his booty.[44] He triumphed *de Vulsiniensibus* on 1 November, and the temple of Vertumnus was his triumphal *monumentum*.[45]

Excavation at the S. Omobono site in 1961 revealed the remains of a circular base in peperino, evidently intended to display some of the statues. The inscription on it reads 'M. FOLV[IO. Q.F. COS]OL. D. VOLSI[NIO. CAP]TO'.[46] Like the two peperino altars on either side of it, it originally stood on level 4 in the stratigraphic series, a pavement of thick blocks of Monteverde tufa, but was demolished and its pieces used in the laying of level 5, a pavement of thin slabs of the same stone.[47] The great podium that was raised after the destruction of the archaic temple(s) on the site—on which the twin temples of Fortuna and Mater Matuta were built—may have been paved first in *cappellaccio* (level 3), unless this was merely a foundation for the tufa-block pavement.[48] At any rate, Fulvius' inscription now gives 264 BC as a firm *terminus ante quem* for the latter.

Much more interesting is the fact that level 5, which buried the remains of Fulvius' monument, must be dated to the reconstruction programme begun in 212, after the disastrous fire the previous year which ravaged the whole area from Salinae to the Porta Carmentalis and destroyed the twin temples.[49] The consuls of 212 were Q. Fulvius Flaccus (for the third time) and Ap. Claudius Pulcher, respectively son and great-nephew of the consuls of 264; they had been elected under the dictatorship of C. Claudius Cento (*cos.* 240), who was Claudius' uncle and had just named Fulvius as his *magister equitum*; Fulvius' brother Gnaeus was elected praetor at the same time.[50] The following stemmata show the essential relationships:

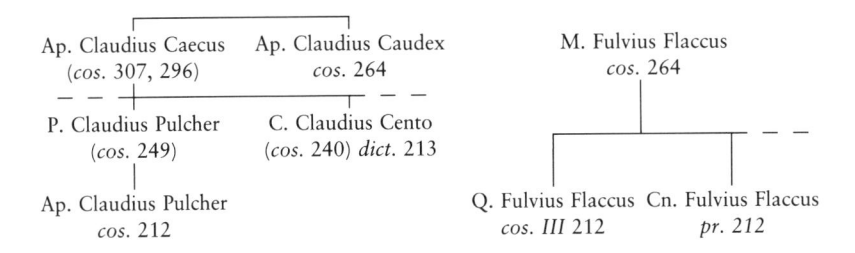

```
┌────────────────────┬────────────────────┐              M. Fulvius Flaccus
Ap. Claudius Caecus    Ap. Claudius Caudex              cos. 264
  (cos. 307, 296)           cos. 264                          │
– – –┼– – – – – – – – – – –┤                            ┌─────┴─────┐– – –
P. Claudius Pulcher    C. Claudius Cento                │           │
    (cos. 249)         (cos. 240) dict. 213      Q. Fulvius Flaccus   Cn. Fulvius Flaccus
       │                                            cos. III 212         pr. 212
Ap. Claudius Pulcher
    cos. 212
```

The bronze statues on M. Flaccus' *monumentum* were presumably destroyed in the fire; all the same, it is striking that so powerful a figure as his eldest son, now in his third consulship, failed to replace it and allowed it to be completely dismantled and buried under the new pavement. It cannot have been anything but a blow to the *dignitas* of the Fulvian house. Perhaps the explanation lies in the defeat of the praetor Cn. Fulvius Flaccus by Hannibal in Apulia that year. His brother the consul was busy with the siege of Capua at the time—it was Appius who returned to conduct the elections—and in his absence the *triumviri* entrusted with the job of rebuilding the temples may not have felt it necessary to replace the Fulvian monument.[51]

'Alas, how difficult is the protection of glory!' That *sententia* of Publilius Syrus finds another such example, I think, in the *area sacra* of the Largo Argentina: A. Postumius Albinus' beautifully inscribed altar, erected in front of the temple of Feronia at some time in the second half of the second century BC, was covered over by L. Minucius Rufus in 106 with the paving of his triumphal monument, the Porticus Minucia; four years earlier an A. Albinus had been humiliatingly defeated by Jugurtha, so the dedicator and his family were in no position to protest.[52] Later examples of the destruction of *monumenta* are more familiar: for instance Sulla's removal of the trophies of Marius from the

Capitol, or Clodius' demolition of the Porticus Catuli on the Palatine in order to build a shrine to Libertas on the site, or the senatorial proposal in AD 41 to abolish the memory of the Julii Caesares by pulling down their temples.[53]

It is a pity that we do not know who the *triumviri* were who dealt this blow to the prestige of the Fulvii in 212 BC. Nor do we know what Q. Flaccus' consular colleague Ap. Claudius thought about it. There is no hint of rivalry between them in Livy's narrative on the campaigns of 212/11; on the other hand, there are indications that at some point in the annalistic tradition an attempt was made to exalt Appius at Flaccus' expense. Livy's story of the execution of the Campanian prisoners after the fall of Capua shows clearly that at least one of his sources had made a great melodramatic scene out of Flaccus' brutality, either contrasting it with Appius' moderation or making it happen only after Appius' death from his wound.[54] (It is also clear from Silius Italicus—and an echo in Livy—that there was one version which emphasized Appius' heroism in the engagement that led to his death.)[55] In the light of these indications it is worth looking at a curious passage in the anonymous work *De viris illustribus* on the war against the Volsinian 'slaves' in 264:[55a]

> 36 Vulsinii, Etruriae nobile oppidum, luxuria paene perierunt. nam cum temere servos manumitterent, dein in curiam legerent, consensu eorum oppressi. cum multa indigna paterentur, clam a Roma auxilium petierunt, missusque Decius Mus libertinos omnes aut in carcere necavit aut dominis in servitutem restituit. 37 Appius Claudius victis Vulsiniensibus cognomento Caudex dictus frater Caeci fuit. consul ad Mamertinos liberandos missus . . . [etc.]

> (36) Volsinii, a famous city of Etruria, almost perished as a result of its extravagance. For when it rashly freed the slaves, and then admitted them to the senate, it was overwhelmed by their unanimity. After suffering many indignities, it sought help secretly from Rome. Decius Mus was sent, and either killed all the freed slaves in prison or restored them to the servitude of their masters. (37) After the victory over Volsinii, Appius Claudius, brother of Caecus, was given the nickname 'Caudex'. As consul he was sent to liberate the Mamertines . . . [etc.]

I think the modern section numbers are misleading in treating the first three sentences as a separate item on Decius Mus, presumably the consul of 279. He is given no *praenomen*, his command against Pyrrhus at the battle of Ausculum is not mentioned, and no cross-reference is made, as would be expected, to his father and grandfather, already dealt with in sections 26 and 27.[56] On the other hand, several items in the collection begin not with the name of the protagonist, but with an introductory passage setting the scene for his exploits.[57] In the case of Ap. Claudius Caudex, the explanation of his *cognomen*—one of the author's favourite themes[58]—requires just such a preliminary account of the punishment of the Volsinienses. For a *caudex* was the log of wood to which imprisoned slaves were shackled.[59]

The word also meant 'blockhead',[60] which is perhaps more in character with Roman habits of bestowing *cognomina*. It may be that the association of Appius with the capture of Volsinii—and the consequent misdating of that event to before his consulship—was the work of a historian anxious to find a more honorific explanation of the name.[61] Certainly the *res gestae* of both Ap. Caudex and Decius Mus were narrated and interpreted in widely differing terms by different annalists. Was it Caudex or M'. Valerius Maximus (*cos*. 263) who defeated King Hiero of Syracuse and celebrated a triumph for it?[62] Did Decius Mus imitate the example of his father and grandfather by sacrificing himself on the field of Ausculum, or at least announce that he would, in order to damage the morale of Pyrrhus' troops?[63] Such questions, and the answers that could be offered to them, clearly mattered to the historians of the second and first centuries BC, and to their readers, who included the descendants of the great men themselves.

What matters here is that Decius Mus and Ap. Caudex get the credit for what was really M. Fulvius Flaccus' achievement. The Fulvii certainly had some dramatic ups and downs: Cn. Flaccus' defeat in 212 BC, M. Nobilior's triumph from Aetolia in 189 and his censorship ten years later, the execution of M. Flaccus and his son after the Gracchan *seditio* of 121, and the power and influence of Fulvia in the late forties as the wife of Antony. There is no difficulty in imagining a context in which a historian might wish to take M. Flaccus' *res gesta* away from him and give it to someone else. The point that concerns us here, however, is that the destruction of the *monumentum* itself must have made it much easier for the false version to gain currency, and much more difficult for the Fulvii to nail the lie.[64]

And yet—we must remember the *virgo regia* and the diademed statue. It is possible that even if M. Flaccus' *monumentum* had survived, the malicious ingenuity of a hostile historian might have found a way to misinterpret it as meaning something quite different.

IV

Malice is not at all an inappropriate concept to invoke when considering the motivation of first-century historians. The circumstantial evidence for it is abundant, and there is one example that happens to be explicitly attested: the allegation in Theophanes of treasonable correspondence between P. Rutilius Rufus and Mithridates.[65] We can be sure that some at least of Theophanes' Roman contemporaries, who were quite familiar with the standards of Hellenistic historiography,[66] were capable of equally unscrupulous invention if it suited their purpose.

As we saw at the beginning, works of historiography were *monumenta litterarum*, designed like other *monumenta* to preserve the glory of great deeds. But the corollary of glory is rivalry and *invidia*. When a historian attacked the record of such deeds, by attributing them to others or turning them into criminal acts (like the occupation of Italy *per clientelas*), that was simply the equivalent of defacing or destroying the physical monument of a rival *triumphator*. Glory could be preserved in words as well as in stone or bronze, and attacked as effectively by the pen as by the pickaxe.

4

Lucretius, Catiline, and the Survival of Prophecy

I

From the very beginning, says Cicero in the introduction to his code of laws, we must convince our citizens of this: the gods control everything; whatever happens, happens by their will; they observe each man's character and behaviour, and take note of the pious and the impious. Such beliefs are both true and useful. True, according to the Stoic belief in a rational and beneficent universe; useful, because they sanction oaths, treaties and lawful behaviour. Just think how many people are saved from committing crimes by the fear of divine punishment.[1]

Despite this passage, and many others which could be quoted,[2] it is widely believed that the gods of the Romans were indifferent to moral behaviour and cared only for ritual. Ogilvie's forthright statement of that view ('Roman religion was concerned with success not with sin') was challenged, rightly in my view, by Liebeschuetz; but even he inferred from our surviving sources that 'fear of divine displeasure was very rarely a motive when a Roman decided on a course of action whether in a public or a private capacity'.[3] Wardman, ignoring Liebeschuetz, endorsed the Ogilvie view ('the tie between gods and men was formed by results, the success which requires certain practical virtues, not by the attempt or intention to be virtuous'), and Beard and Crawford agree; they find Liebeschuetz's defence of the relevance of morality 'ultimately unconvincing'.[4]

I should like to draw attention to two items which have not yet, I think, been exploited in this debate. One of them (Lucretius I 62–111) is very well known—indeed, it is one of the greatest passages in the whole of Latin literature. The other (Dionysius of Halicarnassus V 53–8) is an obscure and patently unhistorical episode which may nevertheless cast light on Roman attitudes in the first century BC.

II

First, the Lucretius:[4a]

Humana ante oculos foede cum vita iaceret	I 62
in terris oppressa gravi sub religione	
quae caput a caeli regionibus ostendebat	
horribili super aspectu mortalibus instans,	65
primum Graius homo mortalis tollere contra	
est oculos ausus primusque obsistere contra,	
quem neque fama deum nec fulmina nec minitanti	
murmure compressit caelum, sed eo magis acrem	
irritat animi virtutem, effringere ut arta	70
naturae primus portarum claustra cupiret.	
ergo vivida vis animi pervicit, et extra	
processit longe flammantia moenia mundi	
atque omne immensum peragravit mente animoque,	
unde refert nobis victor quid possit oriri,	75
quid nequeat, finita potestas denique cuique	
quanam sit ratione atque alte terminus haerens.	
quare religio pedibus subiecta vicissim	
obteritur, nos exaequat victoria caelo.	
Illud in his rebus vereor, ne forte rearis	80
impia te rationis inire elementa viamque	
indugredi sceleris. Quod contra saepius illa	
religio peperit scelerosa atque impia facta.	
Aulide quo pacto Triviai virginis aram	
Iphianassai turparunt sanguine foede	85
doctores Danaum delecti, prima virorum.	
cui simul infula virgineos circumdata comptus	
ex utraque pari malarum parte profusast,	
et maestum simul ante aras adstare parentem	
sensit et hunc propter ferrum celare ministros	90
aspectuque suo lacrimas effundere civis,	
muta metu terram genibus summissa petebat.	
nec miserae prodesse in tali tempore quibat	
quod patrio princeps donarat nomine regem.	

```
nam sublata virum manibus tremibundaque ad aras      95
deductast, non ut sollemni more sacrorum
perfecto posset claro comitari Hymenaeo,
sed casta inceste nubendi tempore in ipso
hostia concideret mactatu maesta parentis,
exitus ut classi felix faustusque daretur.          100
tantum religio potuit suadere malorum.
   Tutemet a nobis iam quovis tempore *vatum*
terriloquis victus dictis desciscere quaeres.
quippe etenim quam multa tibi iam fingere possunt
somnia quae vitae rationes vertere possint          105
fortunasque tuas omnis turbare timore!
et merito. nam si certam finem esse viderent
aerumnarum homines, aliqua ratione valerent
religionibus atque minis obsistere *vatum*.
nunc ratio nulla est restandi, nulla facultas,      110
aeternas quoniam poenas in morte timendumst.
```

When human life lay grovelling in all men's sight, crushed to the earth under the dead weight of superstition whose grim features loured menacingly upon mortals from the four quarters of the sky, a man of Greece was first to raise mortal eyes in defiance, first to stand erect and brave the challenge. Fables of the gods did not crush him, nor the lightning flash and the growling menace of the sky. Rather, they quickened his manhood, so that he, first of all men, longed to smash the constraining locks of nature's doors. The vital vigour of his mind prevailed. He ventured far out beyond the flaming ramparts of the world and voyaged in mind throughout infinity. Returning victorious, he proclaimed to us what can be and what cannot: how a limit is fixed to the power of everything and an immovable frontier post. Therefore superstition in its turn lies crushed beneath his feet, and we by his triumph are lifted level with the skies.

One thing that worries me is the fear that you may fancy yourself embarking on an impious course, setting your feet on the path of sin. Far from it. More often it is this very superstition that is the mother of sinful and impious deeds. Remember how at Aulis the altar of the Virgin Goddess was foully stained with the blood of Iphigeneia by the leaders of the Greeks, the patterns of chivalry. The headband was about her virgin tresses and hung down evenly over both her cheeks. Suddenly she caught sight of her father standing sadly in front of the altar, the attendants beside him hiding the knife and her people bursting into tears when they saw her. Struck dumb with terror, she sank on her knees to the ground. Poor girl, at such a moment it did not help her that she had been first to give the name of father to a king. Raised by the hands of men, she was led trembling to the altar. Not for her the sacrament of marriage and the loud chant of Hymen. It was her fate in the very hour of marriage to fall a sinless victim to a sinful rite, slaughtered to her greater grief by a father's hand, so that a fleet might sail under happy auspices. Such are the heights of wickedness to which men are driven by superstition.

You yourself, if you surrender your judgement at any time to the blood-curdling declamations of the *prophets*, will want to desert our ranks. Only think what phantoms they can conjure up to overturn the tenor of your life and wreck your happiness with fear. And not without cause. For, if men saw that a term was set to their troubles, they would find strength in some way to withstand the hocus-pocus and intimidations of the *prophets*. As it is, they have no power of resistance, because they are haunted by the fear of eternal punishment after death.

Who or what are the 'prophets' (*vates*)? They represent *religio*, as is clear from the cross-references: *vita* 62/105, *religio(nes)* 63/109, *obsistere* 67/109, *minitanti/minis* 68/109. Religion looms over human life like a thundery sky; the terrifying words of the *vates* threaten punishment after death for what they call *scelus* and *impia facta*; only Epicurus, or those possessed of his *ratio*, have the power to resist, and show where the true *scelus* lies.

Philip Hardie describes the *vates* as 'religious quacks', but that is to trivialize them. His later formulation is more to the point: 'spokesmen of traditional religion . . . leaders and manipulators of society.'[5] But we know Lucretius' society—the world of late-republican Rome—better than any other period in ancient history; where do these men belong in it? What sort of people, in the fifties BC, were preaching hell-fire for sinners?

Before we attempt an answer, let us see if we can hear their threatening sermons a little more clearly. Hardie draws attention to a later passage which is clearly relevant, at the beginning of book V.[6] Lucretius is going to prove that the universe is mortal, and will one day end 'in a hideous crash':

>   Qua prius aggrediar quam de re fundere fata   V 110
>   sanctius et multo certa ratione magis quam
>   Pythia quae tripode a Phoebi lauroque profatur,

> multa tibi expediam doctis solacia dictis;
> religione refrenatus ne forte rearis
> terras et solem et caelum, mare sidera lunam,   115
> corpore divino debere aeterna manere,
> proptereaque putes ritu par esse Gigantum
> pendere eos poenas immani pro scelere omnis
> qui ratione sua disturbent moenia mundi
> praeclarumque velint caeli restinguere solem   120
> immortalia mortali sermone notantes.

Before I attempt to utter oracles on this theme, with more sanctity and far surer reason than those the Delphic prophetess pronounces, drugged by the laurel fumes from Apollo's tripod, I will first set your mind at rest with words of wisdom. Do not imagine, under the spell of superstition, that lands and sun and sky, sea, stars and moon, must endure for ever because they are endowed with a divine body. Do not for that reason think it right that punishment appropriate to a monstrous crime should be imposed, as on the rebellious Titans, on all those who by their reasoning breach the ramparts of the world and seek to darken heaven's brightest luminary, the sun, belittling with mortal speech immortal beings.

The reference to the Pythia reminds us of the *vates* (the same two lines are used of the prophet-poet Empodocles at I 738–9);[7] the word-play of *religione refrenatus* (114) is reminiscent of [*superstitio*] *super instans* at I 65;[8] *moenia mundi* (119), a favourite Lucretian phrase,[9] appeared first at I 73; and the key words *poenae*, *scelus* and *ratio* (118–9) are repeated from I 81–2 and 111.[10]

It seems clear enough that in the idiom of the *vates*, those who use their reason to defy religious orthodoxy are like the impious Giants who dared to attack the gods;[11] and like the Giants, they will suffer eternal punishment for it in Hades. For a good Epicurean, the Giants were just fantasy, no more than shapes in the cloud (IV 136f.). But the rest of humanity had no defence against these 'nightmares' conjured up by the *vates*,[12] and the very vehemence of Lucretius' polemic is evidence for their impact.

What Lucretius gives us is the obverse of Cicero's argument in the *De legibus*. If the citizens are to believe in the gods' power, so that they will act virtuously from fear of it, they must be told what will happen if they do not. The *vates* may be mysterious to us, hard to identify in the late-republican world we know, but at least they have an intelligible role.

III

In the ninth year after the expulsion of the kings, which he defines as the seventieth Olympiad,[13] Dionysius of Halicarnassus reports a conspiracy at Rome. A large number of slaves, he says, plotted to seize the heights and set fire to the city, but information was given to the consuls, the strong-points of the city were occupied by the *equites*, the ringleaders were arrested, tortured, and put to death by impalement.[14]

The following year was the consulship of Ser. Sulpicius and M'. Tullius, on which Livy comments 'nothing worth mentioning happened'. Dionysius however, this time at much greater length, reports a second conspiracy.[15] The exiled Tarquin plots with his son-in-law Octavius Mamilius of Tusculum to stir up a civil war in Rome. Their agents exploit popular discontent at the debt crisis and the brutality of creditors; but besides the free poor, slaves are again involved. Again, the plan is to seize the heights; again, information betrays the plot; again, the *equites* are stationed at the strategic points; this time the guilty are executed by the sword.[16] Whether or not this conspiracy is merely a doublet of the first, it is abundantly clear that both of them are late inventions, based on the events of 63-2 BC.[17]

The parallels are obvious. One particular detail, for instance, is the complaint of the free debtors at being chained and beaten like slaves, exactly as C. Manlius complained to Q. Marcius Rex in 63.[18] Another is the Senate's reaction to the consul's report of his information: full authority (*exousia autokratōr*) to discover and punish the offenders, just like the *senatus consultum ultimum* of October 63.[19] Even the aftermath of the Catilinarian affair is reflected, as Ser. Sulpicius the consul avoids the 'harsh and tyrannical' measures which earned Cicero his reputation for *regnum*.[20]

That last detail is very revealing. Dionysius explains at length, as an explicit example of the value of history to statesmen,[21] how Sulpicius took care to have the conspirators apprehended in the forum with maximum publicity, how he summoned the entire populace to a dawn assembly and got the Senate's decree for execution ratified by the Roman People before it was carried out.[22] All that was done with the deliberate intention of avoiding civil bloodshed;[23] Cicero's policy in 63, by contrast, had alienated the populace and failed to avoid civil war.[24]

Both the consuls of '500 BC' had names that were very familiar to an audience in the first century, and it is striking that the hero of Dionysius' narrative is Ser. Sulpicius. His colleague Tullius is not disparaged (he brings his army from the siege of Fidenae), but a detail at the end suggests that Dionysius' source may have been more hostile: at the *ludi Romani* after the suppression of the conspiracy, M'. Tullius falls from the sacred chariot and dies three days later. It looks as if some historian deliberately recast the story of the Catilinarian conspiracy in such a way that M. Tullius Cicero would get no reflected credit.[25] The chronological context was probably the triumviral period, when Cicero was reviled as a traitor. The identity of the historian can be guessed: Dionysius' friend Q. Aelius Tubero, whose father-in-law was the jurist Ser. Sulpicius Rufus, unsuccessful candidate for the consulship of 62 BC.[26]

IV

With that analysis completed, we can turn to the second of our passages on Roman religion. It is at the point in Dionysius' narrative where the quasi-Catilinarian conspiracy is betrayed to the consul (V 54.1–3):

> But the divine providence which protects the city at every crisis, and endures down to my own time, uncovered their plans when information was given to Sulpicius, one of the consuls. It was provided by two brothers, P. Tarquinius and M. Tarquinius from the city of Laurentum, who were very prominent in the membership of the conspiracy.
>
> They were forced to it by divine compulsion,[27] for whenever they slept, horrifying dream visions threatened them with great punishments if they did not stop and abandon their attempt; they ended up believing that demons were beating them, gouging out their eyes, and inflicting many other horrors on them. These things kept them in panic fear and trembling while awake, and they could not sleep because of the terror of them.
>
> At first they tried to beg for release from the demons' persecution of them by certain apotropaic and remedial sacrifices. When that failed they turned to *manteia*, keeping secret the purpose of their enterprise and asking only to know whether it was yet the right time to do what they had in mind. But the *mantis* replied that they were travelling a road of wickedness and ruin: unless they reversed their intentions they would suffer a most dishonourable death. Afraid that someone else would get in first and bring the secret to light, they themselves informed the consul who was in Rome.

I have left *mantis* untranslated. If, as is likely, Dionysius was using a Latin source here, it probably represents *vates*, as in Lucretius. Certainly there are noticeable similarities with the Lucretius: 'Travelling a road of wickedness and ruin' is very close to *viam indugredi sceleris* (I 81f.),[28] and the demon-ridden nightmares were indeed *somnia quae vitae rationes vertere possint* (I 105). So I think it is reasonable to infer that in this passage—supposedly about an event in the tenth year of the Republic, but in reality a thinly disguised piece of contemporary history—we can see in action the same arbiters of moral and religious orthodoxy against whom Lucretius directed his contempt and indignation.

I suppose it is just conceivable that Tubero, or whoever the author was, included this passage as something appropriate only to the distant past and not to his own time. But the late-republican annalists were not given to historicism; on the contrary, their inventions and elaborations were dependent on the assumption that the distant past was like their own time, and could be recreated in its terms.[29] So are we to believe that even in the cynical days of the late Republic, unscrupulous and power-hungry men could really be deterred from crime, as Cicero puts it, by the fear of divine punishment? Our triumviral historian seems to indicate that the idea was not an absurd one. And Dionysius, a serious author for all his shortcomings, evidently assumes that it will be of value for the *politikoi* among his readers.[30]

It is worth remembering that Sallust's analysis of Catiline's character emphasizes *flagitia, facinora, culpa, nefas* and *scelus*; like the Tarquinii in Dionysius' narrative, he could not free himself from the torments of conscience either awake or asleep.[31] Moreover, the question of divine punishment was explicitly addressed in the senatorial debate on the conspirators. Caesar argued that death was no punishment since it puts an end to misery, an Epicurean view attacked by both Cato and Cicero as a rejection of traditional teaching:[32]

> ... credo falsa existumans ea quae de inferis memorantur, divorso itinere malos a bonis loca taetra inculta, foeda atque formidulosa habere.
>
> Itaque ut aliqua in vita formido improbis esset proposita, apud inferos eius modi quaedam illi antiqui supplicia impiis constituta esse voluerunt.
>
> ... disbelieving, I suppose, the account that is given of the underworld, that the wicked go a different way from the good, and inhabit places that are dreadful and desolate, foul and terrifying.

It was in order that the wicked might have something to fear in this life that the men of old believed that certain punishments of that sort were appointed for the impious in the underworld.

There is no reason to suppose that the senators thought the issue irrelevant to their deliberations.

V

It would be worth knowing how Cicero in his epic *De consulatu suo*, with its elaborate mythological apparatus,[33] dealt with the conspirators' posthumous fate. On the shield in *Aeneid* VIII, a glimpse into the underworld shows two figures—Cato giving judgements among the pious, like Minos in the *Odyssey*, and Catiline hanging tormented by the Furies, like the rebellious Giants in the theodicy of the Lucretian *vates*.[34] In Lucan's necromantic Tartarus, one of the effects of the news of civil war was that Catiline had broken his chains, and with the other great revolutionaries of Roman history was hoping to seize the Elysian Fields.[35] Where does this notion come from, of Catiline as one of the great sinners, the Roman equivalent of Tityos and the Giants? Surely from Cicero's epic, which before greater poets overshadowed it was a famous and influential work.[36]

In the first century BC, as in the fifth, the poets were used as guides to morality; Horace's view on the ethical value of Homer was essentially the same as Xenophon's.[37] Moreover, Diodorus is explicit that it was the poet's 'invented myths' of Hades that caused men to act with piety and justice.[38] So if Cicero did put Catiline in Hades, it was no doubt as a moral deterrent, like the example of the Giants used by the *vates* in Lucretius.

At this point we must be careful to avoid confusion. Virgil and Lucan both call themselves *vates*,[39] but the Augustan appropriation of the word to mean 'inspired poet' probably goes back no further than Varro.[40] For Cicero, as for Plautus and Ennius, *vates* means 'prophet', whether inspired or fraudulent, and I believe the same is true for Lucretius as well.[41]

There was a long history of inter-relation between the poet and the prophet, and it is likely that at some very early stage of Greek culture they were identical.[42] Certain types of archaic poetry—for example Hesiodic wisdom literature, the Orphic poems, the *Katharmoi* of Empedocles—certainly imply a poet who is very similar to a *mantis*, if not identical.[43] In Homer, however, the *mantis* and the *aoidos* are separate examples of experts (*dēmioergoi*) who are welcome in the community, and Demodocus and Theoclymenus clearly practise different—if related—skills.[44]

Progressive specialization separated the prophet from the poet, but the poets continued to exploit the common ground,[45] and both professions claimed to offer guidance on questions of ethics and eschatology. It was a soothsayer, Diopeithes, who proposed the decree against atheists that forced Anaxagoras out of Athens;[46] it was a tragic poet, Critias, who put the rationalist view of belief in the gods into the mouth of Sisyphus, one of the famous sinners punished in Hades.[47]

It is easy to see why Varro was tempted to combine the concepts of *vates* and *poeta*, and why the Augustans took over *vates* as their standard term for an inspired poet. But it is not helpful to apply that concept to the Lucretian *vates*; the Dionysius passage suggests that they were *manteis* in the proper sense, more like Diopeithes than Critias.

VI

But were there such *manteis* at Rome? In his brilliant chapter in the new *Cambridge Ancient History*, John North identifies the absence of prophets and holy men as one of the defining characteristics of Roman religion.[48] Elsewhere, he puts the point more cautiously: 'It cannot be assumed that no great prophets or holy men ever existed in Republican Rome, though there is no serious evidence that they did.'[49] I am not sure what would count as 'greatness' in this context; for prophets in general, however, the serious evidence is, in fact, surprisingly plentiful.

The obvious place to look is in Cicero's dialogue *De divinatione*,[50] where the subject is defined in the first sentence as *mantikē*. The Romans themselves, remarks Cicero in his preface, have embraced many different types of divination, not only the *artes* of augury and haruspicy but also prophecy by direct inspiration (and its near relative, the prophetic dream):

> Et cum duobus modis animi sine ratione et scientia motu ipsi suo soluto et libero incitarentur, uno furente, altero somniante, furoris divinationem Sibyllinis maxime versibus contineri arbitrari eorum decem interpretes delectos e civitate esse voluerunt. ex quo genere saepe hariolorum etiam et vatum furibundas praedictiones, ut Octaviano bello Cornelii Culleoli, audiendas putaverunt.

> And since there are two ways—frenzy and dreams—in which minds are inspired by their own free and unchecked impulse without any rational knowledge, [our ancestors] considered that the divination of frenzy was preserved above all in the Sibyl's verses, and it was their will that there should be ten interpreters of them chosen from the citizen body. Also in that category were the frenzied prophecies of soothsayers and prophets which they often thought worth hearing, such as those of Cornelius Culleolus during the Octavian war.

Cornelius Culleolus was no doubt one of the 'Chaldaeans, sacrificers and *sibyllistai*' on whom the consul Cn. Octavius in 87 BC depended for advice.[51] He gets a mere five lines in Paully-Wissowa, enough for Münzer to point out the essential fact: the *cognomen* is otherwise attested only in L. Culleolus, a late-republican proconsul to whom Cicero addressed two letters of commendation.[52] The prophet whose frenzied predictions were listened to, presumably by the Senate, in the civil war of 87 was evidently himself of senatorial family.

In the dialogue itself, 'natural' divination by inspired prophecy (and prophetic dreams) is carefully marked off from 'artificial' divination by augury, haruspicy and other specialist interpretations of phenomena. In book I, following the Peripatetics Dicaearchus and Cratippus, Quintus regards it as a superior form, precisely because it is natural.[53] The divine inspiration that produces it is described as madness (*furor*)[54] or disturbance of the mind,[55] and it only comes when the mind is free from association with the body.[56] This type of prophecy is called *vaticinatio*, and those who practise it are *vates*.[57]

What sort of people were they? The examples given are: 'the oracles of Apollo', later specified as the Pythia at Delphi;[58] the Erythraean Sibyl, evidently identified as the Sibyl of Cumae;[59] Bacis, the Boeotian prophet;[60] Cassandra;[61] Epimenides the Cretan;[62] Cn. Marcius and his brother;[63] Publicius;[64] and a Rhodian sailor in 48 BC, whose prophecy was reported by C. Coponius.[65] The Marcii, whose prophetic books are mentioned (and quoted) by other sources, are described as *nobili loco nati*:[66] evidently they belonged to the great plebeian *gens* (consular from 357 BC). I have suggested elsewhere that both they and Publicius probably date back to the first college of plebeian augurs in 300.[67] True, Cicero is contemptuous of *Publicius nescio quis* at II 113; but that is part of his rhetorical strategy, and not at all inconsistent with Publicius also having been of senatorial rank.[68]

It is quite possible, as Aristophanes and the Attic tragedians show, for prophets to be both held in honour and despised as charlatans in the same society at the same time.[69] Indeed, it is arguable that that is the normal state of affairs:[70]

> Faith and scepticism are alike traditional. Scepticism explains failures of witch-doctors, and being directed towards particular witch-doctors even tends to support faith in others.

At the conclusion to book I of the *De divinatione*, Quintus announces that he does not recognize fortune-tellers (*sortilegi*), necromancers, and those whose prophesy for money; he cares nothing for Marsic augurs, street-corner *haruspices* or astrologers from the Circus Maximus, who have no true skill but are merely 'superstitious prophets and shameless soothsayers'. He goes on to quote a damning speech from Ennius' *Telamo* on mercenary soothsayers—and yet, because he believes in the gods' care for humankind, he approves of divination when it is free from *levitas*, *vanitas* and *malitia*.[71]

Quintus is clearly talking about contemporary practitioners, and specifies, in the case of the necromancers, that Ap. Claudius often consulted them.[72] Appius, consul in 54 and censor in 50, was an augur and the author of books on augury. If we had *his* works and correspondence, instead of Cicero's, our view of the late Republic and its attitude to prophecy might be rather different. Even Cicero, however, can show us how things were if we read him carefully enough. As a character in the dialogue, he concludes his attack on divination in book II with a careful distinction between *religio* and *superstitio*.[73] The latter must be rejected and rooted out. For, as he tells Quintus, it is everywhere:

> Instat enim et urget et, quo te cumque verteris, persequitur, sive tu vatem sive tu omen audieris, sive immolaris sive avem aspexeris, si Chaldaeum, si haruspicem videris . . .
>
> It pursues you and urges you on, it follows you wherever you turn, whether you listen to a prophet or an omen, whether you sacrifice or watch the flight of birds, see an astrologer or a *haruspex* . . .

'Listening to a prophet' is something Quintus might well find himself doing, like Lucretius' readers and the sleepless conspirators in Dionysius.

VII

Divination, as Cicero points out at the very beginning of the work, was both a public and a private phenomenon.[74] As far as the private category is concerned, it is clear that no meaningful distinction could be drawn between Greek and Roman. Just as Theophrastus' superstitious man turned at the least excuse to the dream-interpreters, prophets and augurs,[75] so Cato assumed that the bailiff on his estate would want to consult *haruspices*, augurs, prophets and astrologers.[76] Similarly among the élite: Nicias employed the *mantis* Stilbides for consultation on matters both public and personal, just as Marius' Syrian prophetess Martha picked the winners in gladiatorial contests as well as advising him in the war with the Cimbri and Teutones.[77]

Where Rome conspicuously differed, certainly from Athens and Sparta and no doubt from most other ancient societies,[78] was in the strictly limited role allowed to divination in public decision-making. The story about Themistocles before Salamis—that at the insistence of Euphrantides the prophet he had three Persian princes sacrificed at the altar[79]—could not have been told about a Roman consul. The Roman Republic carefully restricted its consultation of the divine will; as Cicero points out in *De divinatione*, Roman public augury was quite different from that of other nations, and inspired *vaticinatio* was tolerated only through the strictly controlled medium of the Sibylline books.[80]

This, of course, is what John North means about the absence of prophets and holy men. But it is, as he points out, a specifically republican phenomenon. In regal Rome, the augur and miracle-worker Attus Navius had a role perfectly intelligible in Greek terms—as it were, Calchas to Tarquin's Agamemnon.[81] North argues convincingly that 'a very close association existed between the character of the activity of diviners and the Republican system itself'. The implication is that the restricted type of public divination peculiar to Rome dates from the end of the monarchy in the late sixth century—'the only event of which it can certainly be said that it radically changed the nature of the city's religious and political life.'[82]

However, now that we understand better the evolving nature of Roman religion and its sensitivity to changing circumstances,[83] it may be too schematic to look for a single moment when the Roman system of public divination was fixed once and for all.

As an analogy, it is worth considering the miracle stories which—like prophecy by inspiration—attested the direct action of the gods' power in human life.[84] Some of them, like the conception, suckling and deification of Romulus, belong in what is for us the wholly mythical context of the foundation legend. But they continue throughout the 'history' of the kings and the early and middle Republic: Numa's capture of Faunus and Picus and his bargaining with Iuppiter;[85] Attus Navius' miracles in the reign of Tarquinius Priscus;[86] the Dioscuri in the Forum on the day of the battle of Lake Regillus;[87] Genucius Cipus, the praetor who grew horns (an explicitly republican story);[88] Tuccia, the Vestal Virgin who carried water in a sieve in 230 BC;[89] and the Great Mother's miraculous intervention on behalf of Q. Claudia at the Tiber mouth in 204.[90] I think a similar continuity can be shown in the history of the *vates* in Roman public religion.

VIII

With Tanaquil, the Sibyl, and the voice in the Arsian Wood,[91] the stories of prophecy in early Rome display precisely the combination of Etruscan, Ionian Greek and native Latin that we should expect for the sixth century BC;[92] nor is the consultation of Delphi by Tarquin's sons and Brutus necessarily anachronistic for the period.[93] Precisely the same elements recur in Livy's account of Camillus the *fatalis dux* in book V: the Sibylline books, an Etruscan *vates*, Delphi, and the voice in Vesta's Grove.[94] The transition from monarchy to Republic does not seem to have been decisive here.

It is of course impossible to know how accurately these stories represent the historical reality of divination at Rome in the late sixth or early fourth centuries BC. (As for the fifth century, what does it mean that one of the Decemviri carried the *cognomen* 'Vaticanus'?)[95] With the late fourth and early third centuries, however, we are on somewhat firmer ground—and this was a period of very rapid change in Roman political and religious life. The two categories should not be distinguished: as North rightly observes, 'the religion of Rome has to be seen as the construction of a ruling élite',[96] and such events as the takeover of the cult of Hercules in 312 and the extension of the college of augurs to admit plebeians in 300 equally attest the emergence of a new élite and the beginning of a period of radical innovation in Rome's dealings with the gods.[97]

In 296 BC, just before one of the great turning-points in Roman history, the battle of Sentinum, we see a republican *vates* in action.[98]

Alarming portents had been reported. On the altar of Capitoline Iuppiter, blood had appeared for three days, followed by honey one day and milk the next. In the Forum, a bronze statue of Victory had descended from its pedestal of its own accord, and was now standing on the ground, facing the direction from which the Gauls (allies of the Etruscan–Samnite coalition) were already approaching the city. The populace was in a state of panic, exacerbated by the 'ill-omened responses of the prophets'.

At this point 'a certain Manius, by birth an Etruscan', interpreted the portents more encouragingly: Victory had gone forward as well as down, and was now set more firmly on the ground. So the Romans would win, and sacrifice to Iuppiter in thanksgiving, which is what the blood on the altar portended. But after that would come disease (for honey is what sick people need), and famine (for milk would be all the food they could find). Sure enough, the great battle was a Roman victory, but followed by three years of continual epidemic.[99] Manius' reputation for *manteia* was enhanced, but the new crisis demanded a remedy. The answer came 'from the books of fate and the responses of the prophets':[100] bring Aesculapius from Epidaurus.

The narrative seems to presuppose a surprisingly open, and even competitive, climate of prophecy. Perhaps we should compare it not with the more strictly controlled divination of the later Republic but with the situation in Metapontum a few decades earlier, startlingly revealed by a fragment of Theopompus. A young woman called Pharsalia, mistress of the Phocian general Philomelus, was visiting Metapontum; a voice from the oracular bronze bay-tree denounced her as being in possession of sacred property; whereupon she was torn to pieces by 'the prophets in the *agora*'.[101] At Rome too, as we shall see, there were prophets in the Forum.

In 276, despite the presence of Aesculapius, Rome was afflicted by an epidemic of still-births and fatal miscarriages. A ritual remedy was found: the flagellation of women at the Lupercalia as a purification rite.[102] Like other events of the time—the vowing of the Iuppiter Stator temple in 294, the incorporation of the Sabines as *cives sine suffragio* in 290[103]—this crisis was mythologized as an item in the history of Romulus. In Ovid's account of it, the voice from Juno's Grove is interpreted by an Etruscan prophet:[104]

> Augur erat, nomen longis intercidit annis,
> nuper ab Etrusca venerat exul humo.

There was an augur—his name has dropped out in the long years,
but he had come recently as an exile from the Etruscan land.

Since Ovid normally uses *augur* as a synonym for *vates*,[105] I suggest that this Romulean character represents a third-century Etruscan prophet like the Manius of twenty years before: a named individual, not merely an anonymous member of the board of *haruspices*.

The prophets continued to order innovations at times of crisis.[106] Usually our sources mention only the Sibylline books,[107] but Livy's narrative in book XXV shows how much more complex the situation was. In 213 the Senate ordered the urban praetor to control the 'sacrificers and prophets' in the Roman Forum; sacrificial manuals and *libri vaticinii* were confiscated.[108] The following year, however, the Senate discussed two prophecies of Cn. Marcius which had emerged as a result of this police action; one of them recommended the institution of *ludi Apollinares*. The *Xviri s.f.* were instructed to consult the Sibylline books, and as a result the games were set up 'from the Sibylline books and the prophecy of Marcius the prophet'.[109]

What was unusual in 213 BC was not the presence (and popularity) of prophets, but the Senate's determination to control them. If we are looking for the origins of Roman restrictions on divination, this seems to me a more likely moment than the beginning of the Republic. The prophets had one more success, the bringing of the Great Mother from Phrygia in 204,[110] but after that the climate changed radically. The Etruscan-Greek 'sacrificer and prophet' who popularized the mysteries of Dionysus at Rome provoked in 186 an astonishingly repressive demonstration of state authority, as the cult's organization was ruthlessly eradicated throughout Italy.[111] The burning of the Pythagorean 'books of Numa' in 181 and the expulsion of 'Chaldaean' astrologers in 139 are more evidence of the same attitude: uncontrolled prophecy was politically suspect, and could not now be tolerated.[112]

IX

In the *Knights* of Aristophanes, Demos is an enthusiast for prophets and prophecies. Thucydides and Plato on the other hand, Athenians hostile to the democracy, were contemptuous of them.[113] It is reasonable to infer a similar political polarity at Rome; the prophets in the Forum, answerable to no-one but their infallible gods, offered the populace a source of authority and power independent of the Senate and magistrates.

We know that in the second century BC consultation of prophets was regarded as a threat to military and domestic authority;[114] it is clear enough that the same attitude applied with political authority as well. And not without reason. In each of the Sicilian slave wars, the insurgents were led by a prophet—the Syrian Eunus at Enna in the 130s (he was also a miracle-worker), and Salvius at Morgantina in 104.[115]

Although the limitations of our evidence make it difficult to be certain, it seems that the heyday of public prophecy at Rome coincides with the period—the late fourth and third centuries BC—when the Republic was characterized by a degree of genuine popular sovereignty; that it disappears during the senatorial dominance of the second century; and that the first sign of its resumption (the Syrian prophetess who advised Marius) comes at the point when, as Sallust put it, 'the arrogance of the *nobilitas* was first challenged'.[116]

It would be a mistake, however, to think of the *vates* as a purely *popularis* phenomenon. It was the optimate consul Cn. Octavius who was dependent on prophets and sacrificers during the civil war of 87 BC.[117] What mattered was the state of political crisis: as in the war with Hannibal, now once more it seemed to make sense to look for guidance from those who claimed direct contact with the gods. And when on 6 July 83 BC the temple of Iuppiter was burnt to the ground, and the Sibylline books destroyed, there was all the more need of them.

The Senate took serious note of the prophecies of *vates* in 78, when M. Lepidus was in rebellion,[118] and evidently also in May 63, when a lunar eclipse occurred at a time of political tension leading to civil war:[119]

> Multaque per terras vates oracla furenti
> pectore fundebant tristis minitantia casus.

> And many oracles throughout the lands the prophets poured from frenzied breasts, threatening dire calamities.

By then the Sibylline books had been replaced,[120] but other types of inspired prophecy could not be ignored in a time of crisis.

The potentially subversive nature of *vaticinatio* was still very much in evidence. P. Lentulus, an ex-consul and patrician, believed that the Sibyl had prophesied that he would hold regal power in Rome; he was executed by decree of the Senate.[121] Small wonder that when Augustus became *pontifex maximus* he collected all the books of prophecy he could find and burnt them, keeping only a selection of the Sibyllines for preservation in the Palatine temple of Apollo:[122]

> Quidquid fatidicorum librorum Graeci Latinique generis nullis vel parum idoneis auctoribus vulgo ferebatur, supra duo milia contracta undique cremavit ac solos retinuit Sibyllinos, hos quoque dilectu habito.
>
> Whatever Greek or Latin prophetic books were in public circulation, either anonymous or by unsuitable authors, he collected from every source and burned, over two thousand in all; he kept the Sibylline books alone, and even them only after a process of selection.

No doubt Marcius, Publicius and Cornelius Culleolus were among the 'unsuitable authors'.[123]

X

But though the collected prophecies of the past were clearly regarded as dangerous, contemporary *vates* might even be helpful to the policies of the new regime. Maecenas, in the speech of advice attributed to him by Cassius Dio, urges Augustus to ban foreign cults, atheism, sorcery and magic, but allows prophecy as a necessary art.[124] If Lucretius' diatribe and the story of the repentant conspirators (sections II and IV above) do indeed accurately represent their idiom, the prophets in the Forum in the first century BC were a conservative force, preaching traditional piety enforced by threats of punishment in Hades.

The contrast with the provocatively radical *vates* of 213 BC is reflected in the attitude of the poets. Ennius had rejected the Latin metre traditionally associated with prophecy and given his characters, both epic and tragic, opinions contemptuous of the *vates*.[125] By contrast, Horace, Virgil and even Propertius take on the *persona* of the *vates* in order to denounce the wickedness of civil war or to hail the greatness of the man who ended it.[126]

From Augustus onwards, a *vates* is more often a poet than a prophet. But his business is still with revelation, as the greatest of the *vates*-poets shows us in book VI of the *Aeneid*. If we are ever tempted to doubt whether the Romans took seriously the fear of the gods and the moral demands of traditional religion, we should remember Phlegyas' despairing cry in Virgil's underworld:[127]

'Discite iustitiam moniti et non temnere divos!'

'Be warned! Learn justice and not to scorn the gods!'

5

Satyrs in Rome?
The Background to Horace's *Ars Poetica*

Nil intemptatum nostri liquere poetae. (AP 285)

I

At the central point of Horace's epistle to the Pisones (lines 220–50 out of 476) is a lengthy passage on the history and composition of satyr-plays. At the central point within that passage (234–5), with emphatic use of the vocative and the first-person pronoun, Horace presents himself and his addressees as actively involved in writing satyr-plays:

> non ego inornata et dominatia nomina solum
> verbaque, Pisones, satyrorum scriptor amabo.

> As for me, dear Pisos, when writing satyr-plays I shall not favour only the plain nouns and verbs of normal usage.

'Nothing,' says Gordon Williams, 'could seem less relevant to the contemporary Roman literary scene.' And C.O. Brink, who differs sharply from Williams in his interpretation of the *Ars Poetica*, is at one with him on this passage: 'it presents a major puzzle in Roman literary history... There is no evidence for Roman Satyric drama.'[1]

Earlier, Brink had hinted at a possible solution to the problem: 'I doubt if [Horace] would have spoken as he did if he had not considered satyric drama a viable genre, at any rate for recitation.'[2] But recitation offers no escape. Horace is explicit throughout the poem that he is talking about writing for the stage, for performance before a real Roman audience; recitation comes only at the end, where the playwright is imagined as trying out a first draft of his work on friends or clients.[3]

Recent research has done little to resolve the dilemma. Elizabeth Rawson's important article on theatrical life in Rome and Italy allows only a dismissive footnote to the idea of Roman satyric drama; in her view, if satyr-plays were ever seen at Rome, they were performed in Greek by companies visiting from Magna Graecia. Similarly Richard Seaford, in the introduction to his *Cyclops* commentary which is now the standard work on the genre: 'there is no real evidence for satyr-play in Rome .. satyric drama has remained virtually exclusively Greek.'[4]

Certainly it is hard to imagine anything less consistent with Roman *mos maiorum* than the anarchic hedonism of satyrs. It was precisely *libido*, that morally subversive aspect of the Bacchic cult, that led to its brutal suppression by the Roman state in 186 BC.[5] And if no satyrs, then no satyr-plays. Yet Horace's poem quite clearly presupposes a Calpurnius Piso, the elder son of a morally exemplary Roman aristocrat,[6] proposing to write a satyr-play for production before the *equites peditesque* in a Roman theatre. Now, oblique and even devious as his style may be, Horace does not write nonsense. As Brink rightly says, it seems that Horace 'meant to give precisely the emphasis to this subject which many moderns stoutly deny it'.[7] Could it be that the moderns are simply wrong, and that satyr-play was, after all, a living genre on the Roman stage?

II

There is, in fact, some evidence for it, but it is evidence which needs careful scrutiny. The argument must begin with the grammarian Diomedes, in the fourth century AD, who identified four *genera* of dramatic poetry:[8]

> apud Graecos tragica comica satyrica mimica, apud Romanos praetextata tabernaria Atellana planipes.
>
> Among the Greeks, tragic, comic, satyric, mimic; among the Romans, 'purple-bordered', 'tavern-style', 'Atellan', 'flat-footed'.

When, after a lengthy account of the non-dramatic genres, Diomedes returns to tragedy and comedy and expands on his schematic parallel of Greek and Latin dramatic forms, he makes it clear that *fabulae Atellanae* are similar to Greek satyr-plays in that they employ 'argumenta dictaque iocularia', but differ from them in that their characters are not satyrs but 'Oscan characters'—i.e. Maccus, Pappus, Dossennus and the rest.[9]

So it is clear that Diomedes, at least, knew of no Roman satyr-plays. Their absence from the tradition he was following is, in fact, the main reason for believing that Horace in the *Ars Poetica* could not have been referring to a living genre. But Diomedes is not the only witness.

According to Nicolaus of Damascus, a contemporary of Horace, Sulla composed 'satyric comedies' in Latin. Since satyr-play and comedy were different genres, it is universally assumed (remembering Diomedes) that Nicolaus was referring to *Atellanae*.[10] But surely a Greek author knew what he meant by *saturikos*? Nicolaus would hardly mistake the Atellan cast of Oscan rustics for satyrs; and his phrase 'in his native language' suggests that he thought Sulla was using Latin for what would normally be written in Greek. We must remember Horace's strictures against satyrs behaving like comedy characters, 'velut innati triviis et paene forenses' (*AP* 245f.) Perhaps Sulla's 'satyric comedies' were examples of the sort of generic contamination Horace was attacking.

The next piece of evidence is more explicit. Porphyrion, commenting on *Ars Poetica* 221 ('mox etiam agrestes satyros nudavit'), observes:

> Hoc est: satyrica coeperunt scribere, ut Pomponius Atalanten, vel Sisyphon, vel Ariadnen.
>
> That is, they began to write satyr-plays, like Pomponius' *Atalanta* or *Sisyphus* or *Ariadne*.

L. Pomponius, of course, was best known as a writer of *Atellanae*.[11] But he was an innovator, and wrote in more than one genre.[12] If Porphyrion says he wrote satyr-play, and even knows three very plausible titles,[13] I do not think we can simply assert that he is mistaken. Of Pomponius' seventy known plays, only twenty were certainly *Atellanae* (from the presence of the stock characters in title or fragments); three—*Agamemno suppositus*, *Armorum iudicium* and *Pytho Gorgonius*—were mythological burlesques in which satyrs would certainly be more at home than yokels from Campania; and two others—*Marsyas* and *Satura*—can surely be added to Porphyrion's list as satyr-plays. For one of the surviving fragments of *Satura* featured Liber Pater, which makes it likely that the title meant 'Satyr-woman'.[14] (Lucretius uses *satura* in that sense, and the masculine *satur* is attested in the company of Liber Pater on a tomb-decoration from Ostia.[15])

The direct evidence, then, is not so clear-cut as is sometimes thought. It is not, perhaps, strong enough to prove conclusively that Horace had contemporary satyr-plays in mind; but neither is it strong enough to disprove it. What seems to tilt the balance against the idea is the inherent improbability of satyrs in Rome—especially the ordered, puritanical Rome of Augustus' restored Republic. So what we must look at now is the circumstantial evidence.

III

To begin at the beginning. The man who first 'brought satyrs on stage speaking verse' was Arion of Methymna, whom Herodotus portrays returning from a profitable sojourn in Italy and Sicily late in the seventh century BC. That was about the time the hut dwellers of Rome started putting up rectangular buildings with tiled roofs in the newly drained valley of the Forum. Their terracotta revetment plaques were decorated with Gorgons' heads and Minotaurs; whether they knew of satyrs yet, we cannot tell.[16]

Three generations later they certainly did. When satyric drama was evolving at Athens in the late sixth century, and satyrs' antics were a regular theme in red-figure vase-painting, the Latin communities, like their Etruscan neighbours, were decorating their temples with antefixes in the form of satyrs' faces.[17] The find-spots of two of the examples known from Rome suggest that they came from the temple of Iuppiter on the Capitol and the temple of the Dioscuri in the Forum [fig. iv]. (Their habits were as familiar as their faces: another antefix type used on the Capitoline temple showed a satyr seizing a maenad.)[18] No remnants happen to survive from the contemporary temple of Liber, Libera and Ceres (Dionysus, Kore and Demeter), but since their cult was—and remained—Greek, it is quite possible that Liber Pater-Dionysus was attended by his satyr-servants.[19]

The late fifth and early fourth centuries are a dark age for Rome. Contracting cultural horizons may be suggested by the fact that when Apollo the Healer was vowed a temple in 433 BC, it was built in the *prata flaminia* outside the *pomerium*, as the shrine of a foreign god.[20] But there is no reason to suppose that satyrs had suddenly become alien creatures. Vase-painting attests their continued ubiquity in Campania, Lucania and Apulia, and Etruscan art shows an efflorescence of Dionysiac themes in precisely this period.[21] The Etruscan evidence is particularly interesting for our purposes in that it clearly shows actors and dancers impersonating satyrs, scenes which János Szilágyi convincingly interprets as at least an embryonic form of satyric drama.[22] It is

Figure iv

Antefix with the face of a satyr/silenus, from the temple of Castor and Pollux in the Forum, early fifth century BC (Rome, Antiquario forense). The temple of the Dioscuri was supposedly founded after the battle of Lake Regillus (traditional date 499 or 496 BC), when 'the Great Twin Brethren who fought so well for Rome' were seen watering their horses at the nearby spring.
[Photo by courtesy of the Soprintendenza di Roma.]

hardly surprising that Attic drama in the late fifth century associated Dionysus with Italy[23]—and we should not suppose that Rome was somehow immune from such influences.

By the end of the fourth century, Roman power extended as far south as the Greek cities of Campania. For Heraclides of Pontus, Rome was a Greek city; statues of Alcibiades and Pythagoras were erected in the Comitium; a leading member of the new plebeian élite chose *Sophos* as his *cognomen*.[24] At some time around 320 BC, a Campanian mastercraftsman working in Rome made a bronze chest for a Praenestine lady to give to her daughter (no doubt at her marriage). On it he engraved a scene from the tale of the Argo: Amykos, the tyrannical pugilist of the Bebrykes, is bound to a tree after his defeat by Polydeukes [fig. ii].[25] Now, *Amykos* was a Sophoclean satyr-play; and Novius Plautius not only included Silenus in his scene, laughing at the Argonauts' boxing practice, but also made the handle of the chest lid in the form of Dionysus (or Liber Pater) supported by two satyrs.

It was very probably in Novius Plautius' lifetime that the Romans erected a statue of a satyr in the Comitium itself (possibly even on the Rostra). This was Marsyas, from whom the plebeian Marcii claimed descent, and Mario Torelli has very plausibly argued for 294 BC, the censorship of the plebeian hero C. Marcius Rutilus (*cos.* 310), as the date when his statue was set up.[26] Marsyas was the inventor of augury, and Marcius Rutilus was one of the first plebeian augurs, elected in 300.[27] Marsyas was also the minister of Liber Pater, and his statue was the *signum liberae civitatis*; in the 290s, *nexum* had recently been abolished, and the plebeian aediles were busy exacting fines from money-lenders and other oppressors of the *plebs*.[28]

In a strikingly similar political context half a century later, the temple and *ludi scaenici* of Flora were established by plebeian aediles (appropriately called Publicii) who had punished powerful landowners illegally occupying *ager publicus*. The temple was next to that of Liber, Libera and Ceres, and the games provided a stage for Greek drama in Latin, as recently introduced by Livius Andronicus.[29] Rome was now firmly in the Greek world, her origins and history of interest as much to Callimachus and the poets as to Theophrastus, Eratosthenes and the historians.[30] Whether satyr-plays were ever shown at the new *ludi scaenici* we do not know, but drama was certainly performed in the Forum (that is, in the presence of Marsyas); and the plebeian Iunii now start using 'Silanus' as a *cognomen*.[31]

It is important to remember that Silenus is not just the father of the satyrs; he is the source of arcane wisdom, if he can be caught and made to divulge it. Similarly Marsyas, though the symbol of liberty, is not a licentious hedonist; on the contrary, his Phrygian myth (in which he is associated with the Magna Mater) attributes to him sagacity and self-control.[32] His gift of augury was handed on to his descendants, the Marcii, whose prophetic verses led to the institution of the *ludi Apollinares* in 212 BC.[33] His chastely-loved Cybele was brought from Phrygia to the Palatine in 204, and the *ludi Megalenses* instituted in her honour in 191.

Marsyas was important for Italian legends too. He was the eponymous founder of the Marsi,[34] and he sent his ambassador Megales (whose name recalls the Magna Mater) to Tarchon the Etruscan.[35] The Etruscans had their own historical legends, intersecting with those of Rome in the persons of Aulu and Caile Vipinas (Vibenna).[36] A late fourth-century mirror from Bolsena shows the brothers about to attack Cacu the seer; a *satyriskos* watches from behind a rock, and a grapevine surrounds the whole scene [fig. v].[37] Could the allusions be to Dionysus as a god of drama?

Certainly the Etruscans had a dramatic tradition of their own. The clearest evidence for it is in the first century BC, when Varro knew a certain Volnius who wrote *tragoediae Tuscae*,[38] but there is no reason to suppose it was a late innovation. The Livian excursus on the origin of *ludi scaenici* (supposedly in 364 BC) clearly presupposes a longstanding Etruscan tradition of mimetic dance and embryonic drama; Szilágyi has made a very powerful case for accepting at least the essentials of Livy's account, and for interpreting his mysterious phrase 'impletae modis saturae' as linking the satyric dances attested in Etruscan vase-painting with the later tradition of Roman satire.[39]

Whether or not the Etruscan word for an actor (*ister*, whence *histrio*) was derived from *histor*,[40] we may reasonably guess from the Cacu-Vibennae scene that the subject matter of the performances might well be quasi-historical. And not only in Etruria. Most of the 'historical' legends of the towns and peoples of Italy were Greek in origin—foundation stories attached to wandering heroes like Odysseus and Diomedes. That is a familiar phenomenon in historiography and learned poetry,[41] but it is less often remembered in the context of drama. In a brilliant recent article, Stephanie West has very convincingly interpreted as interpolations for dramatic recitation the 200 or so lines in Lycophron's *Alexandra* that refer to Roman and Italian legendary origins; 'deutero-Lycophron . . . is to be sought among the artists of Dionysos in southern Italy', probably in the second century BC.[42]

Figure v

Etruscan mirror from Bolsena (London, British Museum), late fourth century BC. The seer Cacu sings his prophecy, and his boy assistant Artile transcribes it on to tablets. The brothers Caile (left) and Aule Vipinas—Caeles and Aulus Vibenna, heroes from the Etruscan city of Vulci—approach to capture him. A little satyr peeps over the rock behind. [From *Etruskische Spiegel* V (1897), pl. 127.]

Wandering heroes are also a regular feature of satyr-play, and it is striking how far satyric plots overlap with Italian foundation stories. Aeschylus' satyr-play *Circe*, for instance, belonged to a tetralogy which featured Telegonus, Circe's son by Odysseus;[43] Telegonus was said to have founded Tusculum and Praeneste. Other versions of Circe's offspring by Odysseus included the eponymous founders of Antium, Ardea, and Rome itself.[44] Sophocles wrote a satyr-play on Amphiaraus the seer, whose sons were the founders of Tibur. Danae, mother of Perseus, was said to have founded Ardea; she and her infant son were rescued from the sea by the satyrs in Aeschylus' *Diktyoulkoi*.[45]

Also Aeschylean, and probably from a satyr-play, is the aetiology of Rhegion from *rhēgnumi*, comparable with the later derivations of Tusculum from *duskolon* ('difficult of access'), Bauli from *boauloi* (where Herakles kept the cattle of Geryon), and Pompeii from *pompē* (Herakles' triumph).[46] No etymology happens to survive for the Latin town of Satricum at the edge of the Pomptine marsh, but it can hardly have been anything other than *saturikon*. Already in the sixth century BC, as recent excavations have shown, the temple of Matuta at Satricum was decorated with a conspicuous variety of satyr-motif antefixes [fig. vi].[47] Virgil refers to the neighbouring marsh as *Saturae palus*; and a context for the aetiology is provided by the story of Dionysus' war against the Etruscans, after which he left the oldest and youngest of his satyrs in Italy to teach the natives viticulture.[48]

The first literary evidence for satyrs in Rome comes from Fabius Pictor at the end of the third century BC. Describing the original *ludi Romani*, 'not just from what he had heard but from what he knew at first hand',[49] Fabius begins with the *pompa circensis* from the Capitol to the Circus Maximus. It included dancing choruses of *satyristai*, imitating and making fun of the other participants in a dance like the Greek *sikinnis*.[50] Szilágyi is surely right to see this as the old Etruscan custom still surviving, and to adduce in support Appian's description of Scipio's triumphal procession in 201, where the Etruscan origin is explicitly attested.[51] (In Appian the satyr-dancers appear as *tityristai*: we know from Aelian and Strabo that *tityroi* were 'creatures like *silenoi* and *bacchoi*'.)[52]

It seems, then, that from the end of the sixth century to the end of the third the Romans were quite familiar with satyrs and their ways. In the second century, the increasing Hellenization of Roman culture added a new dimension—with tragic results for the worshippers of Dionysus in 186 BC. Against the persecution of the Bacchanals, however, we may set

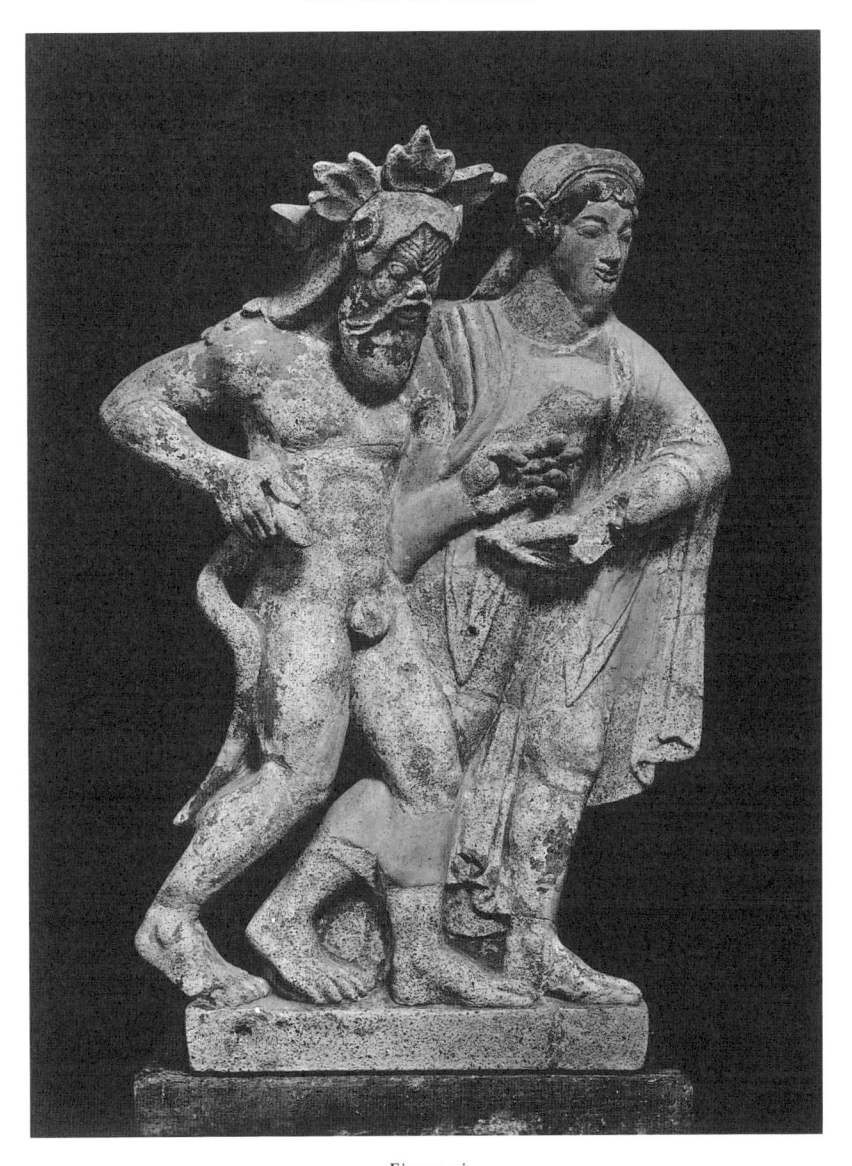

Figure vi

Antefix with satyr and maenad from the temple of Mater Matuta at Satricum, early fifth century BC (Rome, Villa Giulia). The Latin city of Satricum was about 50 km south of Rome, between Antium (Anzio) and the Pomptine marshes. [Photo by Anderson, Rome.]

the second-century temple decoration from Civitalba in Umbria, the ancient Sentinum. The frieze of fleeing Gauls shows that the temple was a monument to the great Roman victory over the Gauls and Samnites 150 years earlier; on the pediment, however, is Dionysus with his satyrs, uncovering the sleeping Ariadne.[53] Since Ariadne was an important figure in the mystic cult of Dionysus (her awakening evidently interpreted as the initiate's entry into everlasting life),[54] this scene reminds us that the suppression of the Dionysiac mysteries in 186 represents only one side of the polarized culture of second-century Rome. The conflict it reveals is attested also by the building and subsequent demolition (in 154) of a permanent theatre below the temple of the Magna Mater, and by the censors' expulsion of Greek stage performers from Rome in 115.[55]

Even in Rome the god of drama and his satyrs were in only temporary retreat. It is certain that Greek plays were being performed again in Rome very soon after the censors' ban: they are attested at Marius' triumphal games in 101, and referred to casually several times in the first century BC.[56] Moreover, Silenus and Marsyas suddenly become popular as coin types at the time of the *Bellum Italicum*, along with Pan, who now joins them as the ancestor of a senatorial family, the Vibii Pansae.[57] Satyrs were present when the war itself broke out (at the fateful *ludi scaenici* at Asculum in 91, the Latin actor Saunio was a 'satyric character'), and Sulla even had a wild one brought before him at Apollonia in 83.[58]

That familiarity with satyrs was not restricted to the Hellenized élite is suggested by the passage in Lucretius on *loca sola*—remote places believed by the country people to be the haunts of satyrs, nymphs and *fauni*. In Horace's lifetime, therefore, as in practically every generation of Rome's history, the conditions necessary to satyric drama were part of the experience of Roman citizens from top to bottom of the social scale—from the 'lofty Ramnes' to the 'buyer of roasted nuts'.[59]

IV

Before proceeding to the next stage of the argument, it may be worth pausing for a moment to consider, firstly the genre itself as it had developed by the first century BC, and secondly the nature of Roman drama as it was performed at the *ludi scaenici* of the late Republic.

As Richard Seaford points out with reference to *Cyclops*, already by the last decade of the fifth century BC satyr-play had evolved some way from its original form and content. Influence from another dramatic genre is tantalizingly suggested by a fragmentary calyx *krater* of the Talos painter, about 400 BC: in a scene interpreted by Erika Simon as illustrating Achaeus' satyr-play *Hephaestus*, Dionysus reclines at a banquet to the piping of a *satyriskos* called 'Mimos'. Our best evidence for contemporary mime is the final scene of Xenophon's *Symposion*, where the dancers impersonate Dionysus and Ariadne.[60] Old Comedy was also an influence, as may be inferred from personal and contemporary references in satyr-play fragments. Indeed, by the late fourth century, when Old Comedy was obsolete, we find satyric drama which is explicitly satirical: Python's *Agen*, staged at Alexander's camp on the Hydaspes in 324, attacked Harpalus and his mistress, while Lycophron's *Menedemos* mocked the banquets of contemporary philosophers.[61] That provoked a reaction, with Sositheos of Alexandria taking the satyrs out of the city and back into their ancestral wilds;[62] whether Horace's distaste for urban satyrs with their sophisticated wisecracks is merely a reflection of this Alexandrian controversy (as the critics think), or actually refers to his own time (which is what he says),[63] either way it is clear that by the first century BC the composer of satyr-play, long since freed from the Athenian tragic tetralogy format, had a wide variety of styles open to him to choose from.

Certainly it seems there was a demand for the genre. Satyric drama was thriving at the festivals of the Hellenistic world, particularly in Delos, with its important population of Roman and Italian *negotiatores*, and in Boeotia, where Sulla set up the new *Amphiaraia* at Oropos in or about 84 BC.[64] At that time of unprecedented cultural Hellenization at Rome, it is, I think, inconceivable that this genre alone should have failed to tempt Latin poets to rival the Greeks.[65]

What actually went on at the *ludi scaenici* of the Roman festivals?[66] About fifty days every year—not counting *ad hoc* shows for triumphs, funerals and so on—were devoted to stage performances of one sort or another. They were organized by ambitious aediles who had to provide the best possible entertainment in order to impress the citizen body with their munificence. What sort of works did they commission, or revive? Comedies and tragedies, of course—and since the standard work denies it, it is worth insisting on the perennial popularity of themes from Roman history: the house of Tarquin was as rich in tragic plots as the house of Atreus.[67] But it took more than just comedy and tragedy to keep the chestnut-munching audience of a Roman theatre attentive for day after day at the Megalesia or the Floralia.

One rare and precious fragment of evidence comes from a lost speech of Cicero delivered in 66 BC.[68]

> His autem ludis—loquor enim quae sum ipse nuper expertus—unus quidam poeta dominatur, homo perlitteratus, cuius sunt illa convivia poetarum ac philosophorum, cum facit Euripiden et Menandrum inter se, et alio loco Socraten atque Epicurum disserentes, quorum aetates non annis sed saeculis scimus fuisse disiunctas. atque his quantos plausus et clamores movet! multos enim condiscipulos habet in theatro qui simul litteras non didicerunt.
>
> At this year's games (for I speak from recent experience) there is one particular dominant poet—a very cultured man, the author of those *Poets' and Philosophers' Dinner-Table Discussions* in which he has Euripides arguing with Menander and another time Socrates with Epicurus, though we know that their lifetimes were not years but centuries apart. And what thunderous applause he gets for them! There are plenty of his fellow-pupils in the theatre audience, who like him never learned their lessons at school.

What sort of performances were these? The *convivia philosophorum* are reminiscent of Lycophron's satyric *Menedemos*, and also of Varro's Menippean satire *Eumenides*.[69] (Varro seems to have described his satires as 'hic modus scaenatilis'. Were they written for theatrical performance?)[70] What is clear is that our ignorance should discourage dogmatism about what could or could not be shown on a Roman stage.

We know from Cicero about the recent introduction of Alexandrian mime in the fifties BC, perhaps to be associated with the *pantomimi* and the tragic ballet which became so popular with Bathyllus and Pylades in the twenties.[71] We know from Ovid of stage plays that celebrated, in the manner of *aretalogoi*, the miraculous deeds of the gods at whose festivals they were shown.[72] The first century BC was evidently a period of vitality and innovation in Roman drama. Why deny the satyrs a place in it? It seems to me that Horace's purist plea for 'genuine' satyr-play presupposes exactly the kind of creative mixture of genres the other evidence leads us to expect.

To text the hypothesis, let us apply it to three items which are otherwise hard to explain.

First, an elliptical comment by Cicero in a letter to his brother in August 54:[73]

> Συνδείπνους Σοφοκλέους, quamquam a te actam fabellam video esse festive, nullo modo probavi.
>
> I don't at all approve of Sophocles' *Fellow-Banqueters*, though I can see your performance of the play was enjoyable.

Quintus, writing from Caesar's camp in Gaul just before the crossing to Britain, had evidently reported his own production of, or performance in, Sophocles' satyric play *Syndeipnoi*.[74] (Remember Python's *Agen*, staged before Alexander at the Hydaspes: perhaps satyr-play was particularly appropriate for highbrow horseplay in the officers' mess.) In Sophocles' drama, the Greeks at Tenedos snub Achilles by not inviting him to dine. If Quintus had adapted that to mock the *boni* and their treatment of Caesar, the great conqueror, we can understand Cicero's disapproval in a letter which emphasizes the need not to offend anyone. So perhaps this passage counts as evidence for the use of satyr-play as a vehicle for topical comment.[75]

Second, Virgil's Tityrus. The enigmatic herdsman who seems to personify Vigil's early work, and certainly represents the poet himself at one point in the *Eclogues*, is named after a species of satyr.[76] The *Eclogues* imitate Theocritean mime-sketches, and were certainly performed in the theatre.[77] One of Virgil's herdsmen is explicitly a rustic mime—'saltantes satyros imitabitur Alphesiboeus'—and performs the Theocritean dramatic monologue in *Eclogue* 8. Though the details escape us, we seem to be in the world of the satyr called Mimos.[78]

The third passage also joins satyrs with mime. It is in the long digression at the end of book VII of Dionysius of Halicarnassus' *Antiquitates Romanae*, where he uses Fabius Pictor's account of the *ludi Romani* procession to prove his constant theme that the Romans were really Greek in origin.[79] He quotes Fabius on the satyr-dances, and then adds that he himself had seen such *satyristai* dancing the *sikinnis* in aristocratic funeral processions, where the jesting and mockery is elsewhere attributed to *mimi*.[80] Moreover, Aristonicus of Alexandria, a contemporary of Dionysius, claimed that 'the satyr-rout called *sikinnis*' was one of the elements out of which Bathyllus and Pylades fashioned their new form of mime. A connection with the Megalesia may be implied by the theory that the dance was Phrygian in origin, named after one of Cybele's attendant nymphs.[81]

V

So I think we may conclude that Roman satyr-play did exist after all—largely, no doubt, in generically contaminated forms like 'satyric comedy' (as written by Sulla) and 'satyric mime'. What Pomponius' satyr-plays were like, whether they would have satisfied a purist like Horace, we cannot tell; but there is certainly no reason to suppose that they were *fabulae Atellanae* like most of his *oeuvre*. He and his audience knew perfectly well what satyrs were, and that they were not Campanian rustics like Maccus and his friends.

Now that we know what we are looking for, we can even find some plausible plots to add to those three titles of plays by Pomponius. Ovid gives us the hint in that precious line already referred to from his story of Q. Claudia and the Magna Mater: 'mira sed et scaena testificata loquar'. That tells us, first, that Ovid used drama as a source (a fact recently exploited in excellent articles by J.C. McKeown and Elaine Fantham); second, that the plays he knew used historical material; and third, that they celebrated the *hieroi logoi* of the divinities honoured at Roman dramatic festivals.[82] Let us look more closely at Ovid's *Fasti*.

In book VI, Cybele throws an *al fresco* party on Mount Ida. Among the guests are satyrs, nymphs, Silenus and Priapus. Priapus' attempt on the sleeping Vesta is frustrated by the braying of Silenus' ass. Elsewhere in Ovid we have allusions to Priapus' lecherous designs on Pomona, and in Martial to his pursuit of Flora, in the goddess's own grove. Any one of these would be good for a one-act satyric mime at the Floralia or the Megalesia.[83]

On a more ample scale is the story, also in book VI, of Ino and Melicertes and their reception at the site of Rome. No satyrs here, but the Dionysiac background is proved by the 'Ausonian Maenads' in the grove of Stimula, and all the topographical references are to the Forum Bovarium and the Circus Maximus, close to the temple of Liber Pater.[84]

Ino and Melicertes were rescued by Hercules—the god of the Forum Bovarium, but also a favourite character in satyr-play. He appears most clearly in that guise in the aetiology of the naked Luperci in book II of the *Fasti*. Here, instead of a Theban story in a Roman setting, we have a Roman god at large in Lydia: Faunus falls in love with Omphale, but in the dark puts his hand up the skirt of the transvestite Hercules instead. Which is why his worshippers come naked to the Lupercalia. Faunus was the Roman Pan, 'Nympharum fugientum amator', a quasi-satyric figure like Priapus; and Hercules and Omphale had long been material for satyr-play plots.[85]

In book III, Faunus is joined by Picus for the aetiology of Iuppiter Elicius (a story told also by Valerius Antias, that most stage-struck of historians).[86] Ovid calls them *silvestria numina*; in Plutarch's version of the story they are '*daimones* who may be likened to satyrs or Pans', and Numa's capture of them (at Egeria's suggestion) is an exact doublet of the capture of Silenus by Midas of Phrygia.[87] Revealed wisdom, magic, and secret spells like the charm against thunder that Iuppiter is tricked into revealing—all these are familiar satyr-play motifs.[88] And *Picus* was the title of a play by Novius, who like Pomponius wrote both *Atellanae* and mythological burlesque.[89]

Like Janus and Saturn, Picus and Faunus could be regarded either as timeless gods or as kings in the history of an aboriginal, pre-Arcadian Latium.[90] Like Marsyas, they were augurs and prophets.[91] Picus, as a young king, was loved by Circe, that familiar satyr-play character, who turned him into a woodpecker when he remained faithful to his wife. (In another version, Circe *was* his wife.)[92] The wife of king Faunus was Fatua the prophetess, whose story was used as an *aition* for the Bona Dea cult: she was a secret drinker, beaten to death by her husband, who then made her a goddess. Alternatively, she was Faunus' daughter, whom he lusted after and ravished in the form of a snake, having first got her drunk.[93] Sex, wine, and an ogre are certainly plausible satyr-play material.

Faunus was not always an ogre: his name could be derived from *favere*, and it was his friendly welcome which enabled Evander and his Arcadians to settle at Pallantion, the site of the future Rome.[94] He was still king of Latium when Hercules came with the cattle of Geryon, and among the stories attached to that episode were several that celebrated the hero's sexual prowess with various aetiologically significant partners—Palanto, the eponym of Pallantion; a daughter of Faunus; Lavinia the daughter of Evander, and so on.[95] The most interesting is that which derived the name of the patrician Fabii from *fovea*, a pit for trapping animals, in which Hercules ravished the ancestress of the *gens*.[96] (A different version alleged that the first Fabius invented such pits, and was named after them: 'first inventions' are also a theme of satyr-play.)[97] Did the Marcii, the Iunii Silani and the Vibii Pansae have similar stories about their origins?[98]

One family whose legendary genealogy seems made for satyr-play was that of the Aelii Lamiae. Their home was Formiae, which some identified as the land of the Laestrygonians,[99] and their ancestor was Poseidon's son Lamos, the Laestrygonian king.[100] The wanderings of Odysseus were full of satyr-play plots—*Cyclops*, *Circe*, *Nausicaa* and so on—and Lamos and his people fit perfectly into the generic theme exemplified by Aeschylus' *Kerkyon*, Sophocles' *Amykos*, and Euripides' *Skiron* and *Busiris*, all 'persecutors of mankind'.[101] Queen of the Laestrygonians was the ogre Lamia, who ate children; she is attested in Euripidean satyr-play and actually mentioned as a stage character in the *Ars Poetica* itself.[102]

Like the primordial kings of Latium, so too the dynasty of Alba Longa provided suitable satyr-play material. (They were Silvii, 'men of the forest', and true satyrs, according to Horace, had to be *silvis deducti*.)[103] The childhood of Proca is Ovid's context for the sex comedy of Janus and Crane, and his reign as king of Alba for the story of Pomona and Vertumnus, in which the satyrs, Silenus and Priapus play a minor (possibly choral?) role.[104] Proca, of course, was the father of Numitor and Amulius. Here we approach the most famous satyr-play plot of all, for which it is necessary to set the scene.

Vitruvius, writing in the twenties BC, described the three different types of theatrical scene appropriate for wall painting: columns and pediments for tragedy, balconies and windows for comedy, and for satyr-play 'trees, caves, mountains and other rustic features'. We may add a spring, from Ovid and the other authors: what counts as satyr country is a wooded glen with running water and a cave.[105] Like this one:

> There is not far off a holy place, arched over by a dense wood, and a hollow rock from which springs issued: the wood was said to be consecrated to Pan.

Pan Lykaios, that is, for 'this place the Romans call Lupercal'. Here they celebrated the Lupercalia, with young men running around laughing, naked but for goatskin loincloths; hilarity and drunkenness were a necessary part of the ritual.[106]

That in itself is appropriate to satyr-play, as we have seen already, the Ovidian aetiology of the Lupercalia involves the quasi-satyr Faunus. But even the story itself falls into a familiar satyr-play category, 'the care of divine or heroic infants'.[107] Plutarch was right to call the story of Romulus and Remus 'theatrical' (see p. 5 above). The particular theatrical aspect he had in mind may have been the capture of Remus and his 'recognition by signs' (in Aristotle's terminology), which was a technique more used in tragedy and comedy than in satyr-play.[108] But the influence of one dramatic genre on another is both explicitly attested, in Sulla's 'satyric comedies', and to be inferred in any case from Horace's argument in the *Ars Poetica*.

VI

If there is after all no reason to deny the existence of Roman satyr-play, whether 'pure' or contaminated, mimic or comic, erotic or patriotic, we need not resist the natural assumption that Horace's advice to young Piso was practical, and concerned with the writing of plays for real stage performance.[109]

As an Augustan purist, Horace called for a return to real classical satyric drama. The intellectual ferment of the first century BC had evidently affected drama like everything else, and in that experimental and innovative atmosphere the satyrs were simply too versatile to be kept corralled inside their traditional genre. The young, urban, lovesick, shameless satyrs Horace objected to sound rather like Encolpius and Giton in the picaresque novel Petronius entitled *Satyrika*. The mixture of genres went on.

I have touched only lightly on one possible aspect of it—the relevance of satyrs to satire. The first of Diomedes' three definitions of *Satura* is generally waved away by modern theorists, but it was evidently taken seriously in the ancient world:[110]

> Satira dicta est a satyris, quod similiter in hoc carmine ridiculae res pudendaeque dicuntur.
>
> Satire is named after satyrs, because in this verse-form likewise funny and disgraceful things are said.

Some satyric drama was certainly satirical; so can we be quite certain that Diomedes was altogether wrong?

6

The Necessary Lesson

Review of: Christian Habicht, *Cicero the Politician* (Baltimore 1990), and Paul MacKendrick, *The Philisophical Books of Cicero* (London 1989).

It is 138 years since Theodor Mommsen published his *Römische Geschichte*, in which he described Cicero as 'a political trimmer ... a statesman without insight, opinion or purpose ... a short-sighted egotist'.[1] Mommsen's verdict, as influential as it was grossly unjust, was the corollary of a hero-worshipping admiration of Caesar which the intervening five generations have shown to have been, at best, optimistic. Now that the Stalinist autocracies have fallen, and half of Europe is facing the risks and responsibilities of constitutional government, our judgement on the man who embodied the *res publica* can surely afford to free itself from the political prejudices of the age of Metternich. Mommsen was a great man, but Cicero was a greater.

Both these excellent books have Mommsen much in mind. Christian Habicht's slim volume, a revision of the 1987 Semple Lectures, concentrates on Cicero's political career and goes a long way—though not far enough—towards refuting Mommsen's slander. Habicht regards Cicero's literary work as a mere 'surrogate for politics', a sort of therapy during his periods in the political wilderness. For Paul MacKendrick, on the other hand, 'his whole life may be said to be a preparation for the philosophical works ... [I]t is impossible to explain his life without his philosophy.'[2] Mommsen, of course, dismissed *De oratore, De republica, De officiis* and the rest as mere derivative journalism; MacKendrick's baggy monster of a book,[3] simply by reminding us in detail of what Cicero says and how he transforms the sources he used, provides ample evidence that that judgement too is a travesty of the truth.

Habicht and MacKendrick neatly complement each other, but a synthesis of their two approaches is needed to do justice to the Cicero who inspired such diverse readers as Augustine, Petrarch, Milton, Hume and Jefferson.[4] The statesman *was* the philosopher; the literary works were also political acts.

Cicero's formative years saw Sulla's march on Rome, the civil war, the proscriptions, and the crippling of the tribunate which allowed Sulla's heirs a decade of unchallenged exploitation—in short, a period of right-wing reaction, violent and corrupt. I think Habicht goes seriously wrong here. He sees the *populares* of the Gracchan period as a new phenomenon, and Sulla as restoring traditional senatorial control.[5] But the Republic was always *senatus populusque Romanus*, a balance between the interests of the few and the interests of the many (who were the sovereign People); in Greek theory, it was a 'mixed constitution' with both oligarchic and democratic elements. The new phenomenon was Sulla himself, and the polarization of political conflict he brought about. Cicero never forgot the proscriptions; and when he was a junior senator it was the *populares* who stood for traditional values and the reform of corrupt government.

Neither Habicht nor MacKendrick gets this clear. 'In exposing the corruption of the provincial governor Verres,' writes MacKendrick, 'he showed the keen awareness of the necessary connection between ethics and politics which is also clear in his famous speeches against the vicious upper-class conspirator Catiline.'[6] Yes indeed, but what matters is that Verres was part of the ruling clique, while Catiline was trying to overthrow the government in a *coup d'état*. In 70 BC, Cicero's eloquence was for the opposition; in 63 it was for the establishment. What had happened in the meantime was that the *popularis* reformers had lost the moral high ground; by the time he was consul, Cicero saw the threat to constitutional government as coming now not from the right but from the left.[7]

In executing the conspirators without trial, on the strength of a senatorial decree which could be argued to excuse the illegality, Cicero took firm executive action in a very dangerous situation. The price he paid for it was the understandable hostility of the *populares*, which resulted in his exile four years later; but he was right to be proud of his achievement. He boasted of it, as Seneca said later, 'non sine causa sed sine fine'. MacKendrick is indulgent ('a vanity which most readers find more endearing than annoying'), but Habicht takes an almost Mommsenian line on Cicero's 'megalomania'. Again, I think he has missed the point: *res gestae* conferred *auctoritas*, and Cicero as an ex-consul was hardly expected to 'step back into the ranks', as Habicht puts it.[8] Even his measuring himself against Pompey and Caesar ('I do not rate the achievements of these great warlords above my own') does not deserve Habicht's irony: there was more to leading the *res publica* than extending the bounds of its empire.[9]

But Pompey and Caesar had a popular power base against which mere conservative conscience could not prevail. Their alliance (with Crassus, the 'first triumvirate') saw Cicero politically neutralized, and then exiled. Pompey helped to bring about his recall, but Cicero's subsequent six-month fling of confident independence was brought to an end by the renewal of the 'triumvirate'. Unsupported by those who should have been his allies (the senatorial establishment), he recognized the realities of power and abandoned his opposition. Naturally, he was not proud of his 'palinode', but Habicht greatly overstates his shame and humiliation. It was not his fault if the Republic was finished; and there were other ways of working for its revival.[10]

It seems to me quite wrong to interpret Cicero's first great period of literary work as a mere consolation for political failure. *De oratore*, *De republica* and the unfinished *De legibus* defend and celebrate the ideals of constitutional government in a free republic more powerfully than any fighting speech to Senate or People could have done. It was these brilliantly innovative dialogues that established Cicero as the voice and conscience of the Republic, politically in the wilderness though he was. In his first chapter Habicht rightly notes that 'on the eve of the Civil War, in the fall of 50 BC, no other Roman citizen was courted as much as Cicero by both protagonists, Caesar and Pompey; both recognized him to be a special political force.'[11] A special moral force, MacKendrick might say; but the two are not to be distinguished.

For Cicero, civil war was the worst of evils. When two dynasts fight for power, one of them in the name of the Republic, what do honour and principle demand? Cicero's agonized deliberations in his letters to Atticus represent, as L.P. Wilkinson remarked in 1949, 'familiar stations on the Via Dolorosa of modern Europe'. He refused to lend respectability to Caesar's Senate ('I think better of myself for that'), but then had to spend three miserable and depressed years away from Rome as the power struggle was fought out.[12] There was a moment in the summer of 46, after Caesar's victorious return, when Cicero thought he saw the opportunity of influencing the dictator towards a form of constitutional rule. But it was an illusion. Caesar went off to fight again, and came back to a style of government more openly autocratic and contemptuous of republican forms.

Once again, Cicero turned to his study. The astonishing series of ethical and theological dialogues he now produced—nearly thirty volumes in less than two years, including the major treatises *De finibus* and *De officiis*—was partly conceived as personal consolation for the loss of his beloved daughter. But there was another motive, equally clearly expressed: 'this is now the only way I can serve my country.'[13] Hermann Strasburger, in an unpublished lecture reported by Habicht, argued that the whole series was 'a well planned attack on Caesar's rule'.[14] In a sense, that must be right. There is no overt opposition,[15] but the whole tone and ethos of the essays is a tacit reproach to the world of power politics. And their influence has far outlasted the circumstances of their composition.

It was while Cicero was engaged in this ambitious programme that Brutus and his fellow-conspirators assassinated the dictator. They called out Cicero's name, to symbolize the Republic—but the Republic could not simply resume. It took Cicero's own courage and conscience, six months later, to bring it briefly back to life, in defiance of Antony and the veterans of Caesar's legions.[16] He was composing *De officiis*—on duties—as he rallied the Senate against the man he saw as a new Catiline, a dissolute *popularis* with a private army. 'Antony was worth twenty of you, you bastard,' says the young schoolmaster in Kingsley Amis's novel.[17] It is a 1960s comment on a 1960s hero. Antony was sexy and glamorous—but when he got supreme power he had Cicero hunted down and killed, and nailed his severed head and hands to what had once been the speakers' platform of a free Republic.

Cicero matters, and not just to classical scholars. Habicht and MacKendrick have done well to set out so clearly the two main reasons why he matters: a political career which for all its failings and compromises stood for the rule of law against the rule of force, and a literary corpus that effectively defined our civilization's concepts of *humanitas* and the liberal virtues. Mommsen was wrong. We need to read Cicero's lesson; Caesar's is all too familiar.

7

Who Was Crassicius Pansa?

Suetonius *De grammaticis* 18:

1. L. Crassicius genere Tarentinus ordinis libertini cognomine Pasicles, mox Pansam se transnominavit.
2. Hic initio circa scenam versatus est dum mimographos adiuvat, deinde in pergula docuit donec commentario Zmyrnae edito adeo inclaruit ut haec de eo scriberentur:

    > Uni Crassicio se credere Zmyrna probavit:
    >   desinite indocti coniugio hanc petere.
    > soli Crassicio se dixit nubere velle
    >   intima cui soli nota sua extiterint.

3. Sed cum edoceret iam multos ac nobiles (in his Iullum Antonium triumviri filium), ut Verrio quoque Flacco conpararetur, dimissa repente schola transiit ad Q. Sextii philosophi sectam.

Lucius Crassicius was a Tarentine by descent and a freedman in rank. His *cognomen* was Pasicles, but he soon changed his name to Pansa. At first he was involved with the stage while assisting the writers of mime; then he taught as a schoolmaster until the publication of his commentary on [Cinna's poem] *Zmyrna*. That made him so famous that the following poem was written about him:

> Zmyrna will trust herself to Crassicius only;
>   Unlearned suitors, do not seek her hand!
> Zmyrna will be a bride to Crassicius only;
>   Her secret parts are known to him alone.

But when he had already taught many noble pupils (among them Iullus Antonius, son of the Triumvir), with the result that he was compared even with Verrius Flaccus, he suddenly abandoned his school and went over to Quintus Sextius' philosophical sect.

I

Crassicius was not a common name. The earliest known holders of it are C. Crassicius P.f., *magister* of a *collegium* on Delos in 113 BC; C. Crassicius P.f. C.n. Verris (evidently a close relative, if not the same man), local magistrate at the Latin town of Cora, responsible for approving and dedicating the new temple of Castor and Pollux; and Ti. Crassicius, one of the contractors for the wall in front of the temple of Serapis at Puteoli in 105 BC.[1]

Since the other dedicator of the Cora temple (M. Calvius M.f. P.n.) and the two magistrates who had earlier been responsible for getting it built ([M.] Calvius P.f. P.n., C. Geminius C.f. Mateiclus) were also from families attested at the time on Delos, it has been convincingly argued that at Cora, as elsewhere in Latium and Campania, ambitious new building projects were being financed by the munificence of local aristocracies made rich by intensive cultivation for export to the Greek East.[2] (At Cora, the slopes of the Monti Lepini are well suited to olive cultivation, and we know that Italian *olearii* were already active on Delos by about 100 BC.)[3] It is no surprise, therefore, to find Crassicii also at 'little Delos', as a contemporary author called the port of Puteoli.[4]

They appear comparatively early at Beneventum as well, where a L. Crassicius (no *cognomen*) was *IIvir iure dicundo*.[5] The communications centre of southern Italy, ideal for keeping in touch with Puteoli and the bay of Naples in one direction and Tarentum and Brundisium in the other, Beneventum was a natural base for commercial interests;[6] the Beneventan Crassicii, however, may be there for a different reason, the settlement of legionary veterans in 41 BC.[7]

Our Crassicius seems to attest the *gens* at Tarentum itself—probably in the seventies BC, though the chronology is unclear.[8] The great days of Lacedaemonian Taras had been ended by the Punic Wars; in 122 BC the Roman colony of Neptunia was founded there, and from then on Tarentum was an amalgam of Greek and Roman, where the Latin satires of Lucilius and the Greek poems of Archias were appreciated with equal enthusiasm.[9] Pompey settled some ex-pirates on marginal land there in 67 BC, but the main part of the proverbially fertile Tarentine territory was occupied by great estates, where a landowner of Epicurean tastes could live in luxury.[10] The produce of those estates was shipped out of the great harbour; founded by a dolphin-riding son of Poseidon, Tarentum was always an important port, even after Brundisium had taken much of the traffic to Greece and the East.[11]

However, if Suetonius is right that Pasicles the freedman was Tarentine by *birth*, then he provides no sure evidence that the Crassicii were active in the town. For the most likely way for a Tarentine to be enslaved in the seventies BC was by capture in a pirate raid, in which case a Crassicius could have bought him in the slave market at Delos or elsewhere.[12] No comment in Suetonius, but some such explanation seems called for by the apparent contradiction between '*genere* Tarentinus', a phrase appropriate to a free man, and 'ordinis libertini'; perhaps Pasicles' situation was analogous to that of the grammarian Tyrannio of Amisus, captured and manumitted by L. Murena after the sack of the city in 72 BC.[13]

On manumission, Pasicles turned himself into a plausible-sounding Roman by changing his name. Of more than sixty cases of double nomenclature in the city of Rome—known from the indices of *CIL* VI, and the formula *qui et* (or *quae et*) linking the old name and the new—about half seem to represent a transition from a Greek to a Latin name; a characteristic case is that of Zosimus the trierarch, who on enfranchisement became 'M. Plotius Paulus qui et Zosimus'.[14]

For a man who had to carve out his career in the first generation of Roman Italy, no doubt it was better to be known as Pansa than as Pasicles. But it was precisely because of the Hellenization of Roman culture that his career was possible at all.

II

In a Greek city, the theatre was usually the most conspicuous building, visible from afar to the approaching traveller (as for instance at Miletus, Ephesus, or Pergamum), and symbolizing the *polis* itself as the place where *politai* met to honour their gods and conduct their political business.[15] When the munificent local aristocrats of central Italy used their wealth to adorn their native towns in Hellenistic style, it was theatres as well as temples that they built—or complexes that were temple and theatre all in one, as at Tibur and Praeneste.[16] This *Hellenismus in Mittelitalien* was not merely architectural: theatres, *exhedrae*, and *scholae* were for actors, dancers, rhetors and poets to perform in, and the Hellenized towns of Italy, including Rome itself by the first century BC, became part of the 'circuit' for dramatic performers and literary men who toured the centres of Greek culture from festival to festival, showing off their skills to appreciative audiences.[17]

L. Crassicius Pansa started in the theatre, 'helping the mime-writers.' That puzzling phrase becomes easier to understand when we remember that in the first century BC 'mime' was no longer mere knockabout farce, but sophisticated entertainment appealing to a cultured and Hellenized public. For Cicero's contemporaries, the 'Greek stage' with its voluptuous dancers was something new, associated above all with Alexandria, and to be welcomed or deplored according to one's attitude to Hellenistic cultural innovations in general.[18] One branch of it developed into the tragic ballet of the *pantomimi*, so popular in the Augustan age,[19] and there is clear (though neglected) evidence to show that already in the late Republic scholarly accounts of mime as a genre might include discussion of tragic plots from Greek mythology, and the question of their historicity.[20]

The evidence comes in the Berne scholia to Lucan. Commenting on 'Thyesteae noctem duxere Mycenae' at I 544, the scholiast describes as *fabulosum* the story that the sun hid in horror to avoid seeing Thyestes unwittingly eat his own children whom Atreus had murdered. What really happened was that Atreus predicted an eclipse, and was made king 'because of this skill' in place of his brother. The scholiast had found this version of events 'in libro Catulli qui <in>scribitur †permimologiarum', a title of which the only plausible emendations are *Peri mimologiōn* (Müller) and *Peri mimōn logarion* (Ussani).[21] It is natural to associate this work with 'Catullus the mimographer', author of *Phasma* and *Laureolus* (of which the latter was being performed on the day of Caligula's murder),[22] now convincingly identified with the mimographer Valerius, author of *Phormio*, whom Cicero mentions in a letter of January 53 BC.[23] I argue elsewhere that this person is no other than *doctus Catullus*, the love poet of Verona;[24] if not, then at any rate a contemporary and a relative.

Against this background, it becomes easier to understand why a learned Greek might be 'helping the mimographers' before moving on to teach literature as a *grammaticus* and to write an erudite commentary on the most Alexandrian of Roman poems, Cinna's epyllion *Zmyrna*.[25] The commentary made him famous. Suetonius' account, and the poem he quotes (like those of Bibaculus on Orbilius and Valerius Cato),[26] give an idea of the prominence a successful *grammaticus* might achieve in the world of Hellenized Rome. From the elder Catulus to Hadrian and beyond, Greek culture was an integral part of the life of the Roman élite; and the men who taught it (often ex-slaves, unlike the rhetors and philosophers) could enjoy a prestige quite unrelated to their social origins.[27]

Suetonius' account is not quite the whole of our knowledge about Crassicius Pansa. The fifth-century grammarian Consentius cites him on defective verbs, and the use of the name 'Pansa' in grammatical examples cited by Charisius, Diomedes, and Marius Victorinus is plausibly referred to Pansa's own work.[28] He may also have been a friend of M. Antonius; Cicero names a Crassicius in a list of Antony's *collusores et sodales* that includes Volumnius Eutrapelus, to whose wit, fine literary judgement and profound erudition Cicero himself pays tribute in his correspondence.[29]

Volumnius was the patron of Antony's mistress Cytheris, the mime actress later famous as Gallus' 'Lycoris'.[30] Antony enjoyed the company of actors, and allegedly granted lands in Campania to *mimi* and *mimae* among his cronies; indeed, two members of the land commission itself were connected with the theatre—Numisius(?) Nucula, who wrote mimes, and Caesennius Lento, who had acted in tragedy.[31] Antony was a philhellene, and his tastes (reported for us by hostile witnesses) were those of a substantial part of the Roman élite of his time. Mime was an aspect of Hellenistic culture, not just erotic entertainment for the masses.[32]

Another beneficiary of the land distributions of 44 BC was Antony's tutor in oratory, the Sicilian *rhetor* Sex. Clodius. Like Crassicius, he had adopted a Roman name (Sabinus); like Crassicius, he was bicultural, giving demonstration speeches in both Latin and Greek on the same day—'male *kai kakōs*', said Cassius Severus.[33] He wrote a treatise 'On the Gods' in Greek, which included a comically Euhemerized account of Faunus and the Bona Dea.[34]

III

Crassicius taught Iullus Antonius, presumably in the thirties and early twenties BC. We know from Horace that Iullus was well known as a poet, and the scholiast gives the details: 'He wrote twelve excellent books of *Diomēdeia* in heroic metre, and various prose works as well.'[35] Was the epic in Greek, as the title implies? The Roman aristocrat's poem on an Argive hero takes its place alongside the Veronese scholar-poet's *Peri mimologiōn* (on Mycenaean legend) and the Sicilian rhetorician's *Peri tōn theōn* (on Italian mythology) as part of the extraordinary amalgam of Latin and Greek, Roman and Hellene, that made up the literary culture of the first century BC.[36] One of the most striking aspects of it is revealed in the third stage of Crassicius' career.

Philosophy played an important part in the culture of Hellenized Rome, both privately, with the 'house philosophers' attached to distinguished Romans,[37] and publicly, with the ethical preaching of the various sects to whatever audiences they could find.[38] It was not an esoteric discipline, but integral to literary studies in the broadest sense: L. Piso's tame Epicurean Philodemus of Gadara was a love poet and a literary theorist as well as a philosopher and a historian of philosophy,[39] while in the theatres of the Hellenistic world, which now included Hellenized Italy, you could hear recitations of Empedocles as well as Homer, and even see philosophical works performed as pantomime.[40] It is no accident that Varro describes his work of popular philosophy, the *Menippean Satires*, as 'hic modus scaenatilis'.[41]

Nevertheless, it is startling to find a Roman of distinguished birth not merely studying Greek philosophy, not merely popularizing it, but actually starting a new sect of his own, as if he were Zeno or Epicurus. But that is what Q. Sextius did in the forties BC. Rejecting a senatorial career under Caesar, he turned full time to philosophy (a decision not without mental anguish) and expounded in frank, vigorous and inspiring writings an ethical system with Stoic and Pythagorean features, but independent of both and with a Roman firmness and confidence.[42] He wrote in Greek; one of his best known followers was a Greek (Sotion of Alexandria); and he spent some considerable time in Athens.[43] While he was there he successfully anticipated a poor yield of oil, and made a great profit by buying up the whole olive crop while prices were low.[44]

It may be a coincidence that the Crassicii had been active in Cora, Tarentum(?) and Delos, centres for the export and marketing of olive oil;[45] when Crassicius Pansa abandoned the teaching of literature to follow Sextius, it was no doubt to pursue frugality, temperance and fortitude,[46] not to discuss the economics of cash crop farming. But it is a salutary reminder of what lay behind the cultural Hellenization of the first century BC.[47]

IV

It is just possible that the story of L. Crassicius Pansa had a final chapter unknown to Suetonius. A marginal gloss in a twelfth-century manuscript of a commentary on Donatus' *ars maior* runs as follows:[48]

> *Pandor* similiter inaequaliter declinatur et facit praeteritum *passus sum* et non facit *pansus* differentiae causa, ne videatur eius participium femininum, quod est *pansa*, proprium nomen, videlicet cancellarii Augusti Caesaris qui Pansa vocabatur.
>
> Similarly *pandor* declines differently, making *passus sum*, not *pansus*, as its past tense. This is to distinguish it, so that the feminine past participle *pansa* should not appear to be a proper name, viz. the name of Augustus Caesar's chancellor, who was called Pansa.

The glossator has some other material not found elsewhere, no doubt from grammatical works now lost: one of his derivations of *numerus* is from Numa Pompilius 'who was the inventor of counting [*numerandi*]', comparable to Suetonius' theory that Numa gave his name to coinage (*nummus*); and his aetiological account of the origin of dramatic masks may have come ultimately from some work on *scaenicae origines* which gave an explanation different from those offered by Festus and Gavius Bassus.[49]

As for Pansa, whether the phraseology is the glossator's own (twelfth century) or that of his putative source (fourth to sixth century?), *cancellarius* is likely to be an anachronism. In Augustus' day it meant a doorkeeper; from about the middle of the fourth century onwards, it comes to refer to the confidential official attached to a senior magistrate.[50] The nearest equivalent under the principate was perhaps *a libellis* or *a cognitionibus*,[51] but in Augustus' time those offices had probably not yet evolved; what position would correspond to a *cancellarius* on his staff is anybody's guess. One cannot help thinking, however, of the private secretary's job Horace was offered and turned down.[52] Was that, or something like it, given to L. Crassicius Pansa? If so, then Suetonius was unaware of the fact, despite his familiarity with Augustus' correspondence.[53]

Given the nature of the evidence, all one can do is to draw attention to the possibility.[54] But it is not wholly incredible that Augustus should turn to a distinguished scholar, a follower of the most respectably Roman of philosophical sects,[55] to help him with the burden of his paperwork. The bicultural Pansa would be well qualified for the job, equally at home with either half of Augustus' Greco-Roman empire.[56] So too was another man with a good Roman name—Pansa's younger contemporary, the poet and dramatist Cn. Pompeius Macer. Augustus' librarian in Rome, and subsequently his *procurator* in Asia, Macer was the son of Theophanes of Mytilene.[57] He was a distinguished *eques*, father of a senator; Pansa, with the taint of slavery in his background, could not equal that. But in other respects they had a lot in common.[58]

8

Conspicui Postes Tectaque Digna Deo

The Public Image of Aristocratic and Imperial Houses in the Late Republic and Early Empire

I

> I am building in three places and refurbishing the rest. I live in a rather more expansive style than I used to. It was necessary.

Why was it 'necessary', in March 56 BC, for Cicero to spend extravagantly on building? Because he owed it to his *dignitas*. He had returned gloriously from exile, re-established himself (apparently) as a *princeps civitatis*, and triumphed over his enemies and ill-wishers. As a symbol of that triumph, he was rebuilding the house on the Palatine (and the villas at Tusculum and Formiae) which Clodius had destroyed in 58. Both in its demolition and in its reconstruction, the house represented Cicero's public status, his *existimatio*.[1]

That idea dates back to at least to the second century BC, when Cn. Octavius' Palatine house brought him the *dignitas* of the consulship (165 BC), and when the violent deaths of M. Fulvius Flaccus and L. Saturninus were followed by a kind of *damnatio memoriae* in the demolition of their houses;[2] similar examples of 'public penalty' in the fifth and fourth centuries BC (Sp. Cassius, Sp. Maelius, M. Manlius Capitolinus, M. Vitruvius Vaccus), and the related story of P. Valerius Poblicola's voluntary demolition of his own house on the Velia, may or may not be historical.[3] By the late Republic, at least, it was well understood that a house might perpetuate the fame of its previous owner, and perhaps (by comparison) the shame of its new one, as Cicero alleged of

Antony's occupation of Pompey's house on the Carinae: 'when you see those ships' beaks in the forecourt, do you really think it's your house you're entering?'[4]

The detail he mentions, of the ships' beaks on the walls of the *vestibulum*, is explained by a famous passage of the elder Pliny:[5]

> In the halls of our ancestors, on the other hand, portraits were to be looked at. They weren't statues by foreign artists, they weren't bronze or marble, but faces modelled in wax and set out in individual cabinets. The purpose was to have likenesses to accompany family funerals, and every time anyone died, all the members of the family that there had ever been were present [in the procession]. There were even family-trees, with lines in different directions connecting painted portraits,[5a] and the archive-rooms were full of documents and written records of the acts of magistrates.
>
> Outside and around the entrance doors there were other images of mighty souls, with enemy spoils fixed [to the walls] which no-one who bought the house was allowed to take down: the houses' triumphs continued even when their owners changed. This was a great incentive, as every day the building reproached an unwarlike occupant for entering someone else's triumph.

Ships' beaks were a rather special form of 'enemy spoils', recording Pompey's victory over the pirates. But all *triumphatores* would have trophies of captured arms and armour, like those re-used by the followers of M. Flaccus two years after his Gallic triumph; it is important to remember that after paying his vows to Iuppiter Optimus Maximus, the *triumphator* in his gilded chariot led his procession of captives and wagons of spoil to his own house. He could do what he liked with them, and it is clear from Pliny's description that he used the captured arms to make his *vestibulum*, in effect, a triumphal *monumentum*.[6]

Triumphal *monumenta* were normally temples or porticos—that is, public buildings put up *ex manubiis* (from the sale of booty).[7] But the house of a Roman senator was itself partly public in function,[8] and his *vestibulum* and *atrium* could advertize his glory to the Roman people as effectively as a temple with his name on the architrave.[9] Perhaps even more effectively, to judge by Sallust's phraseology: 'they decorated the temples of gods with honour, and their own houses with glory.'[10]

In fact, there are some striking parallels between house and temple: the *spolia* round the door,[11] the honorific statues in *vestibulum* or *pronaos*,[12] and in all probability also paintings of glorious *res gestae* within.[13] For Scipio Africanus, the Iuppiter temple was like his own *atrium*; his *imago* was kept there, and brought out each time there was a family funeral.[14] And it may not be accidental that great houses were commonly referred to by the names of their one-time owners, just as temples were named after their founders rather than (or as well as) after the divinities they were built for.[15] Both preserved the 'everlasting memory of the name' in the same way.[16]

II

Filippo Coarelli has recently drawn attention to the overlap of private and public functions in the houses of the Roman élite, and to the related overlap of *architettura sacra* and *architettura privata*.[17] The classic example is Caesar's house, the *domus publica*, with its symbolic *fastigium*.[18] Cicero referred to it as the *regia*, and it is particularly in the case of kings' palaces that the interpenetration of private and public functions is most obvious.[19] For instance: when Virgil describes the palace of Latinus, are we to think of a house or a temple?[20]

> Tectum augustum, ingens, centum sublime columnis   170
> urbe fuit summa, Laurentis *regia* Pici,
> horrendum silvis et religione parentum.
> hic sceptra accipere et primos attollere fasces
> regibus omen erat, hoc illis curia *templum*,
> hac sacris sedes epulis, hic ariete caeso   175
> perpetuis soliti patres considere mensis.
> quin etiam *veterum effigies* ex ordine avorum
> antiqua ex cedro, Italusque paterque Sabinus
> vitisator curvam servans sub imagine falcem,
> Saturnusque senex Ianique bifrontis imago   180
> *vestibulo* astabant, aliique ab origine reges,
> Martiaque ob patriam pugnando vulnera passi.
> multaque praeterea sacris *in postibus* arma
> captivi pendent currus curvaeque secures
> et cristae capitum et portarum ingentia claustra   185
> spiculaque clipeique ereptaque rostra carinis.

The *palace* of Laurentine Picus was a majestic building, with its great height supported on a hundred columns, and standing on the highest ground in the city; it was a place of dread, set in clustering trees and charged with traditional awe. Here, if he would have a prosperous reign, every king must on his accession receive the sceptre and lift up the rods of office. The palace was a *temple* and was used by the Latins as their senate-house, and it was also the hall for their holy feasts, when by custom the elders sacrificed a ram and in unbroken lines took their places at table.

There too, near the *entrance court*, stood *statues* made of ancient cedarwood *representing ancestors* of old in sequence: Italus, Father Sabinus, planter of the vine, guarding in effigy a bent sickle, aged Saturn, Janus with his two faces, and other kings from the beginning, and heroes too who had received battle-wounds fighting for their homelands. There were hanging also on hallowed [*door-*] *pillars* many weapons, chariots which had been captured, axes with curved edges, crests from helmets, huge bars from gates, spearheads, shields and rams wrenched off ships.

The last line may make us think of Pompey's house,[21] and the ancestral *imagines* are certainly appropriate to a *vestibulum* or an *atrium*, but Virgil is explicit at line 192 that Latinus' palace is a *templum divum*. No doubt his readers understood: whether house or shrine, or both, Latinus' palace was above all a monument to his ancestral glory.

Aeneas' ambassadors came 'augusta ad moenia regis' and were received in a 'tectum *augustum* ingens'.[22] Nowhere else in the *Aeneid* is that adjective used. The inference is inescapable: somehow, Latinus and his palace are to be associated with Augustus. It has been suggested that Virgil was inspired by the Forum Augustum,[23] but that is chronologically impossible. We must believe Servius, who tells us that the allusion was the the Palatine complex—simultaneously palace, senate-house, and temple, just as in Virgil's description.[24]

But in what sense was Augustus' house a palace? His private quarters were deliberately modest; and the evidence is quite clear that his Palatine property consisted of individual houses with streets and alleys between them, not a vast unitary complex like the 'Golden House' or the Flavian palace.[25] We shall understand it better if we ask ourselves what impression it made from *outside*.

Cicero's Palatine house was 'in sight of practically the whole city';[26] so too was Pompey's house on the Carinae;[27] it was normal, of course, for the houses of great men to be high and dominating.[28] Caesar's *domus publica*, it is true, was on low ground at the base of the hill, but he could still emphasize its grand gabled entrance: on one occasion he covered the Forum with awnings that led up the Sacra Via as far as his house.[29] As to a temple, so to a *regia*, the approach must be impressive.

We know very little of the Augustan complex as it was before the fire of AD 3 (or thereabouts), but its rebuilt version certainly had a conspicuous entrance, hung with *spolia* in the traditional way.[30] The *postes* were bound with laurel, the *corona civica* hung over the door (probably in a *fastigium*), and the *vestibulum* carried the inscription honouring Augustus as *pater patriae*; that is, both the honours Augustus was most proud of, which he records in the final paragraphs of the *Res gestae*, were represented visibly on the entrance to his house.[31] But where was it? And how did one approach it?

III

To simplify description, it is convenient to think of the Palatine as lozenge-shaped, with the sides formed by the Via Triumphalis on the south-east, the Circus Maximus on the south-west, the Velabrum valley on the north-east, and the so-called 'forum adiectum' on the north-west.[32] Thus the western corner faces the Forum Bovarium and the river, the northern corner overlooks the Forum, the eastern corner corresponds roughly with the summit of the ridge leading to the Velia, and the southern corner faces the Porta Capena [fig. vii].[33] We shall, in fact, be concerned with all four of these cardinal points in turn.

The western corner, facing the river, overlooked the slope of the Cermalus, where the vessel carrying Romulus and Remus came to rest.[34] The *scalae Caci*, which descended at this point, probably originated as one of the access points of the ancient Palatine settlement. The so-called 'walls of Romulus', however, of which substantial stretches remain at this corner of the hill, are not earlier than the fourth century BC.[35] They are in fact terracing walls, and it is natural to associate them with the building, at this corner of the hill, of the temple of Victoria, completed in 294.[36] (It may be that the temple of Iuppiter Victor, vowed at the battle of Sentinum in 295, belongs to the same programme.)[37]

It is unwise to be too dogmatic before the completion of Patrizio Pensabene's important excavations around the temple of Magna Mater, but the present state of our knowledge suggests a substantial reorganization of the western corner of the hill in the 290s BC, with the terrace walls incorporating a new means of access, the Clivus Victoriae.[38] The

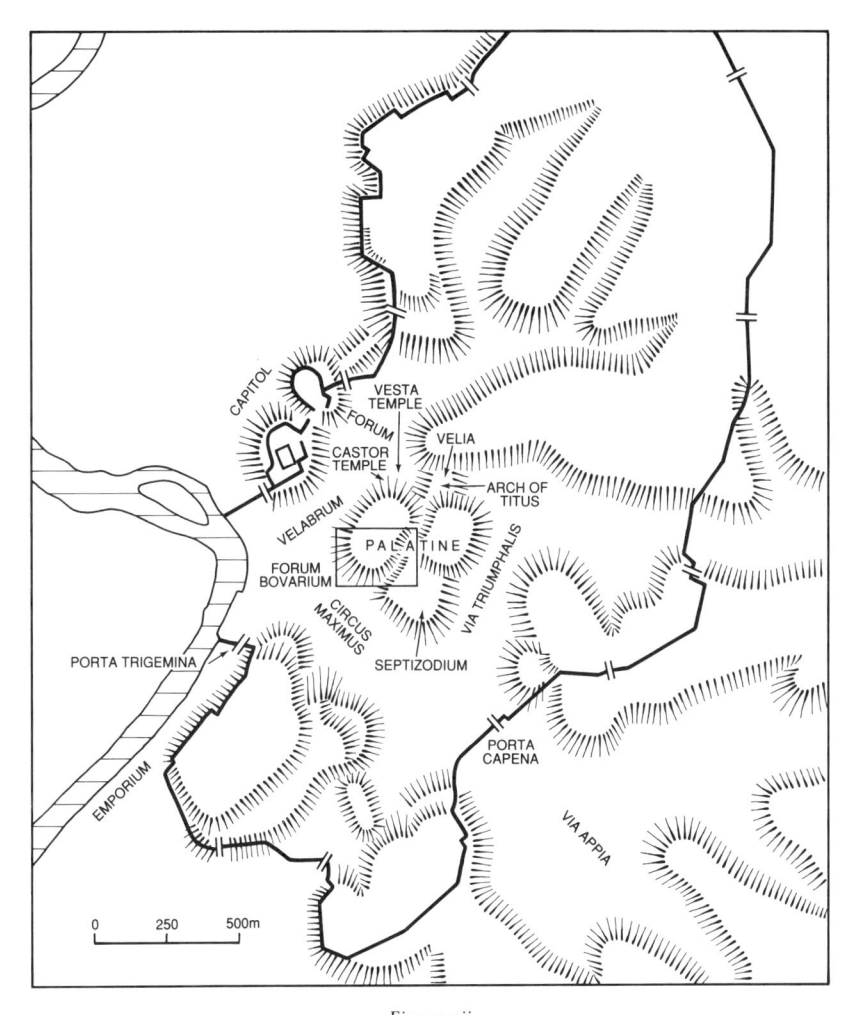

Figure vii

The Palatine and adjacent areas. The rectangle represents the area mapped in fig. viii.

effect must have been like that of the entrance to an acropolis, and the choice of Victoria (Nike) for the temple at the gate suggests that the Athenian acropolis may have been in the architects' minds.

More important, however, is the fact that it faced the river. Rome was a port, and her river harbour was where many travellers first arrived in the city. (From the second century BC onwards, most traffic probably landed at the Emporium below the Aventine, but travellers would enter the city itself at the same place, via the Porta Trigemina.) The bustling commercial area of the Forum Bovarium was therefore where a foreign visitor might well have his first impression of Rome.[39] One thinks of the way Greek city planners liked to provide a grandiose architectural view from the harbour—a theatre, for example, as at Ephesus or Miletus.

It may be no accident that the first proposal for a permanent theatre in Rome, by the censors of 154 BC, envisaged a *cavea* against the slope of the Palatine above the Lupercal.[40] By that time, the precinct of Victoria on the brow of the hill contained the great new temple of Magna Mater (dedicated in 191 BC), in front of which the *ludi Megalenses* were held each April in temporary theatres erected for the purpose.[41] There was a hut or cabin nearby, evidently used as the headquarters of the goddess' eunuch priests, which could be incorporated into the stage structure.[42]

In due course, and before it was much more than two centuries old, the whole complex was given a new significance by historians and antiquarians in search of evidence for the origins of Rome. The temple of Victoria was attributed to Evander and his Arcadians;[43] the terracing walls of *opus quadratum* were identified as the Romulean fortifications of Roma Quadrata;[44] and even the cabin by the Magna Mater temple, at the top of the *scalae Caci*, was called the hut of Faustulus, or of Remus, or of Romulus himself.[45]

Into this amalgam of history and legend, where the gods of victory presided over the relics of the founder,[46] Octavian inserted himself—and Apollo—in the thirties BC. I have tried elsewhere to show how he exploited the associations of the area in which he chose to live, and how Virgil's *Aeneid* reveals the necessary Augustan interpretation of Magna Mater as the Trojan goddess, protectress of Aeneas and of his descendants, the Iulii.[47] What matters here is to recognize that the approach to his house was from the Lupercal (the founder's shrine), up the Clivus Victoriae to the acropolis of Roma Quadrata (*caput imperii*),[48] where Augustus lived between Magna Mater (in the precinct of Victoria) and Apollo of Actium [fig. viii].

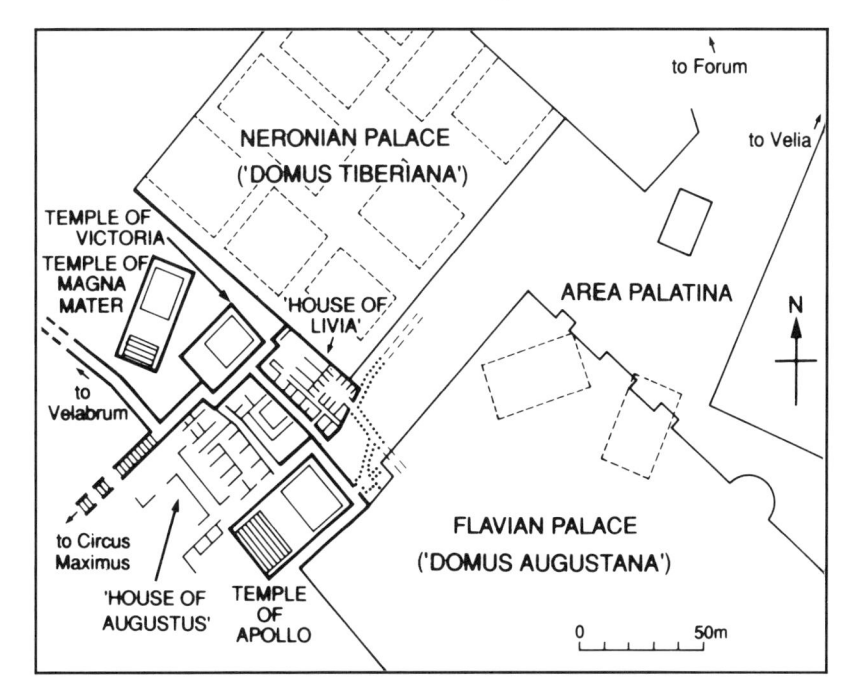

Figure viii

The western quarter of the Palatine. To the left, the steps leading down to the Circus Maximus (and the Lupercal) are the Scalae Caci; the road leading down to the Velabrum is the Clivus Victoriae. At the top right, the route to the Velia is the so-called 'Clivus Palatinus' leading to the Arch of Titus.

Virgil makes an allusion to that approach at a central point in the *Aeneid*, where Anchises in Elysium shows Aeneas his future descendants. After the Alban kings we see, in correct topographical order, Romulus the founder, the walls of his citadels, Magna Mater as a simile for Rome itself, and then the Julian line culminating in Augustus:[48a]

> Quin et avo comitem sese Mavortius addet
> Romulus, Assaraci quem sanguinis Ilia mater
> educet. viden ut geminae stant vertice cristae
> et pater ipse suo superum iam signat honore?   780
> en huius, nate, auspiciis illa incluta Roma
> imperium terris, animos aequabit Olympo,

> septemque una sibi muro circumdabit arces,
> felix prole virum: qualis Berecyntia mater
> invehitur curru Phrygias turrita per urbes   785
> laeta deum partu, centum complexa nepotes,
> omnis caelicolas, omnis supera alta tenentis.
> huc geminas nunc flecte acies, hanc aspice gentem
> Romanosque tuos. hic Caesar et omnis Iuli
> progenies magnum caeli ventura sub axem.   790
> hic vir, hic est, tibi quem promitti saepius audis,
> Augustus Caesar, divi genus, aurea condet
> saecula qui rursus Latio regnata per arva
> Saturno quondam, super et Garamantas et Indos
> proferet imperium . . .   795

> Yes, and Romulus, son of Mars, shall join his grandfather and walk with him. He will be of the blood of Assaracus; the mother who will rear him is to be Ilia. Do you see how on his head the twin crests stand, and how his Father already marks him for the exalted life above with his own emblem? See, my son! It will be through his inauguration that Rome shall become illustrious, and extend her authority to the breadth of the earth and her spirit to the height of Olympus. She shall build her single wall round seven citadels, and she shall be blessed in her manhood's increase; like the Mother of Berecyntus, who rides in her chariot through Phrygian cities wearing her towered crown, happy in the divine family which she has borne, and caressing her hundred grandsons, who are all dwellers in Heaven and have homes on high. Now turn the twin gaze of your eyes this way, and look at that family, your own true Romans. For there is Caesar, and all the line of Iulus, who are destined to reach the brilliant height of Heaven. And there in very truth is he whom you have often heard prophesied, Augustus Caesar, son of the Deified, and founder of golden centuries once more in Latium, on those same lands where once Saturn reigned; he shall extend our dominion beyond the Garamantians and the Indians . . .

I think any reader in the twenties BC would have felt himself unmistakably conducted from the Lupercal, up past the Magna Mater temple, to the *vestibulum* of Augustus' house.

Where were the laurels and the oak-leaf crown? Virgil makes no allusion to them, but it is likely that the doorway they adorned faced westwards, towards this symbolically Romulean approach.[49] By AD 3,

IV

For the later years of Augustus we turn from Virgil to Ovid. In the first poem of *Tristia* III, Ovid's book timidly asks the way of a passer-by, evidently in the Argiletum:[51]

>   Paruit, et ducens 'Haec sunt fora Caesaris' inquit,
>   'haec est a sacris quae via nomen habet,
>   hic locus est Vestae, qui Pallada servat et ignem,
>   haec fuit antiqui regia parva Numae.'   30
>   inde petens dextram 'Porta est' ait 'ista Palati,
>   hic Stator, hoc primum condita Roma loco est.'
>   singula dum miror, video fulgentibus armis
>   conspicuos postes tectaque digna deo.
>   'Et Iovis haec' dixi 'domus est?' quod ut esse putarem 35
>   augurium menti querna corona dabat.
>   cuius ut accepi dominum, 'Non fallimur' inquam,
>   et magni verum est hanc Iovis esse domum . . .'

He did what I asked, and led the way. 'These,' he said, 'are the *fora* of Caesar; this is the road that takes its name from sacred things; this is the place of Vesta, who keeps the Palladium and the fire; this used to be the tiny palace of ancient Numa.' Then, leading to the right, he said: 'That is the gate of the Palatine; here is [Iuppiter] Stator; in this place Rome was first founded.' While I was admiring everything in turn, I saw gleaming arms on a splendid doorway, and a building worthy of a god. 'And is this,' I said, 'the house of Iuppiter?' For the oak wreath gave my mind a divine sign to think that it was so. When I heard whose house it was, I replied, 'I'm not mistaken: it is true that this is the house of great Iuppiter.'

The right turn after Vesta and the Regia is now intelligible, thanks to Coarelli's reconstruction of the course of the Sacra Via:[52] the visitor turned off it at the old Palatine gate, made his way up the road excavated by Boni in 1901 (traditionally identified as the Sacra Via) on to the ridge where the Arch of Titus now stands, and proceeded up the so-called 'clivus Palatinus' to the Area Palatina, the piazza later dominated by the vestibule of the Flavian palace.[53]

For Ovid, it was evidently dominated by the vestibule of Augustus' house; and indeed, *domus August(i)ana* is what the Flavian palace was called.[54] The traditional explanation, that the phrase means 'house of *the* Augustus'—i.e. the emperor—is quite unsatisfactory; Castagnoli must surely be right to infer that part, at least, of Augustus' expanding complex was on ground later used for the Flavian palace.[55] Once he had acquired the splendid house to which the 'Aula Isiaca' belonged (preserved below the northern corner of the Flavian palace), Augustus could present his 'splendid doorway' (*conspicui postes*) where they would be seen across the piazza, facing the street that ran up from the Forum. He had turned his back on the Forum Bovarium and the river harbour, to look towards the heart of the city, the Forum Romanum itself.

No doubt it was for that reason that Ovid associated the foundation of Rome with the Porta Mugionia, and Josephus with the Area Palatina; and that archaizing inscriptions—including the *elogium* of Fertor Resius, who invented the *ius fetiale*—were set up along the 'clivus Palatinus'.[56] The Palatine had been turned round, the historic emphasis moved from the Lupercal and Roma Quadrata to the other side of the hill.

But there was a price to pay for this manoeuvre. It was a walk of more than 300 m from Iuppiter Stator and the Porta Mugionia to the piazza in front of Augustus' new *vestibulum*. What Ovid glosses over with 'while I was admiring everything in turn' was a long succession of grand houses, just as in the heavenly Rome:[57]

> Est via sublimis, caelo manifesta sereno:
> Lactea nomen habet, candore notabilis ipso.
> hac iter est superis ad magni tecta Tonantis   170
> regalemque domum; dextra laevaque deorum
> atria nobilium valvis celebrantur apertis;
> plebs habitat diversa locis; hac parte potentes
> caelicolae clarique suos posuere Penates.
> hic locus est, quem, si verbis audacia detur,   175
> haud timeam magni dixisse Palatia caeli.

There is a road on high, visible when the night is clear, called the Milky Way from its famous whiteness. By this road the gods make their way to the royal house, the palace of the great Thunderer. To left and right the halls of the nobles are thronged, their doors wide open. The plebeians live elsewhere; it is here that the powerful and famous among the dwellers in heaven have made their homes. This is the place, if I may make bold to say it, that I should venture to call the Palatine of the sky.

Augustus had turned the Forum Romanum into a great dynastic *monumentum* dominated by the temple of Divus Iulius.[58] But once the visitor had left the Forum, there was a long sequence of other men's *vestibula*, decorated with other men's triumphal *spolia*, before he came finally to the house of the *princeps*. Was it deliberate? Did Augustus choose to play down the idea of a palace-temple complex on an acropolis,[59] and emphasize instead the house of a Roman *princeps civitatis*, excelling his peers only in *auctoritas*?

It may be so: the original approach to the house via the western corner of the Palatine may well belong, with the Mausoleum and the original plan of the Pantheon, to the 'Hellenistic' ideas of the early twenties BC, from which Augustus was subsequently to retreat.[60] But if the mature Augustus moved from a position of quasi-regal autocracy to a concept of authority more acceptable to the Roman republican tradition, the inherently monarchical nature of the principate made it easy for his successors to go back to the original idea. Again, the imperial property on the Palatine provides the evidence. This time, we must turn our attention to the northern corner of the hill, overlooking the Forum itself.

V

The arch which was voted to Octavian after the battle of Actium was erected just south-west of the temple of Divus Iulius.[61] Like the temple itself, it was no doubt completed at the time of the triple triumph in 29 BC, but it was not on the route of the triumphal procession, like the later arches of Tiberius, Titus and Septimius Severus. Instead, it formed a passage from the Forum to the temple of Vesta and the Regia, which once had been part of the house of the king.[62]

Immediately past the arch, between it and the Vesta temple, a ramp led up to the northern corner of the Palatine. Evidently dating from the second century BC, it was an improved version of the original access to the Porta Romanula, the gate of the archaic Palatine settlement before it incorporated the Velia.[63] I think it was probably Octavian's original idea to link the Forum Romanum directly with his Palatine property by means of the ramp.

Already in the thirties BC his agents had been buying up houses to extend his property; he may have hoped ultimately to extend it right along the north-west side of the hill to the Porta Romanula and the ramp down to the Vesta temple. He had Clodius' example to follow in buying up contiguous sites, and Pompey's in attaching his house to his *monumentum*:[64] the whole Forum Romanum was to be his dynastic monument, and his 'triumphal' arch would act as a formal entrance to the *domus Augusta*.[65] If that was really his intention—and I think it quite possible in the immediate aftermath of the Actium victory—then he was raising the traditional concept of the honorific doorway to a level of unprecedented splendour.

However, as we have seen, he stepped back. He allowed the approach from the Forum to his house to be along a street lined with other men's houses, so that his monopoly of visible glory should not be total. Perhaps 12 BC marks the *terminus ante quem* for his change of mind: in that year Vesta was brought to the house, and not *vice versa*. Perhaps, too, Tiberius' influence had some effect; he would certainly not approve of such grandiose display, and his house lay in the way of the planned extension.[66]

Tiberius detested *magnificentia*, and with one exception did no building, public or private, during his own reign. The exception was the temple of Divus Augustus, to which he was committed by *pietas* but which he never took the trouble to complete.[67] It was left to Gaius to dedicate it with due ceremony[68]—and it was left to Gaius to achieve at last the extension of the Palatine complex to the Forum Romanum.

Suetonius is explicit: 'he brought forward part of the *palatium* as far as the Forum, having transformed the temple of Castor into a *vestibulum*.' And Dio reports Gaius' boast that he had the Dioscuri as doorkeepers for his new entrance to the Palatium.[69] What this must mean is that the way to the imperial residence was to be through Augustus' arch, with the temple of Castor and Pollux on one side and that of Divus Iulius on the other, and thence up the ramp by the temple of Vesta. The trophies on the arch itself, and the *rostra* on the two flanking temples,[70] formed a magnificently grandiose version of the traditional decoration of the house of a *triumphator* (p. 99 above). And now there was to be no competition. The long line of 'rival' houses between the Porta Mugionia and the Area Palatina was by-passed; the visitor could now go straight from the dynastic splendours of the Forum Romanum with only Vesta's temple, symbol of the eternity of Rome, to distract his attention from the glory of the Julian house.

For two reasons, it is appropriate that the completion of Octavian's original plan (if such it was) should fall to Gaius. First, because he put into practice the notion of a 'Hellenistic' autocracy which Octavian and his friends had toyed with in the early days, before Augustus decided to emphasize instead the Roman republican aspect of his power; Octavian as Apollo in the 'banquet of the twelve gods', or as the divinized ruler in the original plan for the Pantheon, was presenting exactly the image of authority that Gaius presented (and would no doubt have met Gaius' fate if he had persevered).[71] Second, because Gaius was the heir of the young Caesar not only in spirit but also by blood: when Augustus had been forced by *atrox fortuna* to adopt Tiberius as his heir in AD 4, he had also arranged that ultimately the power should return, via Germanicus, to his own great-grandsons, the sons of Agrippina. Seianus nearly frustrated that plan, but Gaius survived, to rule as the last of the Iulii Caesares.[72]

The death of Caesar in 44 BC had been symbolized by the fall of the *fastigium*—the symbol of divinity—from his house.[73] When Gaius was killed, the Senate met to restore the Republic after a century of Julian tyranny; now that the last of the Caesars was dead, their memory should be abolished by the destruction of their temples[74]—and that meant their private property as well. For Gaius had gone further even than Octavian had planned. He had incorporated into the imperial complex *both* the dynastic temples of the Caesars—Divus Iulius into his vestibule, Divus Augustus into his passage to the Capitol. Not content with Apollo, Vesta and the Dioscuri, Gaius must bring in Iuppiter Capitolinus as well, and reach out from the *caput imperii* to the *caput rerum*. As Pliny observed, Gaius' property (like Nero's later) seemed to enclose the whole city.[75]

VI

With Nero, we move from the western and northern corners of the Palatine to the eastern corner, the ridge leading to the Velia. That was the way his *domus transitoria* extended from the imperial property on the Palatine, now splendidly refurbished, to the Gardens of Maecenas on the Esquiline.[76] The familiar process of property acquisition must have brought into the emperor's possession those of the sequence of *atria nobilium* that stood along the 'clivus Palatinus'. The others, on the street leading down to the Porta Mugionia (including the house of C. Caecina Largus *cos.* AD 42, which Clodius had once bought from M. Scaurus for nearly 15 million sesterces), were conveniently removed in the great fire of AD 64.[77]

That disaster enabled Nero to rebuild on a grander scale; and the destruction, at last, of those aristocratic houses which stood between the Forum and the Area Palatina made it possible for him to outdo even Gaius with the magnificence of his Palatine entrance.

Nero's *vestibulum* was on the crest of the ridge at the eastern corner of the hill, appropriately central for a house that stretched *a Palatio Esquilias usque*, and at this nodal point stood the hundred-foot bronze colossus of the emperor himself.[78] Leading up to it from the Forum, he planned—and the Flavians probably completed—a grand rectilinear approach, with arcades and pillared halls, that involved the realignment of the whole area from the temple of Vesta to the ridge itself.[79] Where once the old Porta Mugionia had marked the entrance to the Palatine, now a splendid broad avenue led straight up to what was still recognizably the entrance to a house—a *vestibulum* with a statue inside—but on a titanic scale.[80] (Whether it was decorated with appropriate *spolia*, we do not know; according to Suetonius, the crowns Nero won on his Greek tour were hung up in the bedrooms, not the vestibule.)[81]

Vespasian, of course, turned the private pleasure-ground of the *domus aurea* to public use, and converted the colossus into a statue of the Sun.[82] But the great avenue was completed, and for Domitian, at least, served the same purpose of self-glorification. Here is Martial's book, coming past the temple of Vesta just like Ovid's two generations before:

> Quaeris iter, dicam. vicinum Castora canae
>   transibis Vestae virgineamque domum.
> inde sacro veneranda petes Palatia clivo,
>   plurima qua summi fulget imago ducis.
> nec te detineat miri radiata colossi,
>   quae Rhodium moles vincere gaudet opus.
> flecte vias . . .

You ask the way; I'll tell you. You'll go past Castor, neighbour of white-haired Vesta, and the house of the Virgins; then you'll make for the revered Palatine up the sacred slope, where many images of the supreme leader are gleaming. Don't be delayed by the radiate mass of the wonderful colossus, which delights to excel the Rhodian work. Turn aside . . .

Ovid's book, going up the Sacra Via, turned right to approach the Palatine through the Porta Mugionia; Martial's book, evidently continuing on the Sacra Via towards Proculus' house, has to turn left to do so.[83] What had been a side road is now the main thoroughfare. On the Neronian realignment, everything leads the eye to the Palatine and the colossus.

Where Martial's book enters on the great avenue to the Palatine (soon to turn off it, on the old Sacra Via), there are 'many gleaming images of the emperor'. Evidently Domitian marked the entrance with conspicuous statues of himself. This was where the Porta Mugionia had stood, and Coarelli makes the attractive suggestion that the 'arcus in sacra via summa' represented on the Haterii relief is to be identified as the Porta Mugionia—presumably as rebuilt after the fire of AD 64.[84] Did Domitian decorate it with gilded statues of himself?

If so, this too may count as another imperial variation of the *conspicui postes* theme: the arch was not Domitian's *vestibulum* (that was in the Area Palatina, on the site of 'Augustus' house'), but it could be regarded as a formal entrance to the imperial complex, as the Arch of Augustus was in Gaius' scheme. All three of the gates of the ancient Palatine—the Scalae Caci, the Porta Romanula and the Porta Mugionia—had now been metamorphosed into gates of the imperial Palatium.

Finally, the southern corner of the hill. Here Septimius Severus built his great monumental façade opposite the Porta Capena:[85]

> Cum Septizodium faceret, nihil aliud cogitavit quam ut ex Africa venientibus suum opus occurreret et, nisi absente eo per praefectum urbis medium simulacrum eius esset locatum, aditum Palatinis aedibus, id est in regium atrium, ab ea parte facere voluisse perhibetur.
>
> When [Severus] was building the Septizodium, the only thing he had in mind was that his work should present itself to those arriving from Africa. The story goes that he wanted to make the entrance to the Palatine complex—i.e. into the royal hall—on that side [of the hill], but that while he was away a statue of himself was placed in the middle of it by the Prefect of the City.

We may well believe that Severus had contemplated an entrance here; after all, the other three corners had all been used for that purpose at one time or another. Even at this late date, the essential ideological elements are clearly recognizable—a personal monument (*suum opus*), like the decorated *vestibulum* of a republican *triumphator*; a king's hall (*regium atrium*), like the palace of Latinus in Virgil's Augustan vision; and, above all, a grand approach to maximise the visual impact.

As Octavian had engineered his first monumental entrance from the river harbour and the Forum Bovarium, and Gaius his from the Forum Romanum and the monuments of the Julian *gens*, and Nero and Domitian theirs from the site of the ancient Palatine gate, so Septimius Severus placed his great façade where it would strike the eyes of travellers from the Via Appia as soon as they entered the city through the dripping arch of the Porta Capena.[86]

VII

It is no accident that what started out as an investigation into the houses of the republican élite, and their role in projecting the *dignitas* and *gloria* of their inhabitants, should have turned into a study of the palaces of emperors and the very nature of the principate.

However much the republican oligarchs detested the idea of autocracy, there were elements in their own ideology, and in the Greek political theories they adapted to it, that led naturally to the supremacy of a single man.[87] Chief among them was the competitive pursuit of glory, the desire to be first, best, greatest, of which the logical outcome was Pompey the Great, Divus Iulius, and the return of monarchy.[88] Glory was expressed in *monumenta*, public and private. Just as the temples and porticos built *ex manubiis* by republican *triumphatores* develop, via the Pompeian and Caesarian complexes, into the public architecture of the emperors, so too there is a direct line of development from the private houses of the republican *principes civitatis*, their *vestibula* hung with triumphal trophies, to the grandiose palaces of Nero and Domitian.

To understand the 'Roman revolution', we must read not only the authors but the city itself. Topography is not a peripheral subject, but a fundamental source of historical evidence. Nobody understands that better than Filippo Coarelli, whose brilliant and exemplary book on the Forum Romanum has been the basis of several of the arguments used in this chapter. I conclude, therefore, with his explanation of a notoriously controversial passage, as an epilogue on the historical interpretation of 'urban space'.

Festus has two items on *porta Romana*, of which the first, Coarelli plausibly suggests, is his own work and not drawn from Verrius Flaccus. It runs as follows:[89]

> Romanam portam vulgus appellat, ubi ex epistylio defluit aqua; qui locus ab antiquis appellari solitus est statuae Cinciae, quod in eo fuit sepulcrum eius familiae. sed porta Romana instituta est a Romulo infimo clivo Victoriae: qui locus gradibus in quadram formatus est. appellata autem Romana a Sabinis praecipue quod ea proximus aditus erat Romam.
>
> What is commonly called the Porta Romana is where the water flows down from the architrave; the place was usually called 'Cincian Statues' by the ancients, since it contained the tomb of that family. But the Porta Romana was set up by Romulus at the bottom of the Clivus Victoriae; the place is formed with steps into a square. However, it was called 'Romana' by the Sabines in particular, because through it was the nearest entrance to Rome.

Two different sites are mentioned, with a garbled reference to a third. The gate with the water flowing down should be the Porta Capena; Romulus' gate at the bottom of the Clivus Victoriae should be that of the *scalae Caci*; and the reference to the Sabines is only appropriate to the gate Varro calls the Porta Romanula, at the northern corner of the Palatine.

Thus far Coarelli. But we have seen that all three of these gates (and the Porta Mugionia as well) were exploited at different times as access points to the imperial property on the Palatine, or at least—in the case of the Porta Capena—as a focus on that property. Festus probably did not live to see the Septizodium, but the great mass of the Flavian palace must already have dominated the view from the Porta Capena in his day. From the river harbour, from the Forum, from the Via Appia, the 'Roman Gate' was the gate that faced the Palatine. Thanks to the emperors, and the story of Romulus, in a sense the Palatine *was* Rome.

ABBREVIATIONS

For the standard abbreviations of the names and works of classical authors, see (e.g.) *The Oxford Classical Dictionary*.

AE	*L'année épigraphique*
AJA	*American Journal of Archaeology*
AJP	*American Journal of Philology*
Ant. Class.	*L'antiquité classique*
ANRW	*Aufstieg und Niedergang der römischen Welt*
Arch. Anz.	*Archäologischer Anzeiger*
ASNP	*Annali della Scuola normale superiore di Pisa*
Ath. Mitt.	*Mitteilungen des deutschen archäologischen Instituts: athenische Abteilung*
BCH	*Bulletin de correspondance hellénique*
BICS	*Bulletin of the Institute of Classical Studies*
Boll. fil. class.	*Bollettino di filologia classica*
Bull. com.	*Bullettino della Commissione archeologica comunale in Roma*
CAH	*The Cambridge Ancient History*
Class. Ant.	*Classical Antiquity*
CP	*Classical Philology*
CQ	*Classical Quarterly*
CR	*Classical Review*
CSEL	*Corpus scriptorum ecclesiasticorum Latinorum*
Dial. Arch.	*Dialoghi di archeologia*
FGrH	*Die Fragmente der griechischen Historiker*
HSCP	*Harvard Studies in Classical Philology*
IG	*Inscriptiones Graecae*
ILLRP	*Inscriptiones Latinae liberae reipublicae*
ILS	*Inscriptiones Latinae selectae*
JHS	*Journal of Hellenic Studies*
JRA	*Journal of Roman Archaeology*
JRS	*Journal of Roman Studies*
LCM	*Liverpool Classical Monthly*
LIMC	*Lexicon iconographicum mythologiae classicae*
MEFR(A)	*Mélanges d'archéologie et d'histoire de l'École française de Rome: Antiquité*

Ox. Pap.	*Oxyrhynchus Papyri*
PBSR	*Papers of the British School at Rome*
PCPS	*Proceedings of the Cambridge Philological Society*
PIR	*Prosopographia imperii Romani*
PME	*Prosopographia militiarum equestrium*
R-E	*Realencyclopädie der classischen Altertumswissenschaft* ('Pauly-Wissowa')
REL	*Revue des études latines*
Rend. Acc. Linc.	*Rendiconti dell'Accademia dei Lincei*
Rend. Pont. Acc.	*Rendiconti della Pontificia Accademia romana di archeologia*
Rh. Mus.	*Rheinisches Museum für Philologie*
Röm. Mitt.	*Mitteilungen des deutschen archäologischen Instituts: römische Abteilung*
SEG	*Supplementum epigraphicum Graecum*
TAPA	*Transactions of the American Philological Association*
TGF	*Tragicorum Graecorum fragmenta*
TLL	*Thesaurus linguae Latinae*
ZPE	*Zeitschrift für Papyrologie und Epigraphik*

NOTES

Introduction

1. Cic. *De or.* II 36, *Orator* 120; Livy pref. 9–10, Tac. *Ann.* IV 33.
2. Polybius I 1.5 (trans. Ian Scott-Kilvert, slightly adapted).
3. Hor. *Epist.* II 1.156f.: 'Graecia capta ferum victorem cepit, et artes intulit agresti Latio.'
4. E.S. Gruen, *Studies in Greek Culture and Roman Policy* (Leiden 1990), *Culture and National Identity in Republican Rome* (Cornell 1992).
5. Mary Beard, 'Cicero and Divination: the Formation of a Latin Discourse', *JRS* 76 (1986) 33–46; Francis Cairns, *Tibullus: a Hellenistic Poet at Rome* (Cambridge 1979); Andrew Wallace-Hadrill, 'Roman Arches and Greek Honours: the Language of Power at Rome', *PCPS* n.s. 36 (1990) 143–81. Out of many possible examples I choose these three *honoris causa*—and in alphabetical order.
6. Hor. *Epist.* II 1.139: 'agricolae prisci, fortes parvoque beati . . .'
7. M.I. Finley, *Politics in the Ancient World* (Cambridge 1983) 126f.
8. Cic. *Sest.* 123. This paragraph is borrowed from my review of Finley's book: *History of Political Thought* 4 (1983) 396–400, at 399f.
9. Evidence for popular participation collected in Claude Nicolet, *The World of the Citizen in Republican Rome* (Eng. trans. London 1980) 361–73.
10. For Cicero as *rex*, see for instance Cic. *Sull.* 21f., *Ad Att.* I 16.10.
11. L. Pearson, *The Greek Historians of the West* (Atlanta 1987) vii, quoting W.A. Heidel; M.L. West, *The Orphic Poems* (Oxford 1983) 2.
12. D.P. Fowler, *Greece and Rome* 33 (1986) 89, on *Catullus and his World* (Cambridge 1985).

Chapter 1

1. R. Syme, *Tacitus* (Oxford 1958) 132. Cf. 135: 'Roman history originated in the register of bare events before eloquence was known.'
2. Cic. *De or.* II 35–6; translation by A.J. Woodman, *Rhetoric in Classical Historiography* (London 1988) 75.
3. Cic. *De or.* II 51–64. On the whole passage, the indispensable discussion is Woodman, op. cit. 74–95 (q.v. for previous bibliography).

4. Cic. *De or.* II 51–3; trans. A.J. Woodman, op. cit. 76–7.
5. Cic. *De or.* II 54 ('non exornatores rerum, sed tantum modo narratores'); cf. II 55–8 for the eloquent Greeks.
6. Fr. 77 Peter (Gellius *NA* II 28.6).
7. Dion Hal. *Ant. Rom.* I 6.2, *kephalaiōdōs* (cf. Nepos *Cato* 3.4 on Cato's *Origines* I–V: *capitulatim*).
8. Pliny *NH* XIII 87, Cens. *De die nat.* 17.11, Dion. Hal. *AR* II 38.3, 39.1, XII 9.3; G. Forsythe, *Phoenix* 44 (1990) 332f.
9. Dion Hal. *AR* IV 7.5, 15.5, XII 9.3; T.P. Wiseman, *Clio's Cosmetics* (Leicester 1979) 12–18.
10. Gellius *NA* V 18.8–9 (Asellio fr. 1–2 Peter): trans. J.C. Rolfe (Loeb). For Piso's *Annals* as 'sane exiliter scripti', see Cic. *Brutus* 106 (cf. *De legibus* I 6).
11. M. Gelzer, *Hermes* 69 (1934) 46–55 = *Kleine Schriften* III (Wiesbaden 1964) 93–103. See also F. Jacoby, *Atthis* (Oxford 1949) 60–6 and 282–8; F. Bömer, *Historia* 2 (1953) 189–209; J.P.V.D. Balsdon, *CQ* n.s. 3 (1953) 158–64; M. Gelzer, *Hermes* 82 (1954) 342–8 = *Kleine Schriften* III (Wiesbaden 1964) 104–10.
12. E. Rawson, *CQ* n.s. 21 (1971) 158–69 = *Roman Culture and Society: Collected Papers* (Oxford 1991) 1–15. For the pontiff's chronicle, and the later 80-book edition referred to by pseudo-Servius (*ad Aen.* I 373), see B.W. Frier, *Libri annales pontificium maximorum: the Origins of the Annalistic Tradition* (Rome 1979).
13. H. Peter (ed.), *Historicorum Romanorum reliquiae* I (Leipzig 1914) iii: 'historiae Romanae primordia repeti solent a pontificis maximi annalibus.' The most significant contributions since Gelzer have been: D. Timpe, in *Aufstieg und Niedergang der römischen Welt* I.2 (Berlin 1972) 928–69, and the papers of J. von Ungern-Sternberg and D. Timpe in *Vergangenheit in mündlicher Uberlieferung* (ed. J. von Ungern-Sternberg and H. Reinau, Stuttgart 1988) 237–65, 266–86; qq.v. for further bibliography.
14. Fabius Pictor fr. 4 Jacoby (*FGrH* 809), fr. 5 Peter: Dion. Hal. *Ant. Rom.* I 79–83. Plut. *Rom.* 3–8. It is immaterial to my argument whether or not Fabius took the story from the otherwise unknown Diocles of Peparethus, as Plutarch states.
15. Cf. Aristotle *Poetics* 1452a.16–18: 'a complex [plot] is one in which the change is accompanied by recognition or reversal, or both.' It is not enough just to call it 'hellenistische Novellistik', as Dieter Timpe does (opp. cit. [n. 13 above] 944 and 275): as Plutarch points out, it is like *drama*.
16. Plut. *Rom.* 8.7, on the *poiēmata* of the *dēmiourgos*; noted by Macaulay in the introduction to the *Lays of Ancient Rome*.
17. R. Syme, *Tacitus* (Oxford 1958) v; *Fictional History Old and New: Hadrian* (James Boyce Memorial Lecture, Oxford 1986) 10 = *Roman Papers* VI (Oxford 1991) 165.
18. Brief description in *La grande Roma dei Tarquinii* (exhibition catalogue, Rome 1990) 97; topographical consequences developed by N. Terrenato in *Papers of the Fourth Conference of Italian Archaeology* IV (ed. E. Herring, R. Whitehouse, J. Wilkins, London 1992) 31–47.
19. A. Grandazzi, *La fondation de Rome: réflexion sur l'histoire* (Paris 1991), esp. 266–71; quotation from p. 222.

20. D. Ridgway, *The First Western Greeks* (Cambridge 1992); for the wider background, cf. W. Burkert, *The Orientalizing Revolution: Near Eastern Influence on Greek Culture in the Early Archaic Age* (Harvard 1992); O. Murray, *Early Greece* (ed. 2, London 1993), chapters V and VI.
21. Op. cit. 131–2, 137.
22. Op. cit. 55–6, 57.
23. W. Rösler, in *Sympotica: a symposium on the Symposion* (ed. O. Murray, Oxford 1990) 230–7.
24. A. Rathje, in *Sympotica* 279–88.
25. Festus 458–9L, 474L (including also Subura).
26. *SEG* XXXI 875; H. Solin, *ZPE* 51 (1983) 180–2.
27. A.J. Ammerman, *AJA* 94 (1990) 627–45.
28. Justin XLIII 3.4 (from Pompeius Trogus, first century BC); cf. *SEG* XXVII 671, XXXII 940–1017 (Gravisca); Herodotus I 165–7 (Phocaeans).
29. Varro *LL* V 45, Festus (Paulus) 18L, Ovid *Fasti* V 637–62. See F. Coarelli, in *Lexicon topographicum urbis Romae* I (Rome 1993) 120–5.
30. *La grande Roma dei Tarquinii* (n. 18 above) 115–18 (A. Sommella Mura) and tav. IX.
31. Strabo V 2.2 (C219–20), etc. Story already known in the late fourth century: *La grande Roma dei Tarquinii* 18f. on the François Tomb at Vulci.
32. *FGrH* 239 F 43 (Thespis, 535–1 BC); Herodotus V 67.5 (Sikyon); Aristotle *Poetics* 1448a. 33–4 (Epicharmus 'earlier than Chionides and Magnes').
33. Plut. *Numa* 8.9; cf. L. Kaibel, *Comicorum Graecorum Fragmenta* I.1 (Berlin 1899) 133–45 on *pseudepicharmea*.
34. Cicero *De republica* II 36, Livy I 35.9, etc.
35. Fabius Pictor *FGrH* 809 F13(b) = Dion. Hal. *AR* VII 70–3; J.C. Szilágyi, *Prospettiva* 24 (1981) 2–23. See L. Bonfante, *Etruscan Life and Afterlife* (Detroit 1986) 241, 258, 261.
36. O. Szemerényi, *Hermes* 103 (1975) 307–19. Oral transmission: J. Heurgon, *La vie quotidienne chez les Étrusques* (Paris 1961) 302f.; Bonfante, op. cit. 266.
37. F. Coarelli, *Il foro romano: periodo arcaico* (Rome 1983) 123 (fig. 38), 145.
38. T.J. Cornell, in *Roma arcaica e le recenti scoperte archeologiche* (Milan 1980) 31; English text in *JRS* 79 (1989) 132.
39. D. Fehling, *Herodotus and his 'Sources'* (trans. J.G. Howie, Leeds 1989) 210, cf. 248, 254. See in general R. Thomas, *Literacy and Orality in Ancient Greece* (Cambridge 1992) 108–13, and E. Tonkin, *Narrating our Pasts: the Social Construction of Oral History* (Cambridge 1992) 85–90.
40. E.J. Bakker, *Oral Tradition* 8 (1993) 10. On the much-debated question of the historicity of the Trojan legend, the most helpful discussions known to me are: J.K. Davies, in *The Trojan War: its Historicity and Context* (ed. L. Foxhall and J.K. Davies, Bristol 1984) 87–110, and B. Hainsworth, *The Iliad: a Commentary* III (Cambridge 1993) 32–53.
41. N. Zorzetti, in *Sympotica* (n. 23 above) 289–307.
42. Date of foundation unknown (*terminus ante quem* 216 BC: Livy XXIII 30.17) but attributed to the early Republic by pseudo-Asconius on Cic. *Verr.* act. 1.31. See n. 45 below.

43. H. Rix, in G. Vogt-Spira (ed.), *Studien zur vorliterarischen Periode im frühen Rom* (Tübingen 1989) 29–39.
44. *Atellana*: H. Petersmann, in Vogt-Spira, op. cit. 135–59. Mime: E. Rawson, in *Tria Lustra: Essays and Notes Presented to John Pinsent* (ed. H.D. Jocelyn and H.V. Hurt, Liverpool 1993) 255–60, on which see p. 150f. below.
45. Livy VI 42.12–14; I suspect that behind Livy's ruthlessly abbreviated (and thus practically incomprehensible) narrative at VI 42.13 there may lurk a partisan account of the origin of the *ludi plebeii*.
46. Varro's reconstruction is itself brilliantly reconstructed by P.L. Schmidt in Vogt-Spira, op. cit. (n. 43) 77–134. Cf. E. Rawson, *Intellectual Life in the Late Roman Republic* (London 1985) 273f.: 'largely a theoretical construction of the Attic model'.
47. Perhaps the *tabula* of the *pontifex maximus* recorded the epidemic and the *ludi scaenici* that were set up as a result: Augustine *Civitas Dei* II 8 ('auctoritate pontificum'); cf. Schmidt, op. cit. 87. According to another version of the story (Plut. *QR* 107, Cluvius Rufus fr. 4P), it was not an innovation at all: the Etruscan *histriones* were brought in to replace actors who had died in the epidemic.
48. Aristotle fr. 609 Rose (*FGrH* 840 F13).
49. Heraclides Ponticus fr. 102 Wehrli (Plut. *Camillus* 22.2); Callimachus *Aetia* fr. 106 Pfeiffer (*panhellados*); Aristoxenus fr. 124 Wehrli (Athenaeus XIV 632a); Demetrius ap. Strabo V 3.5 (C232).
50. See A. Momigliano, *Settimo contributo alla storia degli studi classici e del mondo antico* (Rome 1984) 437–62; E.S. Gruen, *Culture and National Identity in Republican Rome* (Cornell 1992) 6–51, cf. *Studies in Greek Culture and Roman Policy* (Leiden 1990) 11–20.
51. O. Taplin, *Comic Angels* (Oxford 1993). For *Rhinthonica* at Rome, see Schmidt in Vogt-Spira, op. cit. (n. 43) 121–8.
52. *Cognomina*: Q. Publilius Philo, P. Sempronius Sophus (*coss.* 339, 304). *Cista* (made in Rome, *ILLRP* 1197): T. Dohrn, *Die ficoronische Cista* (Berlin 1972).
53. Dated to 263 BC by F. Coarelli, *Il foro romano: periodo repubblicano e augusteo* (Rome 1985) 11–21, and in *Lexicon topographicum* (n. 29 above) 311–3. But 338 or 318 (C. Maenius as consul or censor) may be preferable: see *JRS* 76 (1986) 307.
54. The evidence is collected and discussed by F. Kolb, *Agora und Theater, Volks- und Festversammlung* (Berlin 1981).
55. Festus 120L, cf. Isidore *Origines* XV 3.11. See in general E.J. Jory in J.H. Betts, J.T. Hooker, J.R. Green (eds), *Studies in Honour of T.B.L. Webster* I (Bristol 1986) 143–52, not refuted by Ramsay MacMullen, *Historia* 40 (1991) 420–3; for the Forum as the site of *ludi* as well as gladiatorial *munera*, see Livy XXXI 50.3 (200 BC).
56. Mastarna: *ILS* 212 (speech of Claudius); A. Momigliano, *Claudius: the Emperor and his Achievement* (Oxford 1934) 11–16. *Praetor maximus*: L. Cincius ap. Livy VII 3.5–7, Festus 276L; A. Momigliano, *Quarto contributo alla storia degli studi classici e del monto antico* (Rome 1969) 403–17. See in general Wiseman, op. cit. (n. 9 above) 45; Andrew Drummond in *CAH* VII.2 (ed. 2, Cambridge 1989) 22f.

57. E. Gabba, in *Bilancio critico su Roma arcaica fra monarchia e repubblica* (Atti dei convegni Lincei 100, Rome 1993) 20–22: 'Questa tappa nella formazione della tradizione, verso la fine del IV e gli inizi del III secolo, deve avere visto una forte selezione dei dati storici trasmessi oralmente ed anche della documentazione ... al momento fra IV e III secolo nel quale tutti questi svariati materiali tradizionali venivano selezionati per entrare a formare il corpo storico, che sarebbe poi trasmesso alla prima annalistica ...'
58. Op. cit. (n. 13 above): von Ungern-Sternberg, 261–5; Timpe, 272f., 283–6.
59. T.P. Wiseman, *Catullus and his World* (Cambridge 1985) 26–38; pp. 36, 79f. above. Our ignorance can have startling results; see for instance Mary Beard in F. Graf (ed.), *Mythos in mythenloser Gesellschaft: das Paradigma Roms* (Stuttgart 1993) 56f. on 'the apparent lack of any arena for myth-making or remaking'—as if fifty days a year of *ludi scaenici* were not enough.
60. Wiseman, op. cit. (n. 9 above) 94 n. 124.
61. *Studies* (n. 50 above) 148–57, on Plautus.
62. Paus. I 3.3 (trans. W.H.S. Jones, Loeb ed.).
63. Plut. *Theseus* 28.2 (trans. Ian Scott-Kilvert, Penguin Classics).
64. Augustine *Civitas Dei* XVIII 10, 12 (from Varro *De gente populi Romani*, frr. 18, 23 Fraccaro); also VI 5 (from Varro *Antiquitates divinae*, fr. 10 Cardauns).
65. Cic. *De legibus* I 47.
66. *Fabulae praetextae*: Festus 249L, Pollio ap. Cic. *Ad fam.* X 32.3, Hor. *AP* 286–8 (who implies they were a regular item). Q. Claudia: Ovid *Fasti* IV 326.
67. Suet. *Aug.* 89.3 (for *commissiones* as stage plays, cf. Cic. *Ad Att.* XVI 5.1, Pliny *Ep.* VII 24.6, Macr. *Sat.* II 7.9); Pliny *Paneg.* 54.1–2 (*ludis et commissionibus*, evidently referring to *pantomimi*).
68. Livy I 46.3: 'tulit enim et Romana regia sceleris tragici exemplum.'
69. Livy V 21.9: 'haec ad ostentationem scenae gaudentis miraculis aptiora quam ad fidem.'
70. Livy II 50.11; Dion. Hal. *AR* IX 22.1–3 (trans. E. Cary, Loeb ed.): like *muthoi* and *plasmata theatrika*.
71. Dion Hal. *AR* III 18.1; for *akribeia* in Dionysius, see C. Gill and T.P. Wiseman (eds), *Lies and Fiction in the Ancient World* (Exeter 1993) 143–5.
72. Theatres: e.g. Aristotheus of Troezen at Delphi (*FGrH* 835 F1); cf. A. Momigliano, *Sesto contributo alla storia degli studi classici e del mondo antico* (Rome 1980) 364f. Large audiences: T.P. Wiseman, *History* 66 (1981) 383–7 = *Roman Studies* (Liverpool 1987) 252–6; C. Schultze, in *Past Perspectives: Studies in Greek and Roman Historical Writing* (ed. I. Moxon *et al.*, Cambridge 1986) 134–6.
73. Duris *FGrH* 76 F1 (cf. F56 for the war of 295 BC). See J.R. Morgan in Gill and Wiseman, op. cit. (n. 71) 184–6, who cites earlier bibliography.
74. Polybius II 56.6–12 (trans. Ian Scott-Kilvert, Penguin Classics).
75. Duris *FGrH* 76 F67 (Plut. *Pericles* 28.1): *Douris ... epitragōdei*. On 'tragic

history' in general, see F.W. Walbank, *Historia* 9 (1960) 216–23 = *Selected Papers: Studies in Greek and Roman History and Historiography* (Cambridge 1985) 224–41; and P. Pédech, *Trois historiens méconnus: Théopompe, Duris, Phylarque* (Paris 1989), esp. 368–82 (Duris), 455–66 (Phylarchus).
76. E.g. Polybius I 2.1, 64.3, III 1.4, IX 9.10.
77. Plut. *Moralia* 345e, 347a (trans. F.C. Babbit, Loeb ed.).
78. Cicero *Ad familiares* V 12.5f. trans. A.J. Woodman, op. cit. (n. 2 above) 72–3.
79. G. Townend, *Hermes* 88 (1960) 98–120, and elsewhere; T.P. Wiseman, in *Flavius Josephus: Death of an Emperor* (Exeter 1991) 110–18.
80. Cic. *De amic.* 97; cf. *Brutus* 290 ('in scaena esse Roscium'), *De or.* I 124 ('gerere personam civitatis'), etc. See in general F. Dupont, *L'acteur-roi* (Paris 1985), esp. 19–40, 413–37; and on the city as the theatre of civic life, Wiseman in I.M. Barton (ed.) *Roman Public Buildings* (Exeter 1989) 151–5.
81. Tac. *Ann.* XIV 48–74; Woodman in T.J. Luce and A.J. Woodman (eds), *Tacitus and the Tacitean Tradition* (Princeton 1993) 104–28.
82. 'Reges ecce vobis et monarchas et velut theatrum hodiernae vitae': quoted by M. Morford in Luce and Woodman, op. cit. 138.
83. R. Syme, *Tacitus* (Oxford 1958) 363.
84. *Proc. Brit. Acad.* 48 (1962) 55 = *Roman Papers* VI (Oxford 1991) 85f.
85. Op. cit. (n. 17 above) 24 = 180.
86. *Tacitus* (Oxford 1958) 132 n. 1: 'Hellenistic theory, better practice (a large subject), cannot here be discussed.'
87. Dion. Hal. *AR* I 73.1 ('old records kept on sacred tablets'), Licinius Macer ap. Livy IV 20.8 (*libri lintei*), Livy IV 16.4, VIII 40.4 (*imaginum tituli*), etc.
88. Op. cit. (n. 17) 8 = 162.

Chapter 2

1. G. Wissowa, *Religion und Kultus der Römer* (ed. 2, Munich 1912) 26f.; K. Latte, 'Über eine Eigentumlichkeit der italischen Gottesvorstellung', *Archiv für Religionswissenschaft* 24 (1926) 244–58: 'für diese unspekulativen phantasielosen Menschen . . .' (256), 'keine mythenbildende Phantasie schlingt ihre Ranken um die Götter' (257).
2. C. Koch, *Der römische Juppiter* (Frankfurt 1937) 30: 'Es gibt auf römischen Boden sichere Spuren einer ausserliterarischen, von dem Einfluss der griechischen Dichtung unberührten Mythologie. Die Spuren verteilen sich gleichmässig auf die altrömischen, etruskischen und griechischen Komponente der historischen römischen Religion.' [For the history of the debate see now Fritz Graf in *Mythos in mythenloser Gesellschaft* (ed. F. Graf, Stuttgart and Leipzig 1993) 31–8.]
3. H.J. Rose, *The Roman Questions of Plutarch* (Oxford 1924) 68; F. Coarelli, *Il foro romano: periodo arcaico* (Rome 1983) 261–82, *Il foro boario* (Rome 1988) 244–53, 328–40.

4. [In 'Mythological Invention and *poetica licentia*' (Graf, *Mythos* [n. 2 above] 131–41, esp. 131–2 n. 3), Nicholas Horsfall offers a rejoinder: 'the author of a review so long and at times so polemical ought to have been more patient in the verification of detail.' I have tried to take account of each of his points in the added notes below.]
5. [Livy pref. 6: 'before the city was founded or its foundation planned.' Dr Horsfall (op. cit. 131 n. 3, on this passage) describes as unfounded my objection to his assertion 'that there never existed a clear scale of credibility applicable to legendary-historical material, chronologically differentiated'; the gloss is certainly welcome. H. appeals to J. Poucet, *Gerion* 5 (1987) 69–85, 'heavily in my favour'.]
6. [Horsfall, op. cit. 132: 'I am sorry to deprive Prof. Wiseman of a dozen local heroes, but *Quellenforschung*, unfashionable though it is, cannot simply be ignored, or be dismissed as utterly discredited.' Cf. 131: 'encumbered by neoromantic nostalgia ... for a primitive Latium where bards chanted tales of ancient heroes'; 132: 'to argue ... for the ghostly presence of some primitive mythological survival, in the teeth of the evidence, does not much advance our studies'; 140f.: 'if the mythography of a Virgil or an Ovid crumbles in our hands and reveals not age-old myth lovingly preserved by wandering bards and banqueting nobles but first-rate Hellenistic scholarly and literary techniques, we do not have the right to complain and we would be ill-advised to try to restore romantic primitivism to the mythology of the *Aeneid*.' I leave it to the reader to decide whether that is a recognizable description of the argument I put forward in the text.

In fact, I agree with much of Dr Horsfall's general case: as he rightly says (op. cit. 135), 'the fluidity of myth is not only extreme, but ancient: invention is integral to the telling of myth as far back as we can reach in the texts available to us.' I object only to the privileging of Virgilian invention in particular, the assumption that so *much* invention took place at precisely *that* point. As for the local stories: (a) were there any? Yes, of course. (b) Did Virgil know them? Some of them, no doubt. (c) Did he nevertheless sometimes have to invent? Yes, of course. (d) Does it follow that he *normally* invents? No.]
7. [Horsfall, op. cit. 131 n. 3: 'My chief difficulties with the idea that Greek myth was widely diffused at Rome in the regal period are the barrier of language and the absence of literary forms suited to widespread diffusion.' ('*Literary* forms' implies a significant tacit premise.) Ibid. 132 n. 3: 'Would one have to posit mythological drama already transposed into Latin?' I would say yes: see pp. 12–20 above.]
8. *SEG* XXVI 1144 [see also p. 7 above].
9. E. La Rocca, *Civiltà del Lazio primitivo* (Rome 1976) 361–71.
10. Kleiklos [p. 7 above]: *SEG* XXXI 875; H. Solin, *ZPE* 51 (1983) 180–2. Aristonothos: B. Schweitzer, *Röm. Mitt.* 62 (1955) 78–106; [see now F.-H. Pairault Massa, *Iconologia e politica nell'Italia antica* (Milan 1992) 19f.].
11. *TLE* 761, cf. 155; D. Ridgway, in *Cambridge Ancient History* IV (ed. 2, 1988) 664.

12. I am grateful to David Ridgway for advice on this and other matters in this section.
13. *SEG* XXVII 671; XXXII 940–1017.
14. G. Colonna, in *Gli Etruschi e Roma* (Rome 1981) 171–2.
15. M. Pallottino, *Studi etruschi* 47 (1979) 319ff.; [illustrated in *Cambridge Ancient History* VII.2 (ed. 2, 1989) 79].
16. [Illustrated in *CAH* VII.2 (1989) 45.]
17. Varro ap. Macr. *Sat.* III 6.17 (*ara maxima*); Plut. *QR* 11 (Saturn); Strabo IV 179, 180 (Diana); Cic. *Balb.* 55 (Ceres).
18. *LIMC* s.v. Aigisthos 50; Serv. *Aen.* II 116.
19. Aristotle *Econ.* 1349b34; [Pairault Massa, op. cit. (n. 10 above) 72–5].
20. A. Sommella Mura, in *Enea nel Lazio* (Rome 1981) 115–22. [Temple illustrated in *CAH* VII.2 (1989) 79. 'I'm not sure, though, that you prove that the Roman in the street knew the stories sculpted by the Greek craftsman' (Nicholas Horsfall, *per litteras* 21 Dec. 1989).]
21. See G.H. Huxley, *Greek Epic Poetry from Eumelos to Panyassis* (London 1969), *passim*.
22. M.L. West, *JHS* 108 (1988) 166–72: quotation from p. 172.
23. T.J. Cornell, in *Roma arcaica e le recenti scoperte archeologiche* (Milan 1980) 33, citing A.M. Snodgrass, *The Greek Dark Age* (Edinburgh 1971) 6ff.
24. *SEG* XXVIII 1596, cf. Herodotus IV 152.3.
25. *Oral Tradition* 1.3 (Oct. 1986) 767–808, 3.1–2 (Jan.–May 1988) 191–228; E. Havelock, *Preface to Plato* (Oxford 1963), *The Literate Revolution in Greece and its Cultural Consequences* (Princeton 1982), *The Muse Learns to Write* (Yale 1986).
26. [So it seemed at the time of writing; but see now *Vergangenheit in mündlicher Überlieferung* (ed. J. von Ungern-Sternberg and H. Reinau, Stuttgart 1988), with essays on Rome by von Ungern-Sternberg and Dieter Timpe (pp. 237–65, 266–86); and *Studien zur vorliterarischen Periode im frühen Rom* (ed. G. Vogt-Spira, Tübingen 1989); also Rosalind Thomas, *Literacy and Orality in Ancient Greece* (Cambridge 1992) 158–70, an epilogue on the Roman world.]
27. [The full sentence reads: 'See too, Scobie, *Apul.* [Alex Scobie, *Apuleius and Folklore* (London 1983)] 4f.: the material here neatly gathered shows that, *carmina* aside, no other pre-literary vehicle for myth is known.' I quote at length because Dr Horsfall describes my treatment in the text as 'improperly distorted by partial quotation' (op. cit. [n. 4 above] 132 n. 3).]
28. D. Ridgway, *The Etruscans* (Edinburgh 1981) 36; A. Rathje, *Analecta Romana* 12 (1983) 7–29, esp. 22–6.
29. See E. Bowie, *JHS* 106 (1986) 15–21.
30. Xenophanes fr. 1 DK (trans. Bowra); Anacreon *eleg.* 2 West; *Poetae melici Graeci* 906 Page (trans. Bowra); Mimnermus 14 West (trans. Bowra, slightly adapted); Theognis 563–6, cf. Plato *Meno* 93a1–2.
31. Plut. *Cato maior* 25.3.
32. Cato *Origines* fr. 118P; Varro *de vita populi Romani* fr. 84 Riposati; Theognis 241–3; A. Momigliano, *JRS* 47 (1957) 110. [See pp. 7, 12 above.]
33. Varro *LL* VII 70; *de vita p. R.* fr. 110 Riposati.

34. Heraclitus fr. 104 DK; Hom. *Od.* VIII 472; E. Havelock, *BICS* 13 (1966) 56 = *The Literate Revolution* (n. 25 above) 243f.
35. Pliny *Ep.* II 20.1: 'get out a penny and hear a golden story.'
36. Excellent collection in Scobie, op. cit. (n. 27 above) 11–16.
37. Pliny *Ep.* IV 7.6. [Horsfall, op. cit. (n. 4) 132 n. 3: 'none of our evidence for *circulatores* (cf. now *Greece and Rome* 36 [1989] 78 n. 84) suggests that they retold myths.']
38. Cf. Petronius *Sat.* 68.6.
39. Nurses: Scobie, op. cit. (n. 27) 16–22; Cic. *De leg.* I 47.
40. Suet. *Div. Aug.* 74; 'aut acroamata et histriones aut etiam triviales ex circo ludios interponebat ac frequentius aretalogos.'
41. See Dio Chrysostom *Or.* 20.10 for such people in the *hippodromos*.
42. W. Starkie, *The Waveless Plain* (London 1938) 278–9. [For analogous performers in the ancient world, see R.J. Starr, *Rh. Mus.* 132 (1989) 411–2 on Gellius *NA* XVIII 5.2–5, Achilles Tatius III 20.4–7, Petr. *Sat.* 59.3.]
43. Cf. N. Horsfall, *JRS* 63 (1973) 68–79.
44. F. Jurgeit, in *Tainia Roland Hampe zum 70. Geburtstag dargebracht* (Mainz 1980) 272–5.
45. F. Coarelli, *Il monumento di Verrio Flacco nel foro di Preneste* (Palestrina 1987) 17–27.
46. Varro *LL* VI 19—though in fact both the text and the meaning of the passage are very uncertain.
47. Ovid *Fasti* IV 326: 'mira sed et scaena testificata loquar.'
48. [Horsfall, op. cit. (n. 4) 131 n. 3: 'Of course my remarks about the lack of mythological mime-titles derive from careful reading of Ribbeck's index (*Com. Rom. Frag.* ed. mai. 505) and it is mere vituperative bluster to suggest otherwise.' I have searched my text in vain for any such suggestion. 'That Laberius' *Caeculi* or *Gemelli* were mythological in context is pure speculation. Nor do I see how an Atellan farce might treat a mythological subject (Novius' *Picus*) or how an event of 204 BC (Ovid *Fasti* IV 326), however romaticized, can be called mythical.']
49. *JRS* 78 (1988) 9 [p. 79f. above]; P.B. Corbett, *The Scurra* (Edinburgh 1986), esp. ch. 3.
50. Livy VII 2.4–10; O. Szemerényi, *Hermes* 103 (1975) 307–19; [pp. 10–13 above].
51. Dio LXII 26.4, Tac. *Ann.* XVI 21; Livy X 2.15. [For the theatre (and the arena) as the site of rituals confirming civic identity, cf. T.N. Habinek, *Materiali e discussioni* 25 (1990) 54–60, on Hypata, Corinth and Cenchreae in Apuleius' *Metamorphoses*.]

Chapter 3

1. Apul. *Met.* VI 28.4 ('honores'), 28.6 ('gaudiis popularium pomparum ovantem'); 29.2: 'nam memoriam praesentis fortunae meae divinaeque providentiae perpetua testatione signabo, et depictam in tabula fugae praesentis imaginem meae domus atrio dedicabo. Visetur et in fabulis

audietur doctorumque stilis rudis perpetuabitur historia "Asino vectore virgo regia fugiens captivitatem".'

2. Cf. Cic. *De or.* II 63 on the subject-matter of history 'in rebus magnis memoriaque dignis'; for *Res gestae* and *Res Romanae* as history-book titles, cf. Nonius 835L, Gell. *NA* XI 8.2, Diodorus VII 5.4, etc.

3. On triumphs as the annalist's subject-matter, cf. Asellio fr. 2P (Gell. *NA* VI 18.9): 'scribere autem bellum initum quo consule et quo confectum sit et quis triumphans introierit ex eo ...' [p. 4 above].

4. Cf. Cic. *Verr.* IV 69 on *monumenta* and the *nominis aeterna memoria*; Pliny *NH* XXXV 22f. on the *tabula Valeria* and other painted records of *res gestae*. For paintings in the *atria* of private houses, cf. L. Bonfante, *American Journal of Ancient History* 3 (1978) 139 on the François tomb, and the bibliography cited by her in n. 19. Trimalchio's *atrium* featured a painted record of his life, including a quasi-triumphal entry ('Minerva ducente Romam intrabat'): Petr. *Sat.* 29.3–6.

5. See esp. A. Scobie, *Rh. Mus.* 122 (1979) 229–59; C. Salles, *Latomus* 40 (1981) 3–20. For history and the novel, cf. A. Momigliano, *Sesto contributo alla storia degli studi classici e del mondo antico* (Rome 1980) 375, and E. Gabba, *JRS* 71 (1981) 53; [see now C. Gill and T.P. Wiseman (eds), *Lies and Fiction in the Ancient World* (Exeter 1993), index s.v. 'history–literature relationship']. For an example of fiction becoming 'history', see J. Winkler, *JHS* 100 (1980) 175–81. There is a lively polemic on the subject in A.J. Woodman, *Omnibus* 5 (1983) 24–7.

5a. [On 'the priority of the pictorial mode of composition', see R. Brilliant, *Visual Narratives: Storytelling in Etruscan and Roman Art* (Cornell 1984) 86f., on the proem to Longus *Daphnis and Chloe*.]

6. Apul. *Met.* IV 23.3, 'virginem filo liberalem et, ut matronatus eius indicabat, summatem regionis'; cf. 23.5 (wealth), 24.4 ('tanta familia'), VII 13.1 (clients, etc.).

7. *Comitium* 'tomb': schol. Hor. *Epod.* 16.13 (quoting Varro), Festus 184L, Dion. Hal. *AR* I 87.2, III 1.2. *Tabulae triumphales*: Livy XL 52.4–6 (L. Aemilius Regillus), XLI 28.8–9 (Ti. Gracchus), cf. *Gramm. Lat.* VI 265, 293 Keil.

8. See previous note; F. Coarelli, *Il foro romano: periodo arcaico* (Rome 1983) 161–78, esp. 166f.

9. Respectively Festus 180L, Val. Max. VI 3.2, Dio V 22.1 = Zonaras VII 17.

10. Tombs of Horatii: Livy I 25.14, Dion. Hal. *AR* III 22.1, Martial III 47.3. *Tigillum sororium*: Livy I 26.13, Dion. Hal. *AR* III 22.8, Festus 380L. Cocles statue: Livy II 10.12, Dion. Hal. *AR* V 25.2, Plut. *Pobl.* 16.7, Gell. *NA* IV 5.1–4. Cloelia statue: Piso fr. 20P (Pliny *NH* XXXIV 29), Livy II 13.11, Dion. Hal. *AR* V 35.2, Plut. *Pobl.* 19.5 and 8 (Valeria). Column of Minucius: Dion. Hal. *AR* XII 4.6, Pliny *NH* XVIII 15, XXXIV 21, cf. Livy IV 16.2 (where read 'bove aurato <et statua> extra portam Trigeminam' with Crévier); M.H. Crawford, *Roman Republican Coinage* (Cambridge 1974) 273, 275. *Busta Gallica*: ILLRP 464.6, Varro *LL* V 157, Livy V 48.3, XXII 14.11.

11. Dion. Hal. *AR* I 6.2, with J.P.V.D. Balsdon, *CQ* 3 (1953) 158–64, and E. Gabba, in *Les origines de la république romaine* (Entretiens Hardt 13,

NOTES TO PAGES 37–41

Geneva 1967) 135–69; E. Badian, in *Latin Historians* (ed. T.A. Dorey, London 1966) 11f.
12. Diodorus XX 36.2, etc. (see also Cic. *Mil.* 37 for the Via Appia as a *monumentum*); Pliny *NH* XXXIV 43; Festus 228L, cf. A. Degrassi, *Inscriptiones Italiae* XIII.1 (Rome 1947) 546. The first coffin in the tomb of the Scipios is that of L. Scipio Barbatus, *cos.* 298, through his *elogium* was evidently not carved on it until two or three generations later (*ILLRP* 309). For the significance of the late fourth-century 'Anfänge römischen Repräsentationskunst', see T. Hölscher, *Röm. Mitt.* 85 (1978) 315–57.
13. Cato fr. 83P (Gell. *NA* III 7.19) on Leonidas: 'virtutes decoravere monumentis: signis, statuis, historiis aliisque rebus.' Cf. Festus (Paulus) 123L: 'monimentum est ... quicquid ob memoriam alicuius factum est, ut fana, porticus, scripta et carmina.'
14. Livy XXXVIII 56.2–4, with F. Coarelli, *Dialoghi di archeologia* 6 (1972) 72f.
15. *Tituli imaginum*: Livy VIII 40.4, cf. IV 16.3–4. Metellus Scipio's *anistorēsia*: Cic. *Ad Att.* VI 1.17 (q.v. also for the possibility of masons' errors).
16. For some possible examples see T.P. Wiseman, *Clio's Cosmetics* (Leicester 1979) 90–103.
17. Suet. *Tib.* 2.1–2: dates (i) 279/8, 264, 207 BC; (ii) 449, 268 (see text), 249 BC.
18. *Cos.* 451, *Xvir* 451/50; *tr. mil. cos. pot.* 403; *dict.* 362, *cos.* 349; see Degrassi, op. cit. (n. 12) under the respective years.
19. Degrassi, op. cit. 5, 40 (fr. xix), 432f.; T.A. Fruin, *Jahrbücher für classischer Philologie* 149 (1894) 103–18; M. Ihm, *Hermes* 36 (1901) 303.
20. Degrassi, op. cit. 547 (triumph), 40 (death *in magitratu*).
21. Livy *Per.* XV, Eutropius II 16, Florus I 19.
22. Florus I 19.2, Varro *RR* I 2.1.
23. Livy XLI 28.10 (Ti. Gracchus), Pliny *NH* XXXV 23 (Mancinus); cf. also Pliny *NH* XXXV 22 (M'. Valerius Messalla), Festus 228L (M. Fulvius Flaccus, T. Papirius Cursor) for contemporary paintings—though not geographical in content—as triumphal *monumenta*. [On maps and glory, see now T.P. Wiseman, *Talking to Virgil* (Exeter 1992) 33f., 40.]
24. *ILLRP* 454, with T.P. Wiseman, *PBSR* 32 (1964) 30–7, 37 (1969) 88–91 [= *Roman Studies* (Liverpool 1987) 108–15, 122–5]; *ILLRP* 335, with M.G. Morgan, *Philologus* 117 (1973) 40–8.
25. Justin XII 3.8, etc. White: Curtius Rufus VI 6.4, Lucian *Dialogues of the Dead* 13.393, Apul. *Met.* X 30, Val. Max. VI 2.7, Festus (Paulus) 28L, Tac. *Ann.* VI 37.2.
26. Duris *FGrH* 76F14 (Athen. XII 536a) on Demetrius Poliorcetes. Coins: N. Davis and C.M. Kraay, *The Hellenistic Kingdoms: Portrait Coins and History* (London 1973), *passim*; also Crawford, op. cit. (n. 10), plates XL.293.1, LXIV.543.1 (Philip V, 113/12 BC; Cleopatra, 32 BC).
27. Crawford, op. cit., plates LI.425.1, LIII.446.1 (Ancus, 56 BC; Numa, 49 BC); Juvenal VIII 259f., 'diadema Quirini'. *Pace* A. Alföldi, *Röm. Mitt.* 50 (1935) 145, there is no reason to think that the statues of the kings on the Capitol were *diadematae*: cf. Hölscher, op. cit. (n. 12) 331f. for the irrelevance of the late-republican coins to the Capitol statues.

28. Livy XXIV 5.4; *contra*, Duris *FGrH* 76F14 (Athen. XII 535e).
29. S. Weinstock, *Divus Julius* (Oxford 1971) 334, cf. 320, attributing the statue (with Mommsen) to Ap. Caecus, and suggesting 'he could have done it under Sicilian influence' (i.e. Dionysius I; but see previous note).
30. Prizes at *ludi* (though not relevant to men of rank after the fifth century BC): Pliny *NH* XXI 5–7, with E. Rawson, *PBSR* 49 (1981) 1–5 [= *Roman Culture and Society* (Oxford 1991) 389–93]. Military decorations: Pliny *NH* XVI 6–14, XXII 4–14, Gell. *NA* V 6, with V.A. Maxfield, *The Military Decorations of the Roman Army* (London 1981), esp. ch. 4.
31. For the development of the triumph see L. Bonfante Warren, *JRS* 60 (1970) 49–66. The classic form—which she attributes to Hellenistic influence—is first attested in 201 BC (triumph of Scipio Africanus, Appian *Pun*. 66); but Festus' item on the *toga picta* (228L: the latest *toga sine pictura* that he knew was from 264 BC) shows that the development was under way two or three generations earlier. For the new ideology of victory in the late fourth and early third centuries (cf. n. 12 above), see S. Weinstock, *Harvard Theological Review* 50 (1957) 211–47 and in *R-E* VIIIA (1958) 2486–7; T. Hölscher, *Victoria Romana* (Mainz 1967) 136–72.
32. Juvenal 10.39f., Tertullian *Coron.* 13.1, Pliny *NH* XXI 6, XXXIII 11. Cf. Dion. Hal. *AR* III 62.2: the golden crown was supposed to have been part of the regalia of the Etruscan kings of Rome. Pompey in 63 (Velleius II 40.4) and Caesar in 45 (Dio XLIII 43.1, XLIV 6.3, 11.2) were given the right to wear it at *ludi*: see K. Kraft, *Jahrbuch für Numismatik und Geldgeschichte* 3–4 (1952–3) 7–97; H.S. Versnel, *Triumphus* (Leiden 1970) 74–7; Crawford, op. cit. (n. 10) 450, 488 n. 1.
33. Varro in Serv. *ad Aen.* V 269 ('magni honoris'), Pliny *NH* XVI 65 ('antiquorum honore'); Plautus *Pseud.* 1265 (convivial garlands).
34. Plut. *Sulla* 27.4; cf. Serv. *ad Ecl.* 9.46 ('Julian star'), Polybius XVIII 46.2, Suet. *Nero* 25.2 (*lemnisci* alone as a sign of triumph). Crawford, op. cit. (n. 10), plates XIV.71.1a (211–208 BC), XXXVI.246.1, XXXVII.247.1, 253.1, 253.3, XXXIX.280.1, XLIX.387.1, LI.419.1e, 419.2, 421.1, LIII.449.4, LXIV.545.1, 546.2a. Ennius *Trag.* fr. 23 Jocelyn ('volans de caelo cum corona et taeniis') has been plausibly attributed to a prologue spoke by Victory (cf. Plautus *Amph.* 41f.): O. Skutsch, *Studia Enniana* (London 1968) 175–7.
35. Pliny *NH* XXI 6; Crawford, op. cit., plates LI.426.4b, LII.435.1 (Pompey's crown, n. 32 above).
36. Crawford, op. cit., plate I.22.1; cf. Cic. *Rosc. Am.* 100 ('palma lemniscata'). Two laurel-wreaths hang in a similar way from a palm-branch carried by an eagle on the Sullan monument from the Capitol: M.H. Crawford, *The Roman Republic* (London 1978), plate 6.
37. *Diadema*: n. 25 above. *Lemnisci*: Festus (Paulus) 102L, Serv. *ad Aen.* V 269; Pliny *NH* XXI 6 (gold).
38. Thus, explicitly, in Nicolaus of Damascus (*FGrH* 90F130.71) and twice in Plutarch (*Caes.* 61.3, *Ant.* 12.2). [Cf. P. Zanker, *The Power of Images in the Age of Augustus* (Ann Arbor 1988) 93: on coins of 19 BC, Augustus' civic crown (an oak wreath) looks like a Hellenistic royal diadem.]
39. Suet. *Div. Jul.* 79.1, Appian *BC* II 108.

40. See n. 32 above; Val. Max. VI 2.7 (Favonius on the *diadema*); Crawford, op. cit. (n. 10), plate LII.435.1 (Pompey's *corona* as a symbol of monarchy); Brutus in Suet. *Div. Jul.* 49.2 (Octavius on Pompey as king); Plut. *Pomp.* 67.3, *Caes.* 41.1 (Ahenobarbus on Pompey as king of kings).
41. E.g. Dion. Hal. *AR* VIII 90.1, XI 28.5, Livy III 44.5, 56.2, IX 46.10f. (cf. Pliny *NH* XXXIII 17), *Per.* XIX (cf. Suet. *Tib.* 2.2). The origin of the theme is the arrival of the first Appius in Rome 'accompanied by a large band of clients' (Livy II 16.4, cf. Suet. *Tib.* 1.1), the elaboration of what was probably a genuine event: for the historical context see Cornell in T.J. Cornell and J.F. Matthews, *Atlas of the Roman World* (London 1982) 24f., [and now *Cambridge Ancient History* VII.2 (ed. 2, 1989) 97–9].
42. Wiseman, op. cit. (n. 16) 104–11; for doubts, see the reviews by E. Rawson (*THES* 378 [18 Jan. 1980] 18) and J. Briscoe (*CR* 31 [1981] 50f.).
43. Sen. *De brev. vit.* 13.4, Suet. *Tib.* 2.1, Florus I 18.5, Sil. It. VI 660, *De vir. ill.* 37.3; cf. Ennius *Ann.* 216 Skutsch, 'Appius indixit Karthaginiensibus bellum'.
44. Volsinii war: Florus I 16, Zonaras VIII 7, Val. Max. IX 1.ext.2, *De vir. ill.* 36. Statues: Metrodorus of Scepsis *FGrH* 184F12 (Pliny *NH* XXXIV 34).
45. Degrassi, op. cit. (n. 12) 74f.; Festus 228L (painting in temple of Fulvius in triumphal dress); cf. Propertius IV 2.3f. (Vertumnus' origin from Volsinii).
46. M. Torelli, *Quaderni dell'Istituto di topografia antica* 5 (1978) 71–5. The original publication was by L. Mercando et al., *Bull. Com.* 79 (1963–4) 35ff.; [see now *Cambridge Ancient History* VII.2 (ed. 2, 1989) 425].
47. I use the numeration of P. Sommella, *Quaderni* (n. 46 above) 63–70, followed by W. von Sydow, *Arch. Anzeiger* 88 (1973) 580–5. Sommella's levels 4 and 5 are labelled respectively V and VI in F. Coarelli, *Guida archeologica di Roma* (Verona 1974) 282f., and on the diagram in F. Coarelli, *Roma* (Guide archeologiche Laterza, Bari 1980) 315, though in the text of the latter (pp. 315–7) Coarelli refers to them as VI and VII respectively.
48. So Sommella, op. cit. 65; cf. E. Gjerstad, *Early Rome* III (Lund 1960) 386, though his dating must be abandoned in the light of the new evidence. However, Coarelli, opp. cit. (1974) 283 and (1980) 317, numbering the *cappellaccio* layer as IV in the former and as V in the latter, believes it to be a separate pavement of the early fourth century; cf. von Sydow, op. cit. 581f.
49. Livy XXIV 47.15 (fire), XXV 7.6 (reconstruction begun); cf. Torelli, op. cit. (n. 46) 74.
50. Livy XXV 2.3–5.
51. Livy XXV 7.6 (*triumviri*), 21 (defeat), 41.10 (elections).
52. Pub. Syr. *Sent.* 203. F. Coarelli et al., *L'area sacra di Largo Argentina* I (Rome 1981) 12–15 (paving levels and altar), 34–42 (identification of portico and temple), 91–6 (date of altar inscription). Sallust *BJ* 35–42, esp. 38.7 and 43.1 ('foeda fuga'), 39.1 ('Aulo omnes infesti'). It is possible, but not certain, that the A. Albinus of the altar inscription was the same man as the unfortunate general (later *cos.* 99) serving as *duumvir lege Plaetoria* at an early stage in his career.

53. Sulla: Velleius II 43.4, Suet. *Div. Jul.* 11, Plut. *Caes.* 6, Val. Max. VI 9.14. Clodius: Cic. *De domo* 112, 137, *De har. resp.* 33 (*Ad Att.* IV 2.5, 3.2 for the restoration of the portico in 57). AD 41: Suet. *Gaius* 60.
54. Livy XXVI 15.1–16.4; on Appius' wound see also Zonaras IX 6.
55. Sil. It. XIII 445–68, Livy XXVI 6.5 ('cui suos ante prima signa adhortanti ... ictum est').
55a. [I quote Pichlmayr's Teubner text (1911, repr. 1966), which is based on the Oxford and Brussels manuscripts (*o* and *p*). However, W.K. Sherwin jr argues that *o* and *p* are too interpolated to be trustworthy, and bases his text (Oklahoma 1973) on the rest of the MSS tradition. Thus Sherwin gives Appius' *cognomen* as 'Audax'; *o* and *p* (and they alone) have 'Gaudex', which Pichlmayr emended to 'Caudex', the consul's nickname as given by Seneca (*De brevitate vitae* 13.4) and in the Capitoline *fasti* (Degrassi, op. cit. [n. 12] 40). 'Audax' is meaningless in the context, and it is hard to see why 'Gaudex' should be a fifteenth-century conjecture, as Sherwin implies; Pichlmayr was surely right to see it as a minor corruption of the true reading.]
56. See esp. *De vir. ill.* 27.1 ('Publius Decius Decii filius ...'). Ausculum: Cic. *De fin.* II 61, *Tusc.* I 89, Eutropius II 13.4, Zonaras VIII 5, Dio X fr. 43.
57. E.g. *De vir. ill.* 11.1, 16.1, 21.1, 25.1, 46.1, 48.1.
58. E.g. *De vir. ill.* 11.1 (Cocles), 19.1 (Coriolanus), 24.1 (Capitolinus), 31.1 (Cursor), 49.1 (Africanus), 60.1 (Achaicus), 61.1 (Macedonicus), 75.1 (Felix).
59. Plautus *Poen.* 1153, cf. 1365 'lignea in custodia'; Propertius IV 7.44, Juvenal 2.57.
60. Terence *HT* 877, cf. Petr. *Sat.* 74.13. On pejorative *cognomina* see I. Kajanto, *The Latin Cognomina* (Helsinki 1965) 68f., 264f.
61. For another suggestion, even more far-fetched, see Sen. *De brev. vit.* 13.4.
62. Narrative sources: Polybius I 11–17, Diodorus XXIII 1–4, Zonaras VIII 8. Caudex is credited with the victory in *De vir. ill.* 37.5, and with a triumph in Eutropius II 18.3 and Sil. It. VI 662 (implied also by Suet. *Tib.* 1.2?), but the Augustan *fasti* list Valerius' triumph only (Degrassi, op. cit. [n. 12] 74f.). No doubt Valerius' version prevailed with the help of the famous picture he put up on the wall of the Senate-house (Pliny *NH* XXXV 22). See now A.M. Eckstein, *American Journal of Ancient History* 5.2 (1980) 181–4.
63. Narrative sources: Dion. Hal. *AR* XX 20.1–3, Plut. *Pyrrhus* 21.5–10, Frontinus *Strat.* II 3.21, Orosius IV 1.19–22. *Devotio*: Cic. *De fin.* II 61, *Tusc.* I 89 (both 45 BC), though in 56 BC Cicero mentions only the two elder Mures (*Sest.* 48); Ennius *Ann.* 191–4 Skutsch, with Skutsch, op. cit. (n. 34) 54–9. Intention only: Dio X fr. 43, Zonaras VIII 5. In Florus I 13.9 Decius is not even at the battle, which is fought 'Curio Fabricioque consulibus': M'. Curius Dentatus was consul in 290, 275 and 274, C. Fabricius Luscinus in 282 and 278.
64. They evidently succeeded, as the Augustan *fasti* show (n. 45 above). But they failed to reverse the usurpation by the Aemilii Lepidi of two of the *monumenta* of M. Fulvius Nobilior, censor in 179: Livy XL 51.5, Plut. *Caes.* 29.3 ('Basilica Fulvia'), Varro *LL* VI 4 ('Basilica Aemilia et Fulvia'),

but thereafter 'Aemilia monumenta' (Tac. *Ann.* II 72.1); Livy XL 51.4 (bridge), Plut. *Numa* 9.6 (attributed to an Aemilius).
65. Theophanes *FGrH* 188F1 (Plut. *Pomp.* 37.4); even Plutarch, usually an ingenuous acceptor of historical fabrications, recognized here a 'malicious action' by Theophanes.
66. See for instance Wiseman, op. cit. (n. 16) 29f., and *History* 66 (1981) 380f. [= *Roman Studies* (Liverpool 1987) 249f.].

Chapter 4

1. Cic. *De leg.* II 15f.: 'utilis esse autem has opiniones quis neget ... quam multos divini supplicis metus a scelere revocarit.'
2. E.g. Plautus *Capt.* 313–5, *Rud.* 26f., Catullus 76.26, Persius 2.73f., Pliny *Paneg.* 3.5. See J.H.W.G. Liebeschuetz, *Continuity and Change in Roman Religion* (Oxford 1979) 39–54.
3. R.M. Ogilvie, *The Romans and their Gods* (London 1969) 17–19; Liebeschuetz, op. cit. 9.
4. Alan Wardman, *Religion and Statecraft among the Romans* (London 1982) 10; Mary Beard and Michael Crawford, *Rome in the Late Republic* (London 1985) 31 and n. 13.
4a. [I have borrowed R.E. Latham's splendid Penguin translation (1951); the italics are mine.]
5. P. Hardie, *Virgil's Aeneid: Cosmos and Imperium* (Oxford 1986) 17f.
6. Lucr. V 110–21 [trans. R.E. Latham]; Hardie, op. cit. 18, 188, 210.
7. Hardie, op. cit. 18f. For Empedocles as a *mantis*, see fr. 102 Wright = 112 DK (Diog. Laert. VIII 61).
8. See R. Maltby, *A Lexicon of Ancient Latin Etymologies* (Leeds 1991) 523, 594: on *religio* and *religare*, Lactantius (*Inst.* IV 28.12) cites Lucr. I 932; on *superstitio*, Servius (*ad Aen.* VIII 187) cites Lucr. I 65.
9. See C. Segal in K. Galinsky (ed.), *The Interpretation of Roman Poetry: Empiricism or Hermeneutics?* (Frankfurt 1992) 139, 145f.
10. Cf. V 160–3 (*nefas*).
11. Cf. Hor. *Odes* I 3.38–40 (*scelus*), III 4.42–8 (*impios Titanas*). [Plato compared materialists to the Giants at *Sophist* 246a–b, and Lucretius may have been alluding to that passage; for Lucretius' knowledge of Plato see P. De Lacy in *Syzetesis: studi sull' epicureismo greco e romano offerti a Marcello Gigante* I (Naples 1983) 291–307. Aristotle too may have used the comparison: see E. Bignone, *L'Aristotele perduto e la formazione filosofica di Epicuro* II (Florence 1936) 414–22 = ed. 2 (Florence 1973) 74–81, who attributes it to *De philosophia* fr. 18 (Philo *De aeternitate mundi* 10f., cf. Plut. *Moralia* 926e, 1119b) and argues that Lucretius had Aristotle in mind. (I am grateful to Prof. Michael Wigodsky for these references.)]
12. I 105 (*somnia*), cf. 133 (dreaming of the dead). [See Pindar fr. 131b Snell (ps.Plut. *Moralia* 120d) on the judgement of souls as revealed in dreams.]

13. Dion. Hal. *AR* V 50.1 (i.e. 499 BC), Varronian date AUC 253 (i.e. 501 BC): Post. Cominius and T. Larcius consuls.
14. Dion. Hal. *AR* V 51.3, a very brief account. Zonaras (VII 13) adds the detail that the slaves were conspiring to seize the Capitol. Livy ignores the episode completely.
15. Dion. Hal. *AR* V 53–7 (summary in Zonaras VII 13); cf. Livy II 19.1.
16. V 53.3 (slaves), 53.4 (seize heights), 54.1–3 (informers), 56.2 (*equites*).
17. So F. Münzer, *R-E* IVA.1 (1931) 747 and VIIA.2 (1948) 1315 (Sulpicius 35, Tullius 41); T.R.S. Broughton, *The Magistrates of the Roman Republic* I (New York 1951) 10.
18. Dion. Hal. *AR* V 53.2 (*sōmata*); Sall. *Cat.* 33.1 (*corpora*).
19. V 55.1; Sall. *Cat.* 29, Plut. *Cic.* 15.
20. V 55.1; Cic. *Sull.* 21f., *Att.* I 16.10, Plut. *Cic.* 23.2 (*dunasteia*).
21. V 56.1; E. Gabba, *Dionysius and The History of Archaic Rome* (Berkeley 1991) 80–5. See T.P. Wiseman and C. Gill (eds), *Lies and Fiction in the Ancient World* (Exeter 1993) 144–5.
22. V 55.3 ('in the sight of all'), 57.2 ('as all the crowd flocked together'), 57.4 ('the assembled crowd having confirmed the decree of the Senate').
23. V 53.1 (Tarquin plots civil war), 55.2, 56.3, 58.5 ('civil bloodshed').
24. For the 'Catilinarian *war*', see Cic. *Cat.* III 25, Sall. *Cat.* 56–61 (esp. 61.5–9).
25. For M'. Tullius as supposed ancestor of Cicero, cf. Cic. *Brut.* 62.
26. Pomponius in *Digest* I 2.2.51; Dion. Hal. *AR* I 80.1, Thuc. 1. Sulpicius Rufus' *popularis* proposal in 63 to change the structure of the *comitia centuriata* is compatible with the consul Sulpicius' speech on liberty and tyranny at Dion. Hal. *AR* V 55.5.
27. Cf. V 56.1 on 'instances of divine intervention' (*to daimonion*).
28. Cf. Ennius *Trag.* fr. 267 Jocelyn on prophets 'qui sibi semitam non sapiunt, alteri monstrant viam'; also *Matthew* 7.13f., *John* 14.5f., *Acts* 9.2, etc.
29. Gabba, op. cit. (n. 21) 159–66.
30. See n. 21 above: *to daimonion* (n. 27) was part of his lesson. [For vatic prophecy as a familiar notion in the late Republic, cf. Nepos *Atticus* 16.4 on Cicero ('futura praedixit ... cecinit ut vates'): e.g. Cic. *Att.* VIII 11.3.]
31. Sall. *Cat.* 14f., esp. 15.4: 'neque vigiliis neque quietibus sedari poterat; ita conscientia mentem excitam vastabat.'
32. Cic. *Cat.* IV 7–8; Sall. *Cat.* 51.20, 52.13.
33. Cic. *De div.* I 17 (Urania), *Att.* II 3.4 (Calliope), ps.Sall. *in Cic.* I 7 (council of the gods).
34. Virg. *Aen.* VIII 666–70, cf. Hom. *Od.* XI 568–71 (Minos), Lucr. V 116f. (*pendere* in a different sense).
35. Lucan VI 793–9 (cf. 665 for bound Giants).
36. Plut. *Cic.* 2.3f., confirmed for the 50s and 40s BC by the controversy over 'cedant arma togae ...' (Cic. *Pis.* 72, *Phil.* II 20, *De off.* I 77).
37. Xen. *Symp.* 3.5f., 4.6; Hor. *Epist.* I 2.1–31. See C.O. Brink, *Horace on Poetry III: Epistles Book II* (Cambridge 1982) 289f.; S.R. Bonner, *Education in Ancient Rome* (London 1977) 241–4.

38. Diodorus I 2.2 (bringing about *eusebeia* and *dikaiosunē*); cf. Polybius VI 56.12, in the context of the Romans' use of religion for social cohesion.
39. Virg. *Aen.* VII 41, Lucan I 64.
40. Varro *LL* VII 36, cf. VI 52 (referring to his *De poematis* or *De poetis*); Isid. *Orig.* VIII 7.3. Schol. Bern. on Virg. *Ecl.* 9.34. See H. Dahlmann, *Philologus* 97 (1948) 337–53; E. Bickel, *Rh. Mus.* 104 (1951) 257–314; J.K. Newman, *The Concept of Vates in Augustan Poetry* (Coll. Latomus 89, Brussels 1967).
41. Cic. *Poet.* fr. 11.28 Traglia (*De div.* I 18); Plautus *Miles* 911; Ennius *Ann.* 207, 374 Skutsch.
42. See G. Nagy in G.A. Kennedy (ed.), *The Cambridge History of Literary Criticism* I (Cambridge 1989) 23–9, and in J.L. Kugel (ed.), *Poetry and Prophecy: the Beginnings of a Literary Tradition* (Cornell 1990) 56–64.
43. Hesiod's *Works and Days* were followed by an *Ornithomanteia* (Schol. on Hes. *Op.* 828); on the *Orphicorum fragmenta* (ed. O. Kern, 1922), see M.L. West, *The Orphic Poems* (Oxford 1983); for Empedocles, see n. 7 above.
44. Hom. *Od.* XVII 381–5. For the similarities, see R. Lamberton, *Homer the Theologian* (Berkeley 1986) 1–43.
45. E.g. Pindar fr. 150 Bergk: the Muse as *mantis*, the poet as *prophētēs* (interpreter).
46. Plut. *Per.* 32.3, Ameipsias fr. 10 K–A, Aristophanes *Birds* 988.
47. Critias fr. 1 Nauck (*TGF* 43F19); Plut. *Moralia* 880e, Galen XIX 250 Kühn (attributed to Euripides, and assumed to represent the dramatist's own view).
48. J.A. North, 'Religion in Republican Rome', in *Cambridge Ancient History* VII.2 (ed. 2, Cambridge 1989) 573–624, at 578: 'the system offered no eschatology, no explanation of creation or man's relation to it; there was no room for prophets or holy men . . .'
49. J. North, 'Diviners and Divination at Rome', in M. Beard and J. North (eds), *Pagan Priests: Religion and Power in the Ancient World* (London 1990) 51–71, at 67; cf. also 66 on the Roman style of divinatory activity: 'It is a style that (a) lacks emphasis on specifically prophetic utterance; (b) lacks identifiable prophets or holy men; (c) produces anonymous teams of diviners who display an oblique or reticent relationship to their divinatory techniques.'
50. On which see A.S. Pease's commentary (Urbana 1920), and the important articles by Mary Beard and Malcolm Schofield in *JRS* 76 (1986) 33–46 and 47–65 (with earlier bibliography).
51. Cic. *De div.* I 4; Plut. *Mar.* 42.4.
52. F. Münzer, *R-E* IV (1901) 1295 (Cornelius 123): Cic. *Ad fam.* XIII 41–2, cf. *Att.* VI 3.6.
53. Dicaearchus fr. 15 Wehrli (Cic. *De div.* I 113, cf. 71, II 100–9).
54. Cic. *De div.* I 34, 66f., 70f.; II 100 (*furor divinus*), 101, 110–12.
55. I 4, 34, 89 (*permotio divina*); II 100, 111.
56. I 4, 34, 66, 113; II 101.
57. I 4, 12, 34, 67, 113–17, 132; II 100, 112, 149. Also *harioli*: I 4, 66 (Accius quotation), 132.

58. I 34, 114f.; II 113, 115–8; J. Fontenrose, *The Delphic Oracle* (Berkeley 1978) 196–232.
59. I 34, II 110–12; the identification goes back at least to the third century (ps.Aristotle *Mir. ausc.* 838a), though Varro distinguishes the Cumaean Sibyl from the Erythraean (*Ant. div.* fr. 56a Cardauns = Lact. *Inst.* I 6.9f.). See H.W. Parke, *Sibyls and Sibylline Prophecy in Classical Antiquity* (London 1988), with the important review-discussion of D. Potter, *JRA* 3 (1990) 471–83.
60. I 34; cf. Herodotus VIII 20, 77, Aristophanes *Peace* 1070 etc.; Parke, op. cit. 180–7.
61. I 66, 114, II 112; cf. Aesch. *Agam.* 1035–330, Lycophron *Alexandra*, etc. On Cassandra in Ennius' *Alexander*, see H.D. Jocelyn, *The Tragedies of Ennius* (Cambridge 1967) 203–33.
62. I 34; cf. Plato *Laws* 642d–e, Diog. Laert. I 109–12; for the background, see G.E.R. Lloyd, *Magic, Reason and Experience* (Cambridge 1979) 10–49.
63. I 89, 115, II 113; cf. Livy XXV 12.3 (*vates inlustris*), Festus 162L (Cn. Marcius), Festus (Paulus) 185L, Isid. *Orig.* VI 8.12.
64. I 115, II 113; cf. *ILLRP* 35 for a very early dedication to Aesculapius by M. Populicius M.f.
65. I 68–9, II 114.
66. I 89, cf. n. 63 above. According to Livy (VI 1.6), a Cn. Marcius was *tribunus plebis* in 389.
67. *LCM* 16.8 (Oct. 1991) 118f., on Livy X 9.2.
68. Cf. Cic. *Att.* VI 3.6, where he is contemptuous of a Culleolus, probably the proconsul (n. 52 above) and therefore perhaps related to the *vates*.
69. For Aristophanes, see N.D. Smith, 'Diviners and Divination in Aristophanic Comedy', *Class. Ant.* 8 (1989) 140–58; for tragedy, cf. the treatment of Tiresias in Soph. *OT* and elsewhere.
70. E.E. Evans-Pritchard, *Witchcraft, Oracles and Magic among the Azande* (Oxford 1937) 193, cf. K. Thomas, *Religion and the Decline of Magic* (London 1971) 401; both cited by Lloyd, op. cit. (n. 62) 18f.
71. I 132, with Jocelyn, op. cit. (n. 61) 128, 396–8 on the extent of the Ennius quotation.
72. For Appius' views, cf. I 105, *Tusc.* I 37, *Brut.* 267, *Ad fam.* III 9.3 etc., and the great scene in Lucan V 64–236.
73. II 148–9, with *religio* interpreted in a Stoic sense.
74. I 3: 'publice privatimque'.
75. Theophr. *Char.* 16.11 (*oneirokritai, manteis, ornithoskopoi*); cf. 11.6 for the third category.
76. Cato *Rust.* 5.4: 'auspicem augurem hariolum Chaldaeum nequem consuluisse velit.'
77. Plut. *Nic.* 4.2, 23.5, *Mar.* 17.1–3. [For prophetesses, evidently not common at Rome, cf. Dio LV 31.2 (AD 6), Suet. *Galba* 9 (Spain, AD 69).]
78. Athens: see the material collected in G.R. Morrow, *Plato's Cretan City: a Historical Interpretation of the Laws* (Princeton 1960) 427–34, and A. Powell, *Athens and Sparta* (London 1988) 383–413. Sparta: e.g. Plut. *Lys.* 22.5–6, *Ages.* 6.5.

79. Plut. *Them.* 13.2f., from Phainias of Eresos. Demanding human sacrifice was characteristic of the *mantis*: e.g. Aesch. *Agam.* 198–204, Eur. *Heracleidae* 401–9, Arnob. *Adv. gent.* II 68 (*Apollinis monitu*).
80. Cic. *De div.* I 26, II 70, 76 (augury); I 4, II 112 (Sibyl).
81. North, op. cit. (n. 49) 69; for Attus Navius, see G. Piccaluga, *Studi e materiali di storia delle religioni* 40 (1969) 151–208.
82. Quotations from North, opp. cit. (n. 49) 70, (n. 48) 610.
83. See North's classic article 'Conservatism and Change in Roman Religion', *PBSR* 44 (1976) 1–12, esp. 8–11.
84. Dion. Hal. *AR* II 68–9, Val. Max. I 8, Tertull. *Apol.* 23.12, Augustine *Civ. Dei* X 16, etc. Cf. North, op. cit. (n. 48) 598: 'There seems no reason to think that Roman gods act typically either by way of direct intervention in human life or as immanent forces realizing themselves through human actors.' But what counts as typical? [Miracles and *divinatio* are associated in the career of Attus Navius, and in the *haruspices*' notion of a miraculous change in the entrails (Cic. *De div.* I 118f., II 35f.).]
85. Valerius Antias fr. 6P, Plut. *Numa* 15.3–6 (two versions), Ovid *Fasti* III 285–348.
86. Cf. n. 81 above. Whetstone: Cic. *De div.* I 31–3, II 80 (Marcus calls it a *commenticia fabula*), Livy I 36.2–4, etc. Fig-tree: Pliny *NH* XV 77.
87. Val. Max. I 8.1, Dion. Hal. *AR* VI 13, Plut. *Aem. Paul.* 25.2–4, etc. The context may be the institution of the *transvectio equitum* in 304: see J. Sihvola in E.M. Steinby (ed.), *Lacus Iuturnae* I (Rome 1989) 76–86. The *aition* of the Ahenobarbi (Plut. loc. cit., Suet. *Nero* 1.1, Tertull. *Apol.* 23.12) is unlikely to pre-date the first known use of the *cognomen*, by the consul of 192 BC.
88. Val. Max. V 6.3, Ovid *Met.* XV 565–621. For a possible context, see Wiseman, loc. cit. (n. 67).
89. Val. Max. VIII 1.abs.5, Dion. Hal. *AR* II 69.1–3, Pliny *NH* XXVIII 12 (giving the date, cf. Livy *Per.* XX).
90. Ovid *Fasti* IV 247–348, Propertius IV 11.51f., etc.; for the different versions of the story see T.P. Wiseman, *Clio's Cosmetics* (Leicester 1979) 94–9.
91. Tanaquil: Livy I 34.9, Dion. Hal. *AR* III 47.4, etc. Sibyl and Tarquin: Varro *Ant. div.* fr. 56a Cardauns (Lact. *Inst.* I 6.10), Dion. Hal. *AR* IV 62.1–4, Pliny *NH* XIII 88, etc. *Arsia silva*: Livy II 7.2, Dion. Hal. *AR* V 16.2f., etc.
92. For Sibyls as an East Greek phenomenon, see Parke, op. cit. (n. 59) 51–70. For Latin oracular shrines in sacred woods, see F. Coarelli, *I santuari del lazio in età repubblicana* (Rome 1987), esp. 12–19 (Gabii); 90f., 105f. (Tibur); 173f, 182 (*nemus Dianae*). For supernatural voices, see Cic. *De div.* I 109 with A.S. Pease's commentary (Urbana 1920) 279.
93. Livy I 56.4–12, Dion. Hal. *AR* I 69.2–4; cf. Herodotus I 167.2–4 (Caere and Delphi).
94. Livy V 13.5f., 15.4–11, 16.8–11, 32.6f. (cf. Cic. *De div.* I 101 for the *lucus*).

95. T. Romilius T.f. T.n. Rocus Vaticanus *cos.* 455 (Fasti Cap., Diodorus XII 5.1); for the *ager Vaticanus*, named from *vaticinia* and *vatum responsa*, see Varro *Ant. div.* fr. 107 Cardauns (Gell. *NA* XVI 17.1f.), Festus (Paulus) 519L.
96. Op. cit. (n. 49) 71.
97. Both events are relevant to the history of prophets: the *aition* of the Hercules cult at the Ara Maxima depended on Carmenta's prophecy of his apotheosis, and one of the plebeian augurs appointed in 300 belonged to the prophetic Marcian *gens* (see nn. 63 and 66 above); for the possible vatic credentials of two of the others, M. Minucius and T. 'Publius', see Wiseman, loc. cit. (n. 67).
98. Zonaras VIII 1; for the context (the completion of the temple of Victory), see Wiseman, op. cit. (n. 67) 120–3.
99. Val. Max. I 8.2, 'triennio continuo' before 291 BC.
100. Arnob. *Adv. nat.* VII 47 (cf. n. 106 below); Livy (X 47.6f.) and Valerius Maximus (I 8.2) mention only the Sibylline books; according to Ovid (*Met.* XV 631–40), Delphi was consulted.
101. Theopompus *FGrH* 115F248 (Athen. XIII 605c–d); the bay-tree was set up at the time of Aristeas of Proconessus' stay in Metapontum after his visit to the Hyperboreans (Herodotus IV 13–15).
102. Livy fr. 14 Weissenborn-Müller (Gelasius *CSEL* XXXV 456f.), Orosius IV 2.2, Augustine *Civ. Dei* III 17 (*CSEL* XL 140); for 'deus Februarius' in the Livy fragment, cf. Festus (Paulus) 75–6L on *februare*. See A.W.J. Holleman, *Pope Gelasius I and the Lupercalia* (Amsterdam 1974) 20f.
103. Livy X 36.11, 37.15 (cf. I 12.3–6, etc.); Velleius I 14.6 (cf. Serv. *ad Aen.* VII 709). See T. Mommsen, *Hermes* 21 (1886) 570–84 = *Gesammelte Schriften* IV (1906) 22–35, endorsed by G. Dumézil, *Archaic Roman Religion* (Chicago 1970) 5–7: the whole story of Romulus and the Sabines probably dates from this period.
104. Ovid *Fasti* II 443f. The goddess' instruction, 'Italidas matres sacer hircus inito' (441) clearly refers to Inuus, one of the names of the god of the Lupercal (Livy I 3.2).
105. E.g. *Met.* III 348f., 511f. (Tiresias), XII 18 (Calchas), *Fasti* VI 751, *Amores* III 2.51. At *Met.* XV 596 (cf. 577), the *augur* is a *haruspex*; at *Amores* III 5.31–3 (cf. 45) he is an *interpres* of dreams. [At Livy I 55.6 and VI 12.8 the *vates* is probably a *haruspex*.]
106. Arnob. *Adv. nat.* II 73 (*a vatibus moniti*), VII 40 (*iussis et monitis vatum*), VII 49 (*iussis vatum*).
107. E.g. Varro in Censorinus 17.8, Verrius Flaccus in Porph. on Hor. *Carm. saec.* 8 (cult of Dis and Proserpina, 249); Pliny *NH* XVIII 286 (*ludi* of Flora, 238); Livy XXII 9.7–10 (cult of Venus Erycina, *ver sacrum*, etc., 215).
108. Livy XXV 1.6–12. For the prophets in the Forum, cf. n. 101 above; also *Epistles of Diogenes* 38.2 (*The Cynic Epistles*, ed. A.J. Malherbe [Missoula 1977] 161: Olympia, fourth century BC); Apul. *Met.* II 13f. (Corinth, second century AD).
109. Livy XXV 12 (cf. n. 63 above), Festus 438L, Macr. *Sat.* I 17.25–30.

110. Arnob. *Adv. nat.* VII 49 (*iussis vatum*), Varro *LL* VI 15 (*ex libris Sibyllinis*), etc.; see n. 90 above (miracle story). For the background, see E.S. Gruen, *Studies in Greek Culture and Roman Policy* (Leiden 1990) 5–33.
111. Livy XXXIX 8–19 (8.3 for the *vates*, 13.12 for inspired *vaticinatio*), *CIL* I^2 581 = *ILLRP* 511; Gruen, op. cit. 34–78 (who however tries to argue away the ideological significance of the event).
112. Books of Numa: Livy XL 29.3–14, Pliny *NH* XIII 84–7, etc.; Gruen, op. cit. 158–70 (with the same reservation as in n. 111). *Chaldaei* (and worshippers of Sabazios): Val. Max. I 3.3 (epitomes of Paris and Nepotianus); cf. E.N. Lane, *JRS* 69 (1979) 35–8.
113. Aristophanes *Knights* 61, Thuc. V 26.3, Plato *Rep.* II 364b, etc.; see Powell, loc. cit. (n. 78).
114. Appian *Iber.* 85, on Scipio Aemilianus' army in Spain; Cato *Rust.* 5.4, with North, op. cit. (n. 49 above) 58–60, on the *vilicus*.
115. Diodorus XXXIV/V 2.5–10, XXXVI 4.4. Cf. also Plut. *Crass.* 8.3: the wife of Spartacus was a prophetess (and a Dionysiac initiate). For the importance of this element in slave rebellions, see K.R. Bradley, *Slavery and Rebellion in the Roman World* (Indiana 1989) 113–5.
116. See n. 77 above; Sall. *Jug.* 5.2, on the Jugurthine war. Cf. Pliny *NH* XV 120f. for the Senate's dominance giving way to that of the people before the Marsic War (91 BC).
117. See n. 51 above.
118. Sall. *Hist.* I 67.3M (speech of Philippus): 'vatum carmina'.
119. Cic. *Poet.* fr. 10.28f. Traglia (Cic. *De div.* I 18), emphasizing the consul's involvement.
120. Varro *Ant. div.* fr. 56a Cardauns (Lact. *Inst.* I 6.11), Dion. Hal. *AR* IV 62.6, Fenestella fr. 18P (Lact. *Inst.* I 6.14).
121. Cic. *Cat.* III 9 ('ex fatis Sibyllinis haruspicumque responsis'), Sall. *Cat.* 47.2.
122. Suet. *Div. Aug.* 31.1; cf. Dio XLIV 17.2, Tac. *Ann.* VI 12. For *fatidici libri*, cf. Livy XXV 1.12 (*libri vaticinii*), Arnob. *Adv. nat.* VII 48 (*fatalia carmina*).
123. See above, nn. 51, 63, 64.
124. Dio LII 36.2f. (*anankaia*). But he has only haruspicy and augury in mind; see F. Millar, *A Study of Cassius Dio* (Oxford 1964) 102–18 on the speech of Maecenas, of which 'the entire content (with trivial exeptions) relates to the early third century and not to the time of Augustus' (140). On magic, astrology, etc., see R. MacMullen, *Enemies of the Roman Order* (Harvard 1967) 85–162.
125. Ennius *Ann.* 206f. Skutsch: 'scripsere alii rem vorsibus quos olim Faunei vatesque canebant'. Cf. ibid. 374, *Trag.* fr. 266–9 Jocelyn (n. 71 above).
126. Hor. *Epod.* 16.66 (cf. 7.13–20), *Odes* I 31.2, IV 6.44, etc.; Virg. *Aen.* VII 41–5; Prop. IV 6.1 (at IV 1 Propertius ironically juxtaposes the *vates*-poet with the *vates*-prophet, Horus the astrologer). See Newman, op. cit. (n. 40).
127. Virg. *Aen.* VI 620; cf. n. 38 above.

Chapter 5

This is the revised and annotated text of a lecture given to the Roman Society in June 1987. I am very grateful to the Editorial Committee and to Richard Seaford for suggestions and improvements. The following works are referred to by the author's name alone:

Brink: C.O. Brink, *Horace on Poetry II: the Ars Poetica* (Cambridge 1971).
Frassinetti: *Atellanae fabulae*, ed. P. Frassinetti (Rome 1967).
Rawson: E. Rawson, 'Theatrical Life in Republican Rome and Italy', *PBSR* 53 (1985) 97–113 [= *Roman Culture and Society: Collected Papers* (Oxford 1991) 468–87].
Seaford: R. Seaford, *Euripides Cyclops* (Oxford 1984).
Steffen: *Satyrographorum Graecorum fragmenta*, ed. V. Steffen (Poznań 1952).
Szilágyi: J.C. Szilágyi, 'Impletae modis saturae', *Prospettiva* 24 (1981) 2–23.

1. G. Williams, *Tradition and Originality in Roman Poetry* (Oxford 1968) 354; Brink 273–4, cf. 286 and 496 on the vocative at line 235. [Professor Brink's reaction to the argument in this chapter will be found in his article 'Second Thoughts on Three Horatian Puzzles', forthcoming in a book of essays for Prof. R.G.M. Nisbet (ed. S.J. Harrison, Oxford 1995). As he rightly says, the indirect evidence 'points to Roman satyrs, but not, or not necessarily, to satyr-drama'. But if Horace seems to refer to satyr-drama, where does the onus of proof lie? I am very grateful to Professor Brink for allowing me to see the relevant part of his article in advance of publication.]
2. *Horace on Poetry I: Prolegomena to the Literary Epistles* (Cambridge 1963) 228. In 1971 Brink criticized his own suggestion as going beyond the evidence, but still wondered whether 'the withdrawal of much tragic production into the reciter's hall' might be relevant to the problem (Brink 275, 276).
3. Stage: *AP* 125, 179ff. Audience: *AP* 113, 153–5, 248–50. Trial *recitatio*: *AP* 419–76, esp. 420, 427, 474.
4. Rawson 111 n. 86, cf. 102f. [= 484 n. 86, cf. 475]; Seaford 21 n. 59, 29f.
5. Livy XXXIX 8–19; *CIL* I² 581. For the reality behind Livy's hostile travesty, see R. Seaford, 'The Mysteries of Dionysos at Pompeii', in H.W. Stubbs (ed.), *Pegasus: Classical Essays from the University of Exeter* (Exeter 1981) 52–68.
6. Hor. *AP* 36, 366f. For the identity of the father (Cn. Piso *cos. suff.* 23 or L. Piso *cos.* 15), see R. Syme, *The Augustan Aristocracy* (Oxford 1986) 379–81 and Table XXV, citing previous bibliography and arguing firmly for Piso the Pontifex (*cos.* 15).
7. Brink 496.
8. Diomedes *Ars. gramm.* III (*GL* I 482K).
9. Ibid. 490K:
    Similarities: 'The first type is toga-plays (*togatae*) which are called "purple-bordered"; in these the subject is the deeds of commanders and public affairs, and Roman kings or generals are presented; they are like

tragedies in the dignity and high status of their characters . . . The second type is toga-plays which are called "tavern-style"; they are like comedies in the low status of their characters and the similarity of their plots . . . The third type is Latin plays which are named after the Oscan town of Atella, where they originated; in their plots and jokes they are like Greek satyr-plays. The fourth type is "flat-footed" drama, which in Greek is called mime.'

Differences: ' "Purple-bordered" toga-plays differ from tragedy in that in tragedy [Greek] heroes are presented; for instance Pacuvius wrote tragedies with heroic names—*Orestes, Chryses* and such-like—as did Accius; in what is entitled "purple-bordered" drama [the characters are] Brutus or Decius, likewise Marcellus. "Tavern-style" toga-plays differ from comedy in that in comedy Greek customs are presented, and Greek characters like Laches and Sostrata; in the other, Roman ones . . . Latin "Atellan" drama differs from Greek satyr-plays in that in satyr-plays the characters presented are satyrs, or absurd and satyr-like, such as Autolycus and Busiris; in "Atellan" drama the characters are Oscan, like Maccus.' (No differentiation is offered between *planipes* and *mimus*.)

10. Nic. Dam. *FGrH* 90F75 (Athen. VI 261c); Rawson 110f. [= 484]. [In his forthcoming article (see n. 1 above), Professor Brink points out that the Greek phrase 'satyric comedy' is used by John Lydus (*De mag.* I 41) to describe Lucilius' Latin satire.]
11. Jerome *Chron.* 150H (89 BC, 'L. Pomponius Bononiensis Atellanorum scriptor clarus habetur'); Gell. *NA* X 24.5, XII 10.7, XVI 6.7; Macr. *Sat.* I 4.22, VI 4.13, 9.4; Nonius 75L.
12. Velleius II 9.5 ('verbis rudem et novitate inventi a se operis commendabilem'); ps.Acro on *AP* 288 (*praetextae* and *togatae*).
13. Steffen 117, 139–41, 221f.: Aristias' *Atalante*, Aeschylus' *Sisyphos*, Euripides' *Sisyphos*. For *Ariadne*, parallels are hardly required (cf. n. 54 below).
14. Frassinetti 23–67 for Pomponius' fragments. *Marsyas*: Arnob. *Adv. nat.* II 6. *Satura*: Priscian *GL* II 200K for Liber.
15. Lucr. IV 1169; *CIL* XIV 5303, cf. F. Matz, *Dionusiakē Teletē: archäologische Untersuchungen zum Dionysoskult* (Wiesbaden 1964) Taf. 25. (At Catullus 32.10f. the phrase '*satur supinus*' immediately precedes an allusion to a satyr-play: see Seaford 166 on Eur. *Cyclops* 327f.).
16. Suda s.v. 'Arion'; Herodotus I 24.1f.; archaeological synthesis in J.C. Meyer, *Pre-Republican Rome* (Rome 1983) 157–60.
17. Athens: Seaford 12–16. Rome: E. Gjerstad, *Early Rome* III (Lund 1960) 139, 144, 189; IV.2 (Lund 1966) 458–62, 597. Elsewhere: A. Andrén, *Architectural Terracottas from Etrusco-Italic Temples* (Lund 1940) clxv–vii, clxxiii–iv (Signia, Velitrae, Satricum, as well as many Etruscan sites); *Enea nel Lazio: archeologia e mito* (Rome 1981) 15, 197 (Ardea, Lavinium).
18. Gjerstad, op. cit. III 202, IV.2 463–6; cf. Andrén, op. cit. clxxxiii–v for Caere, Città Castellana, Velitrae, Lanuvium, and the 'magnificent series' of antefixes from Satricum. For Etruria in particular, see J. Heurgon, 'Le satyre et la ménade étrusques', *MEFR* 46 (1929) 96–114.

19. Dion. Hal. *AR* VI 17.2; Vitr. *Arch.* III 3.5; Tac. *Ann.* II 49.1; Cic. *Balb.* 55 on the *sacra Graeca*. See A. Bruhl, *Liber Pater: origine et expansion du culte dionysiaque à Rome et dans le monde romain* (Rome 1953) 30–45, and now also de Cazanove, op. cit. (n. 23 below).
20. Livy IV 25.3, 29.7, cf. III 63.7.
21. See A.D. Trendall, *The Red-figured Vases of Lucania, Campania and Sicily* (Oxford 1967), index p. 707; A.D. Trendall and A. Cambitoglou, *The Red-Figured Vases of Apulia* (Oxford 1978–82), partial index p. 1293 (cf. 1279: 'genre scenes of no special significance not included'); Y. Bomati, 'Les légendes dionysiaques en Étrurie', *REL* 61 (1983) 87–107. It may not be irrelevant that Aristophanes was evidently being performed in Apulia in the first half of the fourth century (O. Taplin, *PCPS* 33 [1987] 96–101).
22. Szilágyi 2–4, 8–11 (late sixth to mid-fourth centuries BC).
23. Soph. *Ant.* 1118. See now O. de Cazanove in *L'association dionysiaque dans les sociétés anciennes* (Coll. de l'École fr. 89, Rome 1986) 177–97—though he sees it as a 'dionysisme sans Dionysos'.
24. Her. Pont. in Plut. *Cam.* 22.3; Pliny *NH* XXXIV 26; Plut. *Numa* 8.20; consular and triumphal *fasti* for 304 BC (P. Sempronius Sophus). Cf. A. La Regina, *Dial. arch.* 2 (1968) 176 on *ILLRP* 309, the *elogium* of L. Scipio Barbatus, *cos.* 298: 'quoius forma virtutei parisuma fuit' translates *kalos kagathos*.
25. *ILLRP* 1197: 'Dindia Macolnia fileai dedit, Novios Plautios med Romai fecid'; T. Dohrn, *Die ficoronische Cista* (Berlin 1972). For the iconography see A. Weis, *AJA* 86 (1982) 22–38, who suggests it was 'ultimately based on a monumental painting . . . created in central Italy in the fifth or early fourth century BC' (p. 29).
26. Hor. *Sat.* I 6.115–7 and scholiasts ('in rostris', ps.Acro); Servius *ad Aen.* IV 58 ('in foro'); M. Torelli, *Typology and Structure of Roman Historical Reliefs* (Ann Arbor 1982) 98–106, for Marsyas on the 'Anaglypha Traiani'; F. Coarelli, *Il foro romano: periodo repubblicano e augustea* (Rome 1985) 91–119. [See now C.F. Giuliani and P. Verduchi, *L'area centrale del foro romano* (Florence 1987) 101–3, identifying the Marsyas statue as monument no. 11, next to the praetor's tribunal in the middle of the piazza.]
27. Servius *ad Aen.* III 359 ('a Marsya rege missos e Phrygia regnante Fauno, qui disciplinam auguriorum Italis ostenderunt'), cf. Gellius fr. 7P on Marsyas' ambassador Megales; Livy X 9.2.
28. Servius *ad Aen.* III 20 ('in liberis civitatibus simulacrum Marsyae erat, qui in tutela Liberi patris est'), IV 58; see Coarelli, op. cit. (n. 26) 95–100 on Marsyas' shackles (presumably with a *broken* chain). Aediles: Livy X 23.11–13, 31.9, 33.9. For the *popularis* tradition of the Marcii (e.g. Sall. *Cat.* 33.2, Virg. *Aen.* VI 815f.), see D.C. Feeney, *PCPS* 32 (1986) 9f.
29. Ovid *Fasti* V 277–94 ('vindicibus laudi publica cura fuit', 290), Tac. *Ann.* II 49.1 (temple); cf. Varro *LL* V 158, Festus 276L. The Publicii may have been prophets as well (Cic. *De div.* I 115, II 113); cf. the Marcii, n. 33 below. For the dates of the Floralia (241? 238?) and of Livius Andronicus' first production (240?), see Velleius I 14.8, Pliny *NH* XVIII 286, Atticus

fr. 5P (Cic. *Brut.* 72, cf. *De sen.* 50, *Tusc.* I 3). For aediles' fines, cf. also Schol. Bob. 90St (249 BC); Gell. *NA* X 6.3, Livy XXIV 16.19 (246 BC, temple of *Libertas*); T.P. Wiseman, *Clio's Cosmetics* (Leicester 1979) 92–4.
30. Callimachus fr. 106–7Pf; Dion. Hal. *AR* I 34.4, 49.2, Plut. *Rom.* 17.6, etc. (poets); Pliny *NH* III 57 (Theophrastus), Strabo I 66 (Eratosthenes), *FGrH* 840F7–23.
31. Drama in Forum: M. Gaggiotti, *Analecta Romana* 14 (1985) 60f.; E.J. Jory, *CQ* 36 (1986) 537f. Iunii: first known Silanus praetor in 212 BC (Livy XXV 20.1); n. 57 below.
32. Silenus: Cic. *Tusc.* I 114; Herodotus VIII 138, Xen. *Anab.* I 2.13 etc. (Midas); Virg. *Ecl.* 6.13ff. Marsyas and Cybele: Diodorus III 58–9 (58.3 for his intelligence and self-control), Pausanias X 30.9, Steph. Byz. s.v. 'Pessinus', etc.; cf. Plato *Symp.* 215a–c for Socrates as Silenus or Marsyas. The satyrs themselves represent the eternal felicity of the initiate: see Seaford, op. cit. (n. 5) 64f.
33. Livy XXV 12 (*carmina Marciana*), Cic. *De div.* I 89 for the Marcii as seers 'of noble birth' [p. 59 above].
34. Sil. Ital. VIII 502–4, Pliny *NH* III 108 (from 'Gellianus'), Solinus 2.6.
35. Gellius fr. 7P (Solinus 1.7). On this text see F. Coarelli in *Gli Etruschi e Roma: incontro di studi in onore di Massimo Pallottino* (Rome 1981) 200f.; J.P. Small, *Cacus and Marsyas in Etrusco-Roman Legend* (Princeton 1982); T.P. Wiseman in *Les 'bourgeoisies' municipales italiennes aux IIe et Ier siècles av. J.-C.* (Paris and Naples 1983) 302–4 = *Roman Studies* (Liverpool 1987) 300–2; and Coarelli, op. cit. (n. 26) 113–7. I am not convinced by Small's attempt to find a sixth-century context for the passage (op. cit. 15f., 45–7, 105–8).
36. *ILS* 212.17–24 (Claudius), Arnob. *Adv. nat.* VI 7, Servius *ad Aen.* VIII 345, Varro *LL* V 47, Festus 38L, 468L, Tac. *Ann.* IV 65, etc. For a full presentation and discussion of the evidence on the Vibennae saga, see F. Buranelli (ed.), *La tomba françois di Vulci* (Rome 1987) 225–33 (M. Pallottino), 234–43; ibid. 79–110 (F. Roncalli) on the paintings of the François tomb. For Etruscan historians (Varro in Censorinus 17.6, *ILS* 212.18), see T.J. Cornell, *ASNP* 6.2 (1976) 411–39.
37. Small, op. cit. (n. 35) 4, 113. [See F. Coarelli, *Il foro boario* (Rome 1988) 135–8, who identifies the satyr as Marsyas or Faunus—very unlikely, since he is not named—and assumes for no good reason that the scene is Rome.]
38. Varro *LL* V 55.
39. Livy VII 2.4–8, Val. Max. II 4.4, with Szilágyi 4f, 12–18; cf. n. 22 above. Earlier accounts—e.g. M. Coffey, *Roman Satire* (London 1976) 18–22, and A.S. Gratwick in *The Cambridge History of Classical Literature* II (Cambridge 1982) 160–2—will have to be modified in the light of Szilágyi's arguments.
40. See O. Szemerényi, *Hermes* 103 (1975) 312–6.
41. The classic account is still E.J. Bickerman, '*Origines gentium*', *CP* 47 (1952) 65–81; for poetic *ktiseis*, see F. Cairns, *Tibullus: a Hellenistic Poet at Rome* (Cambridge 1979) 68–70.
42. S.R. West, 'Lycophron Italicised?', *JHS* 104 (1984) 127–51, esp. 145f.

43. Seaford 22, 24; Plut. *Moralia* 316a (Praeneste), Hor. *Odes* III 29.8 (Tusculum).
44. Xenagoras *FGrH* 240F29 (Rhomos, Anteias, Ardeias); anon. ap. Plut. *Rom.* 2.1 (Romanus); anon. ap. Servius *ad Aen.* I 273 (Latinus, cf. Hesiod *Theog.* 1011–6).
45. Steffen 151–3, 123–7. Tibur: Pliny *NH* XVI 237 (Tiburnus); Sextius in Solinus 2.7 (Catillus), cf. Servius *ad Aen.* VII 670; see F. Coarelli, *Dial. arch.* 1.2 (1983) 60–5 for Amphiaraus and Tibur in the François tomb. Ardea: Pliny *NH* III 56. For lists of Italian foundation legends, see Ovid *Fasti* IV 65–81, Justin XX 1, Solinus 2.5–13.
46. Steffen 147 (Strabo VI 258, from *Glaukos Pontios*?); Festus 486L, Servius *ad Aen.* VII 662. [Add Strabo V 233: Tarracina ('Trachinē') from *trachys* (rugged).]
47. See n. 18 above. For the Satricum excavations, see J.A. De Waele, *Med. Nederl. Inst. Rome* 43 (1981) 7–68, and *Arch Laziale* 4 (1981) 305–16.
48. Virg. *Aen.* VII 801f., Sil. Ital. VIII 379f., Charax *FGrH* 103F31; cf. Sil. Ital. VII 162–211 (Dionysus in the *ager Falernus*).
49. Dion. Hal. *AR* VII 71.1.
50. Fabius *FGrH* 809F13(b) = Dion. Hal. *AR* VII 70–3: to be read in Jacoby's text (*FGrH* IIIC [Leiden 1958] 865–9), where Dionysius' own comments are distinguished typographically.
51. Appian *Pun.* 66; Szilágyi 8–11, 21 n. 90; de Cazanove, op. cit. (n. 23) 190–5.
52. Aelian *Var. hist.* III 40, Strabo X 466.
53. M. Verzar in P. Zanker (ed.), *Hellenismus in Mittelitalien* (Göttingen 1976) 122–6, 133f. Cf. Bomati, op. cit. (n. 21) 90–5 for the popularity of the theme in Etruscan art.
54. In a near-contemporary painting on Delos, Ariadne is shown being awakened by a winged Psyche: *Ricerche di pittura ellenistica* (Quaderni dei DdA 1, Rome 1985) 219 fig. 3. See in general E. Richardson in *Styles in Classical Art and Archaeology: a Tribute to Peter Heinrich von Blanckenhagen* (ed. G. Kopcke and M.B. Moore, Locust Valley 1979) 93–5, and F. Matz (ed.), *Die dionysischen Sarkophage* III (Berlin 1969) 374f. For Ariadne as Libera (cf. n. 19 above), see Ovid *Fasti* III 512, Hyginus *Fab.* 224.2.
55. Theatre: Val. Max. II 4.2, Velleius I 15.3, Livy *Per.* XLVIII, Appian *BC* I 28, Augustine *Civ. Dei* II 5; [see now J.A. North in *Apodosis: Essays Presented to Dr W.W. Cruikshank* (London 1992) 75–83]. *Ars ludicra*: Cassiodorus *Chron.* on 115 BC. Note also the expulsion of 'Chaldaean' astrologers in 139 (Val. Max. I 3.3, Livy *Per. Oxy.* LIV); see nn. 29 and 33 above for the prophets Publicius and the Marcii; Ennius *Ann.* VII 206Sk on 'Faunei vatesque'.
56. Plut. *Mar.* 2.2; Cic. *Ad fam.* VII 1.3 (55 BC), *ILLRP* 803 (late Republic), Nic. Dam. *FGrH* 90F127.19 (46 BC), Cic. *Ad Att.* XVI 5.1 (44 BC), *ILS* 5050.157–61 (17 BC); see Rawson 102f. [= 475].
57. M.H. Crawford, *Roman Republican Coinage* (Cambridge 1974) 336f. (D. Silanus 91 BC, Silenus), 344f. (Q. Titius 90 BC, Liber and Silenus), 346 (C. Vibius Pansa 90 BC, Silenus and Pan), 377 (L. Censorinus 82 BC,

Marsyas). For Pansa's 'double-headed' issues, cf. A. Wallace-Hadrill, *JRS* 79 (1986) 74f. and 82: 'double-headed coins . . . invite the user to discover some special significance.' Pan and Liber are featured on the issues of Pansa's son in 48 BC (Crawford, op. cit. 464f., 467); [cf. n. 75 below].

58. Diodorus XXXVII 12.1f., Plut. *Sulla* 27.2.
59. Lucr. IV 580–9; Hor. *AP* 342, 249.
60. Seaford 16–18; E. Simon, *The Ancient Theatre* (London 1982) 19f. and pl. 8; Xen. *Symp.* 9.2–7. [Overlap of the genres is implied by an early fourth-century red-figure cup from Corinth showing a dancing-girl (a *mima*?) performing before Dionysus, naked except for the hairy pants, with attached tail and erect phallus, usually worn by (male) satyr-play performers: J.D. Beazley, *Attic Red-Figure Vase-Painters* (ed. 2, Oxford 1963) 1519 no. 13; illustrated in *AJA* 34 (1930) 339.]
61. Seaford 18–20; B. Snell, *Scenes from Greek Drama* (Berkeley 1967) 99–138 on Python; Athen. II 55d, X 419d on Lycophron.
62. Dioscorides 23G–P (*Anth. Pal.* VII 707); Seaford 20f. Cf. Meleager 126G–P (*Anth. Pal.* VII 535): Pan comes to town now that Daphnis is dead.
63. Hor. *AP* 244–50, cf. Brink 291f. Roman context at line 248 (*equites*)— and *forenses* at 245 might make Horace's readers think of Marsyas.
64. See G.M. Sifakis, *Studies in the History of Hellenistic Drama* (London 1967) 26f., 30, 53, 124–6; C. Garton, *Personal Aspects of the Roman Theatre* (Toronto 1972) 154f. Records of the *Amphiaraia*: *IG* VII 416, 419–20, etc.
65. See G. Williams, *Change and Decline: Roman Literature in the Early Empire* (Berkeley 1978) 102–52 on 'the dominance of Greek culture'. Cf. also Wiseman, opp. cit. (n. 29) 154–67, (n. 35) 299–307.
66. See E.J. Jory, in J.H. Betts et al. (eds), *Studies in Honour of T.B.L. Webster* I (Bristol 1986) 143–52.
67. Livy I 46.3 [p. 17f. above]; cf. V 21.9, Dion Hal. *AR* III 18.1, IX 22.3, Plut. *Rom.* 8.7 ('theatrical' inventions). W. Beare, *The Roman Stage* (London 1950) 42–4 on the supposed obsolescence of the *fabula praetexta* after Accius; *contra* T.P. Wiseman, *Catullus and his World* (Cambridge 1985) 33f.
68. Cic. *Pro Q. Gallio* fr. 4 Puccioni (Jerome *Ad Nepotianum ep.* 52.8); [the passage is discussed by F. Giancotti, *Mimo e gnome: studio su Decimo Laberio e Publilio Siro* (Messina 1967) 120–8; for table-talk as a genre, see N. Horsfall, *Ancient Society* (Macquarie) 17.1 (1987) 16f.]. Cf. also fr. 6 Puccioni (Nonius 88L) on 'logi qui ludis dicti sunt'.
69. Lycophron, n. 61 above; Varro *Men.* 143–4B = 117, 131 Cèbe.
70. Varro *Men.* 304B (Nonius 259L): 'sed, o Petrulle, ne meum taxis librum,/ si te †pepigat haec modo† scenatilis'. Oehler (1844) emended to *hic modus*.
71. Cic. *Rab. Post.* 35; Wiseman, op. cit. (n. 67) 34f.; cf. also Ovid *Tristia* I 2.79f., Statius *Silvae* V 5.66–9. *Pantomimi*: see E.J. Jory, op. cit. (n. 66) 147–9, and *BICS* 28 (1981) 147–61, esp. 154f. on Livy VII 2 and 157 on mid-first-century innovation.
72. Ovid *Fasti* IV 326 ('mira sed et scaena testificata loquar'), on Q. Claudia

and the Magna Mater. *Aretalogi*: H. Engelmann, *The Delian Aretalogy of Sarapis* (Leiden 1975), esp. 37, 55f.; Philodemus (*De poem*. 13 Dübner) associates *aretalogoi* and *mimographoi*; also Suet. *Div. Aug.* 74 [p. 33 above], Juvenal 15.16, Dio Chrys. *Orat.* 20.493R, etc.

73. Cic. *Ad Q.f.* II 16.3; Shackleton Bailey, following Buecheler, reads *factam*.
74. Steffen 273–6, among the doubtful satyr-plays; but since someone throws a stinking chamber-pot across the room (Athen. I 17d), it is not likely to be a tragedy.
75. Cicero's disapproval: *Ad Q.f.* II 16.1 ('ut tibi placet, damus operam ne cuius animum offendamus'); similar sentiments at II 11.3, 13.2, 14.4. [Topical subjects: cf. Suet. *Div. Jul.* 32: an apparition playing Pan-pipes at the crossing of the Rubicon in 49 BC. Could that be from a satyric drama with a topical plot? Caesar's henchman C. Vibius Pansa (see n. 57 above) may have been aedile in 48: G.V. Sumner, *Phoenix* 25 (1971) 255.]
76. Virg. *Ecl.* 1.1, 6.4, etc., *Georg.* IV 566; see n. 52 above.
77. Servius *ad Ecl.* 6.11; Donatus *Vita Verg.* 26; cf. Tac. *Dial.* 13.2.
78. Virg. *Ecl.* 5.73, 8.62ff.; n. 60 above. (Cf. n.32 above for Silenus in *Ecl.* 6.)
79. Dion. Hal. *AR* VII 70–3 (see n. 50 above), with I 4–5, 89–90.
80. VII 72.10 and 12; cf. Suet. *Div. Vesp.* 19.2 for funerals. Note that Dionysius also cites the soldiers' songs at triumphal processions as analogous to *saturikē paidia* (VII 72.11); the word he uses for their mockery is *iambizein*, and *Iambe* was a satyr-play by Sophocles (on Iambe, see N.J. Richardson, *The Homeric Hymn to Demeter* (Oxford 1974) 213–7). For satyrs and processions in the Hellenistic world, see Callixeinos of Rhodes *FGrH* 627F2 on the grand procession of Ptolemy Philadelphus.
81. Athen. I 20e (Aristonicus); Arrian *FGrH* 156F106; the *sikinnis* was discussed by Accius in his *Pragmatika* (Gell. *NA* XX 5).
82. Ovid *Fasti* IV 326; J.C. McKeown, 'Augustan Elegy and Mime', *PCPS* 25 (1979) 71–84; E. Fantham, 'Sexual Comedy in Ovid's *Fasti*', *HSCP* 87 (1983) 185–216, esp. 187, 197f. on satyr-play (but only as a literary source?).
83. Ovid *Fasti* VI 319–48 (the same story at I 390–440, with Lotis for Vesta, is set at a Greek Dionysiac festival); *Met.* XIV 634–41 (also satyrs, Pan, Silenus); Martial X 92.11f. See Fantham, op. cit. 201–9 on the two versions in the *Fasti*.
84. Ovid *Fasti* VI 480–550, exploiting a myth often featured in satyric drama (Steffen 150, 245, 258 on *Athamas* satyr-plays). Maenads: 503f., 507, 514 (cf. Livy XXXIX 12.4, 13.12 for the *lucus Stimulae* and the Bacchanalia). Topography: 477f., 518 (cf. Tac. *Ann.* II 49.1 for the temple of Liber *ad circum maximum*): [see now F. Coarelli, op. cit. (n. 37) 420f.].
85. Ovid *Fasti* II 303–58, cf. Hor. *Odes* III 18.1 for Faunus (and Dion. Hal. *AR* I 32.3–5 on the Lupercal as the cave of Pan). Steffen 230–4, 241f. for *Omphale* satyr-plays by Ion and Achaeus; cf. E. Simon, *Arch. Anz.* (1971) 199f., and Fantham, op. cit. (n. 82) 192–201.
86. Ovid *Fasti* III 285–348, leading into the *aition* of the Salii and their *ancilia* (349–92, cf. Plut. *Numa* 13); the Salii were presumably the armed dancers imitated by the *satyristai* in the *pompa circensis* (Dion. Hal. *AR* VII 72.6).

Antias fr. 6P, cf. frr. 18, 22, 37, 40, 46, 55P on *ludi*; Wiseman, op. cit. (n. 29) 116f.
87. Ovid *Fasti* III 303, cf. 309, 315 ('di nemorum . . . di agrestes'). Plut. *Numa* 15.3. Midas: n. 32 above.
88. See Seaford 1, 7, 37; for satyrs as magicians, see Snell, op. cit. (n. 61) 106f., on Python's *Agen*.
89. Frassinetti 88; Festus 369L. For Novius as 'Atellanarum scriptor', see Gell. *NA* XVII 2.8; Macr. *Sat.* I 10.3; his titles include not only *Duo Dossenni, Maccus copo, Pappus praeteritus*, etc., but also *Andromacha, Hercules coactor* and *Phoenissae*.
90. See Virg. *Aen.* VII 45–9, 177–91, VIII 319–23.
91. Picus: Pliny *NH* X 40f., Servius *ad Aen.* VII 190. Faunus (and Fauna) *a fando*: Varro *LL* VII 36, cf. Calp. Sic. *Ecl.* 1.33–5. For Marsyas and Faunus as royal contemporaries, see n. 27 above.
92. Ovid *Met.* XIV 320–434, Virg. *Aen.* VII 189–91. Circe: see above, nn. 43–44.
93. Plut. *Moralia* 268d–e, Arnob. *Adv. nat.* V 18, Macr. *Sat.* I 12.24f.; T.P. Wiseman, *Cinna the Poet and other Roman Essays* (Leicester 1974) 135f. Note that the celebrants of the Bona Dea mysteries are called 'Priapi maenades' in Juvenal 6.316f.; and Propertius' grove of the Bona Dea (IV 9.22–70, invaded by Hercules) seems to be the *lucus Stimulae* of Ovid's maenads (n. 84 above). [In general, see now H.H.J. Brouwer, *Bona Dea: the Sources and a Description of the Cult* (Leiden 1989).]
94. Dion. Hal. *AR* I 31.2, Justin XLIII 1.6, *Origo gentis R.* 5.3. Cf. Seaford 6f. on the ambiguity of satyrs and *sileni*.
95. Solinus 1.5 (Silenus of Caleacte), Justin XLIII 1.8f, Servius *ad Aen.* VII 51, Dion. Hal. *AR* I 43.1.
96. Festus (Paulus) 77L, Plut. *Fabius* 1.1, Sil. Ital. VI 627–36 (Evander's daughter).
97. Festus (Paulus) 77L, Plut. *Fabius* 1.2; cf. Seaford 36f.
98. Cf. nn. 26, 31, 57 above. One wonders too (remembering Marsyas and the *popularis* tradition) about the Satureii (tribune of the *plebs* in 133) and the Sicinii (tribunes in '493–2, 499, 387', and 76); see n. 81 above on the *sikinnis*.
99. Cic. *Ad Att.* II 13.2, Hor. *Odes* III 16.34, Pliny *NH* III 59, Sil Ital. VII 276, 410, VIII 529; otherwise, Formiae could be called a Laconian foundation (Strabo V 233), and the Laestrygonians sited in Sicily (Thucydides VI 2.1, etc.).
100. Hom. *Od.* X 81 and scholiasts; Hor. *Odes* III 17.1–9, 'Aeli vetusto nobilis ab Lamo', for whose identification see Syme, op. cit. (n. 6) 394f.
101. Seaford 33f. For the geographical exploitation of *Odyssey* IX–X, see nn. 43–44 above. *Cyclops* was a familiar mime plot in Horace's time (*Sat.* I 5.63). [Whence the story of Polyphemus in love? See E.W. Leach, *JRA* 1 (1988) 105f. for evidence of Roman mime in wall-paintings, including Polyphemus and Galatea at Boscotrecase.]
102. Scholiast on Theocritus 15.40, Diodorus XX 41.6 (Euripides), Hor. *AP* 340; before the association with the Laestrygonians, she was assigned to Libya (Duris *FGrH* 76F17, Pausanias X 12.1, etc.). [Lamia may be the

old woman tortured by satyrs on the Beldame Painter's name-piece (C.H.E. Haspels, *Attic Black-Figure Lekythoi* [Paris 1936] 170, plates 49–51); see M. Hahn-Tisserant, *Kernos* 2 (1989) 67–82 on the story of her capture (Aristophanes *Wasps* 1177).]
103. Livy I 3.7 ('mansit Silviis postea omnibus cognomen'), Hor. *AP* 244.
104. Ovid *Fasti* VI 143, *Met.* XIV 622f.
105. Vitr. *Arch.* V 6.9, VII 5.2; Ovid *Fasti* I 401–4, II 315f., III 295–8; Plut. *Sulla* 27.2, *Numa* 15.3; Calp. Sic. *Ecl.* 1.8–12, etc.
106. Val. Max. II 2.9 ('laetitia exultantes ... epularum hilaritate et vino largiore'); Plut. *Rom.* 21.3–7 (*aition*).
107. See Seaford 38 on Aeschylus' *Trophoi*, Sophocles' *Dionysiskos*, *Herakleiskos*, etc. Note that one of Pomponius' mythological burlesques was *Agamemno suppositus* (Nonius 758L).
108. Plut. *Rom.* 8.7 (cf. n. 67 above); Aristotle *Poet.* 16.1 (1454b21).
109. See the commentary of Kiessling and Heinze on *AP* 220, where the essentials were set out three generations ago: Pomponius' three titles, Q. Cicero's *Syndeipnoi*, the fact that satyr-play still flourished in the Greek East. Cf. also D.F. Sutton, *The Greek Satyr Play* (Meisenheim 1980) 93, where the credibility of Horace (and Porphyrion on Pomponius) is rightly defended.
110. Diomedes *GL* I 485K. See n. 39 above for Szilágyi's heterodox (and convincing) view.

Chapter 6

1. T. Mommsen, *Römische Geschichte* III (Berlin 1856) 168, 597f. = *The History of Rome* (tr. W.P. Dickson, Everyman Library 1901) IV 159, 574. Habicht 4; MacKendrick 288f.
2. Habicht 71 (cf. 3, 'only a second best'); MacKendrick 1.
3. [Professor MacKendrick rightly took me to task for this phrase: 'a monster, yes, but not *baggy*—there's no spare space at all!']
4. MacKendrick 258–315 on his influence.
5. Habicht 9–15 (cf. 7, Sulla as a 'genius of power').
6. MacKendrick 1; cf. Habicht 27f.
7. [See now T.P. Wiseman, 'The Senate and the Populares, 69–60 BC', in *The Cambridge Ancient History* IX (ed. 2, Cambridge 1994) 327–67.]
8. Seneca *De brev. vit.* 5.1; MacKendrick 2; Habicht 34, 44.
9. Cic. *Ad Att.* X 4.4 (49 BC); Habicht 41.
10. Cic. *Ad Att.* IV 5.1 (palinode); Habicht 57, 89.
11. Habicht 6.
12. L.P. Wilkinson, *Letters of Cicero* (London 1949) 19; Cic. *Ad Att.* IX 18.1 ('at ego me amavi').
13. Cic. *De div.* II 1–7: 'in libris enim sententiam dicebamus, contionabamur.'
14. Habicht 74, citing H. Strasburger, 'Ciceros philosophisches Spätwerk als Aufruf gegen die Herrschaft Caesars' (Heidelberg Academy, April 1978).

15. The attacks on Caesar in *De officiis* (I 26, 112; II 23; III 82–5) were of course written after the Ides of March.
16. [See now E. Rawson in *CAH* IX (n. 7 above) 468–90.]
17. Kingsley Amis, *Take a Girl Like You* (London 1960) 67, on the second *Philippic*: 'For a man so long and so thoroughly dead it was remarkable how much boredom, and also how precise an image of nasty silliness, Cicero could generate.'

Chapter 7

1. *ILLRP* 759, 60, 518 ad fin.
2. F. Coarelli, in *Les 'bourgeoisies' municipales italiennes aux IIe et Ier siècles av. J.C.* (Paris and Naples 1983) 217–40, esp. 237f.; for Delos, cf. *BCH* 36 (1912) 24 (M. Calvius A.f.), *ILLRP* 750a (a Geminius among those who financed the north portico of the slave market; cf. Coarelli, *Op. Inst. Rom. Finlandiae* 2 (Rome 1982) 119–45 on the so-called 'Agora of the Italians'). For the phenomenon in general, see also G. Bodei Giglioni, *Riv. stor. ital.* 89 (1977) 72–6.
3. *ILLRP* 344, *BCH* 36 (1912) 140; cf. F. Coarelli, *Lazio* (Guide archeologiche Laterza, Bari 1982) 244 for Cora and olives.
4. Festus (Paulus) 109L, citing Lucilius. On Puteoli, see now M. Frederiksen, *Campania* (London 1984), the final chapter by Nicholas Purcell, esp. 324–30.
5. *CIL* IX 1643: he and P. Cerrinius 'viam straverunt et lacus fecerunt d.d. pro ludis'.
6. See additional note (p. 153–4 below) on *CIL* IX 1781.
7. *CIL* IX 1610, M. Crassicius M.f. Ste. Castellus of the *legio XXX*; see L. Keppie, *Colonisation and Veteran Settlement in Italy 47–14 BC* (London 1983) 157, suggesting that the *IIvir* might be a son or grandson of the veteran.
8. He was a *collusor et sodalis* of Antony in 43 (Cic. *Phil.* XIII 3), but how old he was at the time is anybody's guess; his pupil Iullus Antonius was praetor (i.e. thirty years old?) in 13 BC.
9. Cic. *De fin.* I 7 (Lucilius), *Arch.* 5 (Archias); cf. Gell. *NA* XIII 2.2 (Pacuvius and Accius at Tarentum), Plut. *Cicero* 29.2 ('Thyllus of Tarentum', i.e. the Greek poet Thyillus? T.P. Wiseman, *Cinna the Poet* (Leicester 1974) 141–6). For the cultural amalgam, cf. *CIL* IX 239 ('Cn. Nearchus nepos Fabianus'), Strabo VI 253.
10. Cic. *Ad fam.* VII 12.1, Hor. *Odes* II 6.9–20, *Sat.* I 6.59f.; cf. *Sat.* II 4.34, *Epist.* I 7.45, 16.11, Juvenal 6.297, etc.; R.G.M. Nisbet and M. Hubbard, *A Commentary on Horace: Odes Book II* (Oxford 1978) 94f. Fertility: Strabo VI 281. Pirates: Probus on Virg. *Georg.* IV 125.
11. Produce (especially oil, cf. Hor. *Odes* II 6.15f.): P. Desy, *Ant. Class.* 52 (1983) 187–94. Harbour: Strabo VI 278, 282, Livy XXIII 33.4, XXVII 15.3, etc. Dolphin: [M.H. Crawford, *Coinage and Money under the Roman Republic* (London 1985) 26 fig. 3;] Pausanias X 13.10, etc.

12. Tarentum is not specifically mentioned in connection with pirate raids, but cf. Cic. *Leg. Man.* 32f. (Brundisium, Caieta, Misenum, Ostia), *Verr.* V 90–100 (Syracuse); Plut. *Pomp.* 24.6f., Dio XXXVI 21–22 (Italian ports in general); Strabo XIV 668 (and n. 2 above) for the Delos slave market.
13. Plut. *Luc.* 19.7. For other *grammatici* of ambiguous origin and status, cf. Suet. *Gramm.* 7.1, 11.1, 20.1, 21.1.
14. *CIL* VI 3621; full list at *CIL* VI.7 pp. 4912 (*quae et*), 4940 (*qui et*). Cf. [Virg.] *Cat.* 10.8, 'iste post Sabinus ante Quintio'; Cic. *Ad fam.* XV 20.1 (Sabinus), *Cluent.* 72 (Paetus), *Sest.* 68f. (Ligus), 72 (Serranus). For a change *to* a Greek name, see Suet. *Gramm.* 10 on L. Ateius Praetextatus, 'Philologus ab semet nominatus', following the precedent of Eratosthenes. [See also Frederiksen, op. cit. (n. 4) 301 on the Campanian custom, 'confined to the late Republic and early Empire', of freedmen having two *cognomina*, one Greek and one Latin.]
15. In contrast to the Roman tradition: Cic. *Flacc.* 15–17, on which see L.R. Taylor, *Roman Voting Assemblies* (Ann Arbor 1966) 29–31. The theatre begun in 154 BC 'a Lupercali in Palatium versus' (Velleius I 15.3), and successfully opposed by P. Scipio Nasica as 'inimicissimum . . . bellatori populo ad nutriendam desidiam lasciviamque commentum' (Orosius IV 21.4 cf. Taylor, op. cit. 124f.), would have dominated the harbour of Rome and impressed arrivals there just like the theatres of Ephesus and Miletus. [See p. 104 above.]
16. E.g. *ILLRP* 621 (Paeligni), 646 (Pompeii), 680 (Tibur), 708, 710, 719 (Capua); P. Zanker (ed.), *Hellenismus in Mittelitalien* (Göttingen 1976); J.A. Hanson, *Roman Theatre-Temples* (Princeton 1959); H. Kähler, 'Das Fortunaheiligtum von Palestrina Praeneste', *Annales Universitatis Saraviensis* 7 (1958) 189–240 = F. Coarelli (ed.), *Studi su Praeneste* (Perugia 1978) 221–72.
17. See A. Hardie, *Statius and the Silvae: Poets, Patrons and Epideixis in the Graeco-Roman World* (Liverpool 1983), esp. ch. 2; T.P. Wiseman, in *Les 'bourgeoisies' municipales* (n. 2 above) 299–307, esp. 300f. [= *Roman Studies* (Liverpool 1987) 297–305, esp. 298f.].
18. Cic. *Rab. Post.* 35. Dancers: Antipater of Sidon 61G–P = *Anth. Pal.* IX 567 (Antiodemis), *ILLRP* 803 (Eucharis, *Graeca scaena*), Plut. *Sulla* 2.2f., Varro *Men.* 513B, Lucr. IV 973–83. See J.C. McKeown, *PCPS* 25 (1979) 71–84, on mime in relation to Roman elegy; [also T.P. Wiseman, *Catullus and his World* (Cambridge 1985) 27–35, 44–7, 187f., 192–4; and in opposition, Elizabeth Rawson's essay 'The Vulgarity of the Roman Mime', posthumously published in *Tria Lustra: Essays and Notes Presented to John Pinsent* (ed. H.D. Jocelyn and H.V. Hurt, Liverpool 1993) 255–60: 'I want to reassert the traditional view, that all the publicly staged mimes of which we know anything . . . *were* 'knockabout farce' aimed primarily at the humbler part of the audience. They were watched and often enjoyed by the well-off too, of course, and watched at least even by the well-educated, though these last are consistently deprecating about them.'

Though aiming to prove that Roman mime 'was primarily vulgar slapstick' (p. 259), Rawson's argument also includes, with characteristic honesty and erudition, much evidence that points the other way. And it concludes with a carefully nuanced judgement (p. 260): 'The games in general were a focal point in Roman culture, and I suggest that they were a great unifying social force—even though, as I have argued, the best educated had considerable contempt for what they nevertheless did watch, and perhaps were influenced by.']

19. For the origins of *pantomimus*, see E.J. Jory, *BICS* 28 (1981) 147–61, esp. 154f. and 157 on the late Republic. Cf. B. Helly in *Les 'bourgeoisies' municipales* (n. 2 above) 373 for a Roman organizing 'pantomime' in Thessaly in the first century BC.
20. If mime was defined as the imitation of real people (cf. Diomedes *Gramm. Lat.* I 490K, 'mime is the imitation of life, involving both the permitted and the forbidden'), then perhaps its extension to mythological subjects forced the theorists to ask how much reality such *fabulae* contained.
21. Comm. Bern. pp. 35–6 Usener (cf. Servius *ad Aen.* I 568, Hyginus *Fab.* 258); L. Müller, *Rh. Mus.* 24 (1869) 622; V. Ussani, *Boll. fil. class.* 9 (1902–3) 63f.
22. Juvenal 8.185, 13.110, Martial V 30.3, Suet. *Gaius* 57, Tertullian *Adv. Val.* 44; M. Bonaria, *Romani mimi* (Rome 1965) 133–5.
23. Priscian *Gramm. Lat.* VI 7, 73K, Cic. *Ad fam.* VII 11.2; D.R. Shackleton Bailey, *Cicero Epistulae ad Familiares* I (Cambridge 1977) 338, and *Two Studies in Roman Nomenclature* (New York 1976) 71 [= (Atlanta 1991) 45]; cf. W.S. Watt, *Hermes* 83 (1955) 497f.
24. Wiseman, op. cit. (n. 18) 194–7; *contra*, but without argument, Shackleton Bailey, loc. cit. (n. 23); [also Rawson, op. cit. (n. 18)].
25. See S.F. Bonner, *Education in Ancient Rome* (London 1977) 120–22 on the *pergula* mentioned by Suetonius; ibid. 62f., 217 on *grammatici* as literary scholars. For the *Zmyrna*, see above all Catullus 95, with clear allusions to Callimachus (fr. 398, *Epigr.* 28 Pfeiffer) and the assurance that it will be read in the Greek world where the story is set (the river Satrachus in Cyprus); cf. Wiseman, op. cit. (n. 9) 44–58, esp. 48f. on the influence of Parthenius.
26. Suet. *Gramm.* 9.5, 11.4.
27. Catulus: Suet. *Gramm.* 3.5, Pliny *NH* VII 128 (on Lutatius Daphnis). See A. Wallace-Hadrill, *Suetonius* (London 1983) 30–38, 181–9, on the symbiosis of *studia Graeca* and Roman aristocratic society; E. Rawson, *Intellectual Life in the Late Roman Republic* (London 1985) 66–99 on the status differences among the learned professions; and K. Quinn, *ANRW* II.13 (1983) 104–12, 133f., 150f. on *grammatici* and their significance.
28. Consentius *Gramm. Lat.* V 378K; see J. Tolkiehn, *Berliner philologische Wochenschrift* 13 (1911) 412–6 on Charisius I 25B, Diomedes *Gramm. Lat.* I 510, 516K, Marius Vict. *Gramm. Lat.* VI 113K, Consentius *Gramm. Lat.* V 347, 360, 365K.
29. Cic. *Phil.* XIII 3: 'Eutrapelum, Melam, Coelium, Crassicium, Tironem, Mustelam, Petissium; comitatum relinquo, duces nomino'; *Ad fam.* VII 32 (wit), 33.2 ('limatulo et polito tuo iudicio et illis interioribus litteris tuis'). The 'Classicius'—or 'Cassius', in some MSS—named in company with Tiro and Mustela at *Phil.* V 18, as one of the officers in charge of Antony's armed escort to the temple of Concord on 19 September 44 BC (cf. II 8,

106; VIII 26; XII 14 for the other two), can hardly be the freedman Crassicius Pansa, despite the suggestion of R. Syme, *JRS* 51 (1961) 24 n. 25 = *Roman Papers* II (Oxford 1979) 521 n. 1.

30. Cic. *Ad fam.* IX 26.1f., *Phil.* II 58, *Ad Att.* X 10.5; Servius *ad Ecl.* 10.2.
31. Cic. *Phil.* II 101 (cf. VIII 26): 'agrum Campanum . . . tu compransoribus tuis et collusoribus dividebas; mimos dico et mimas, patres conscripti, in agro Campano collocatos' (cf. Nic. Dam. *FGrH* 90F75 on Sulla). Did Crassicius benefit (*collusor*, n. 29 above)? Antony and mimes: Plut. *Ant.* 9.3–5 (Hippias and Sergius, cf. *Phil.* II 62), 21.2, 24.2, etc. Nucula (cf. R. Syme, *Historia* 13 [1964] 120) and Lento: Cic. *Phil.* XI 13.
32. Rightly emphasized by McKeown, op. cit. (n. 18), esp. 71f. Antony as philhellene: e.g. Plut. *Ant.* 24 (Ephesus), 29 (Alexandria), 56.4–57.1 (Samos, Athens); cf. J. Griffin, *JRS* 67 (1977) 17–26 [= *Latin Poets and Roman Life* (London 1985) 32–47].
33. Cic. *Phil.* II 42f., 101 (cf. VIII 26), Suet. *Rhet.* 29, Sen. *Contr.* IX 3.13f.
34. Arnob. *Adv. nat.* V 18, Lact. *Div. inst.* I 22.11, cf. Plut. *Moralia* 268d–e; Wiseman, op. cit. (n. 9) 136f.
35. Hor. *Odes* IV 2; ps.Acro on *Odes* IV 2.33.
36. Latin as Greek: Philoxenus of Alexandria, *On the Roman Dialect* (*GRF* 443–6 Funaioli). Romans as Hellenes: Dion. Hal. *AR* I 5.1, 89–90, VII 70, etc. See G. Williams, *Change and Decline* (Berkeley 1978) 112–24; T.P. Wiseman, *Clio's Cosmetics* (Leicester 1979) 154–7.
37. E.g. Athenodorus of Pergamum with Cato (Plut. *Cato min.* 10, 16.1, Strabo XIV 674); Diodotus the Stoic with Cicero (Cic. *Acad.* II 115, *Brut.* 309); Staseas of Naples with M. Piso (Cic. *De fin.* V 8, 75, *De or.* I 104). [See now E.D. Rawson in *Philosophia Togata: Essays on Philosophy and Roman Society* (ed. M. Griffin and J. Barnes, Oxford 1989) 233–57.]
38. E.g. Cic. *Cael.* 41 (*scholae*), Varro *Men.* 517B (*acroasis*); cf. Hor. *Sat.* II 3.33–6, Petr. *Sat.* 71.12, etc.
39. Cic. *Pis.* 68–72; see A.S.F. Gow and D.L. Page, *The Greek Anthology: The Garland of Philip* II (Cambridge 1968) 371–4 on his poetry, G.M.A. Grube, *The Greek and Roman Critics* (London 1965) 193–206 on his literary criticism.
40. Athen. XIV 620d (from Dicaearchus), I 20c–d (second century AD, *PIR*[2] A 148).
41. Varro *Men.* 304B (Nonius 259L), cf. Cic. *Acad.* I 8; for the theatre, see especially the fragments of his *Onos luras* (348–69B) and *Parmeno* (394–9B). Cf. also J.-P. Cèbe, *Varron, Satires menippées* VI (Rome 1983) 1027f., and bibliography cited there, on *Men.* 218B.
42. Sen. *Quaest. Nat.* VII 32.2, *Epist.* 59.7, 64.2–5, 98.13 (Caesar), Plut. *Moralia* 77e (anguish); see M.T. Griffin, *Seneca: a Philosopher in Politics* (Oxford 1976) 37–40.
43. Sen. *Epist.* 59.7 ('Graecis verbis Romanis moribus philosophantem'), Jerome *Chron.* 171B Helm (Sotion), Pliny *NH* XVIII 274.
44. Pliny *NH* XVIII 273f. (in imitation of Democritus and Thales? cf. Cic. *De div.* I 111); cf. XVII 11 on the effect of rain and south winds *circa vergilias*.
45. See above, nn. 3 and 11.

46. Sen. *Epist.* 73.15, 'hac itur ad astra'.
47. 'Some day, someone, writing the right book, will crack open the great eggshell still called "Roman civilisation" and show us in full the Greco-Roman creature that we all know lies within; we can then properly study the nature and origins of its hyphenation ... so as to say that the same people who wrote eclogues (or whatever) were also active in commerce (or whatever). So our knowledge of the Hellenizing process might be gradually refined.' R. MacMullen, *Historia* 31 (1982) 484, 502—the beginning and end of his admirable article on 'Roman attitudes to Greek love'.
48. *Gramm. Lat.* VIII (Suppl.) 255 Hagen; pointed out by Tolkiehn, op. cit. (n. 28) 414.
49. Hagen pp. 240 (cf. Suet. in Suda s.v. *assaria*), 248 (cf. Festus 238L, *GRF* 490f.). His own capacities may be gauged from Hagen p. 237, where he cites 'ad balneas Palatinas' as from *quidam poeta*; in fact, it is Cic. *Rosc. Am.* 18 (read 'Pallacinas'), used by Servius and Pompeius (*Gramm. Lat.* IV 431K, V 162K) as an example of *balnea* (f.); presumably the glossator's source did not name the author.
50. O. Seeck, *R-E* 3 (1899) 1456–9.
51. For which see F. Millar, *The Emperor in the Roman World* (London 1977) 232, 249–51.
52. Suet. *Horace* (p. 297 Roth = p. 113f. Rostagni); for the *ab epistulis*, see Millar, op. cit. (n. 51) 224f.
53. See Wallace-Hadrill, op. cit. (n. 27) 91–5, arguing convincingly against the thesis that Suetonius' knowledge of the letters was due to his own tenure of the office *ab epistulis*.
54. Pansa the *cancellarius* does not appear in *PIR* or *R-E*.
55. Sen. *Quaest. Nat.* VII 32.2, 'Romani roboris secta'.
56. See the important chapter on 'Greeks in the imperial service' (many of them were philosophers) in G.W. Bowersock, *Augustus and the Greek World* (Oxford 1965) 30–41.
57. See Bowersock, op. cit. 36–41, and in F. Millar and E. Segal (eds), *Caesar Augustus: Seven Aspects* (Oxford 1984) 176–83. Macer's *Medea* is cited by Stobaeus (617H). [See now P. White, *CQ* 42 (1992) 210–18.]
58. This article benefited substantially from comments made on an earlier draft by the late Elizabeth Rawson, to whom I am very grateful.

Additional note, on Castricii.
Among the funerary inscriptions of Beneventum (cf. above, n. 6) is one of A. Castricius Achilleus and his wife Culcia Isidora (*CIL* IX 1781). Both were evidently ex-slaves of families active in Campania and the Greek East. For 'Culcius', the *TLL Onomasticon* offers only eleven examples, of which four are from Campania (*CIL* X 2354–55, Puteoli; 3768, Suessula; 8074.2, Pompeii?) and three from Asia Minor (*Ath. Mitt.* 1889.94, Smyrna; 1891.438, Cyzicus; 1908.414, Pergamum). A. Castricii are known in Puteoli (*AE* 1978.124, AD 35), Herculaneum (*CIL* X 1403.f.3.14), Capua (X 4607) and Thebes (III 7301); otherwise only at the port of Tarracina (X 6338, cf. Coarelli [above, n. 2] 236), and at Lanuvium (XIV 2105 = *ILS* 2676).

The Lanuvine inscription was copied as follows: 'A. Castricius Myrio/Talenti f. tr.mil. praef.eq./et classis mag. colleg./Lupercor. et Capitolinor./et Mercurial. et paga/nor. Aventin. XXVIvir/[. . .]moni per plures/[. . .]i sortitionibus/[. . .] dis redemptis'; see *PIR*² C 541, Devijver *PME* C 99. For the form of the name, cf. P. Servilius [. . .]cinus Telemaci f., evidently enfranchised by P. Servilius Isauricus *cos.* 48 BC (*ILLRP* 405). Some however read 'Myriotalenti f.'; for a comparable compound name, cf. P.T. Eden, *Seneca, Apocolocyntosis* (Cambridge 1984) 141 on Pheronaotus = *phērōn aōtos* at *Apocol.* 13.5 (neither Talentus nor Myriotalentus appears in L. Pape's *Wörterbuch der griechischen Eigennamen* [1911]). For the social level of the *magistri Capitolini* and *Lupercorum*, cf. *ILLRP* 696 (= *CIL* I² 1004 = *ILS* 1924), the tombstone near Tarracina of the wealthy freedman Geganius Clesippus, whose piquant story is told by Pliny (*NH* XXXIV 11f.); he did not aspire to equestrian officerships or the vigintisexvirate, but held the respectable position of *viator tribunicius* (cf. N. Purcell, *PBSR* 51 [1983] 140f., 152–54). (For the *collegium* named at line 6 of the Lanuvium inscription—really *pagani Amentini?*—see Th. Mommsen, *Hermes* 17 [1882] 44, n. 2, referring to *CIL* VI 251 and Pliny *NH* III 68.)

A Castricius may have been buying and selling slaves in the 40s BC (Cic. *Att.* XII 28.3; cf. II 7.5, 59 BC); the Castricius who was honoured in fulsome terms at Smyrna (Cic. *Flacc.* 75) was no doubt engaged in commercial *negotia*; so too perhaps was M. Castricius, 'summo splendore ingenio gratia praeditus', honoured by Verres in Sicily (Cic. *Verr.* III 185; cf. *Ath. Mitt.* 1881.42, M. Castricius Diadoumenos in Cyzicus). And the elder Pliny used the works of a Castricius who wrote in Greek on market gardening (*kēpourika*, *NH* I 19, index). It seems probable that the Castricii—dealt with in this separate note in order to avoid confusion of the similar names—were a *gens* very like the Crassicii; and that A. Castricius Myrio, a Greek who made himself at home in the military, civil and religious life of Rome, was a figure as characteristic of the Hellenized society of the first century BC as was L. Crassicius Pansa himself.

Chapter 8

The following works are referred to by the author's name alone:

Castagnoli: F. Castagnoli, 'Note sulla topografia del Palatino e del foro romano', *Archeologia classica* 16 (1964) 173–99.
Coarelli: F. Coarelli, *Il foro romano: periodo arcaico* (Rome 1983).
Nash: E. Nash, *Pictorial Dictionary of Ancient Rome* (ed. 2, London 1968).
Wiseman: T.P. Wiseman, 'The Temple of Victory on the Palatine', *Antiquaries Journal* 61 (1981) 35–52 [= *Roman Studies* (Liverpool 1987) 187–204].

1. Cic. *Ad Q.f.* II 5.1; for the house as a status symbol, see R. Saller, *Phoenix* 38 (1984) 351f.
2. Cic. *De off.* I 138 (Octavius), *De domo* 102 (Flaccus); Val. Max. VI 3.1c (Saturninus). For the analogous Greek custom of *kataskaphē*, see W.R. Connor, *TAPA* 115 (1985) 79–102.

3. Cic. *De domo* 100f., Val. Max. VI 3.1a–b; Saller, op. cit. 354. Livy II 7.5–12, 41.11, IV 16.1, VI 20.13, VIII 20.8, etc.; for the Poblicola story see now Coarelli 79–82, arguing for its essential historicity.
4. Cic. *Phil.* II 68f.; cf. *De off.* I 139, quoting an unknown playwright ('O domus antiqua, heu quam dispari/dominare domino') alluded to also at *Phil.* II 105 (Antony and the villa of Varro).
5. Pliny *NH* XXXV 6f.; Trimalchio had his *fasces*, in the form of a ship's prow, hung on the door of his *triclinium* (Petr. *Sat.* 30.1).
5a. [For *stemmata*, see Sen. *Epist.* 44.1, Martial IV 40.1, Statius *Silvae* II 6.11, III 3.44, Suet. *Galba* 2, Juvenal 8.1 and 6, 8.40; E. Courtney, *A Commentary on the Satires of Juvenal* (London 1980) 384–5.]
6. *Spolia*: Plut. *C. Gracchus* 15.1 (Flaccus), cf. Livy X 7.9, Suet. *Nero* 38.2. [See now E. Rawson in *Staat und Staatlichkeit in der frühen römischen Republik* (ed. W. Eder, Stuttgart 1990) 159–61 = *Roman Culture and Society* (Oxford 1991) 583–5.] Procession to the house: Propertius I 16.1–4. Disposal of booty at discretion of *triumphator*: I. Shatzman, *Historia* 21 (1972) 177–205.
7. Festus (Paulus) 123L, 'monimentum est . . . quicquid ob memoriam alicuius factum est, ut fana, porticus . . .'; *TLL* VIII (1963) 1462–4.
8. Pliny *NH* XXXIV 17, on honorific statues: 'Soon a "forum" was created even in private houses.' Vitr. *Arch.* VI 5.2: 'For nobles, whose duty in holding honours and magistracies is to make their services available to the citizens, [the architect] must provide princely forecourts, lofty halls, spacious colonnaded gardens, groves and broad avenues furnished to a standard of majestic elegance; also libraries and basilicas, appointed no differently from public buildings, because often in their houses public consultations as well as private judgements and decisions are carried out.' On the nature of the consultations referred to, see T.P. Wiseman, *Roman Political Life 90 BC–AD 69* (Exeter 1985) 14–16; on public functions in general, see Saller, op. cit. (n. 1) 352f.
9. E.g. Cic. *Verr.* IV 69 on the temple of Iuppiter O.M. (not a triumphal monument, however): 'At this point, Quintus Catulus, I call on you—for I am speaking of your most famous and splendid *monumentum* . . . together with that temple is consecrated the everlasting memory of your name.' Cf. Val. Max. VI 9.5, Tac. *Hist.* III 72.3 for Catulus' inscription; Suet. *Galba* 2 on 'Q. Catulus Capitolinus'.
10. Sall. *Cat.* 12.4, on the great *maiores*.
11. Temple: Gallus (*JRS* 69 [1979] 138), 'multorum templa deorum/fixa legam spolieis deivitiora tueis'; cf. Virg. *Aen.* III 286f., V 359f., XI 778, etc. [See also Rawson, op. cit. (n. 6) 162–4 = 586–8.] House: above, nn. 5 and 6.
12. Temple: e.g. Cic. *Ad Q.f.* III 1.14 (Tellus), Dio LIII 27.3 (Pantheon). House: e.g. Dio XLIV 18.2 (Caesar), Juvenal VII 125, VIII 3 (triumphal chariot), Tac. *Dial.* 8.4, 11.3, Pliny *NH* XXXIV 17 (put up by clients), XXXV 7 ('animorum ingentium imagines'), Virg. *Aen.* VII 177–82.
13. Temple: e.g. Pliny *NH* XXXV 22 (Iuppiter O.M.), Livy XLI 28.10 (Mater Matuta); cf. also p. 40f. above on the temple of Tellus (Varro *RR* I 2.1), and F. Cairns in *Poetry and Politics in the Age of Augustus*

(ed. T. Woodman and D. West, Cambridge 1984) 153f. on the temple of Apollo Palatinus (Propertius IV 6). House: inferred from Petr. *Sat.* 29.3–6, Apul. *Met.* VI 29.2 (p. 37 above), and the 'atrium' of the François tomb: see D. and R. Rebuffat, *Latomus* 37 (1978) 88–104, and F. Coarelli, *Dial. Arch.* 1.2 (1983) 58f. Mosaic floors offered another medium for self-advertisement: see R.I. Curtis, *AJA* 88 (1984) 557–66 on A. Umbricius Scaurus' house in Pompeii.

14. Val. Max. VIII 15.1 ('instar atrii Capitolium est'), Appian *Iber.* 23; cf. Livy XXVI 19.6, Dio XVI 57.39, *De vir. ill.* 49.2f.; on the Scipio legend see F.W. Walbank, *PCPS* 13 (1967) 54–69 [= *Selected Papers: Studies in Greek and Roman History and Historiography* (Cambridge 1985) 120–37].
15. Temples: Pliny *NH* XXXIV 57 ('aedes Pompei Magni'), XXXVI 26 ('delubrum Cn. Domitii'), 40 ('aedes Metelli'), 163 ('aedes Seiani'), Varro *RR* III 5.12 ('aedes Catuli'); cf. also Val. Max. I 7.5 ('aedes Honoris Mariana'), Festus 282L ('aedes Herculis Aemiliana'), Vitr. *Arch.* III 3.5 ('Hercules Pompeianus'), Pliny *NH* XIII 53 ('Apollo Sosianus'), *CIL* VI 4305 ('Diana Cornificiana'), *Rend. Pont. Acc.* 43 (1970–1) 123–8 ('Diana Planciana'). Houses: Nepos *Atticus* 13.2 ('domus Tamphiliana'), Suet. *Gramm.* 17 ('Catulina domus'), *Div. Aug.* 72.1 ('aedes Hortensianae'), *Tib.* 15.1 ('Pompeiana domus'); cf. also Cic. *Ad Att.* I 6.1, 13.6, 14.7, IV 3.3, *Ad fam.* VII 20.1, *Ad Q.f.* II 3.7, where the reference may be merely to the *last* owner.
16. Cic. *Verr.* IV 69 (n. 9 above).
17. F. Coarelli, *Dial. Arch.* 2.2 (1984) 152–4, and in *Architecture et société* (Coll. de l'École fr. de Rome 66, Rome 1983) 191–217, esp. 200–6 on the *horti Lucullani* and the Fortuna sanctuary at Praeneste.
18. Cic. *Phil.* II 110, Livy in Plut. *Caes.* 63.9, Obsequens 67, Florus II 13.91, Suet. *Div. Jul.* 81.3; S. Weinstock, *Divus Julius* (Oxford 1971) 276–81.
19. Cic. *Ad Att.* X 3a; Coarelli 56–72, and in *Architecture et société* (n. 17) 199f.
20. Virg. *Aen.* VII 170–86 [trans. by W.F. Jackson Knight (Penguin Classics 1956), my italics]; cf. W.A. Camps, *CQ* 53 (1959) 54 on the Capitoline temple as a possible influence on Virgil here.
21. Cic. *Phil.* II 69, Hist. Aug. *Gordiani* 3; for the pun on *carinae*, see Velleius II 77.1, Plut. *Ant.* 32.3, Florus II 18.4, *De vir. ill.* 84.3, Dio XLVIII 38.2.
22. Virg. *Aen.* VII 153, 170.
23. H.T. Rowell, *AJP* 62 (1941) 262–71.
24. Servius *ad Aen.* VII 170: 'domum quam in Palatio diximus ab Augusto factam per transitum laudat' (cf. also his comments on VII 173 and 175). Palace and temple: P. Zanker, in *Città e architettura nella Roma imperiale* (Analecta Romana Suppl. 10, Odense 1983) 21–40. Senate-house (i.e. the library of the Apollo temple): D.L. Thompson, *AJA* 85 (1981) 335–9, [cf. R. Talbert, *The Senate of Imperial Rome* (Princeton 1984) 117–8.]
25. Suet. *Div. Aug.* 72.1; Castagnoli 188–90 on Josephus *Ant.* XIX 103f., 116f., 214.
26. Cic. *De domo* 100; cf. 103, 116, 132 ('in pulcherrimo urbis loco ... pulcherrimo prospectu ... in urbis clarissimo loco').
27. Inferred from Cic. *De har. resp.* 49, Clodius' threat to build another portico on the Carinae, 'quae Palatio responderet'.

28. Hor. *Odes* III 1.45f. ('cur invidendis postibus et novo/sublime ritu moliar atrium?'); cf. Martial I 70.12 ('atria excelsae domus'), Sen. *Epist.* 84.12 (*vestibula* approached by steps).
29. Pliny *NH* XIX 23; cf. Servius *ad Aen.* VIII 363 for the *domus publica* 'in radicibus Palatii'.
30. Dio LV 12.4–5, Suet. *Div. Aug.* 57.2 (fire); Ovid *Tristia* III 1.33f. [For Augustus' *vestibulum* and doorway as represented on the 'Sorrento base', see T.P. Wiseman, *Flavius Josephus: Death of an Emperor* (Exeter 1991) 107–9; for Augustus' house and the Apollo temple, see P. Zanker, *The Power of Images in the Age of Augustus* (Ann Arbor 1988) 51f., 67f.]
31. Augustus *Res gestae* 34.2, 35.1, with Mommsen's reading 'laureis postes aedium mearum v[incti]': see E.A. Judge, in *Polis and Imperium: Studies in Honour of Edward Togo Salmon* (ed. J.A.S. Evans, Toronto 1974) 311. *Fastigium*: Sen. *De clem.* I 26.5, cf. Suet. *Div. Claud.* 17.3; Weinstock, op. cit. (n. 18) 280f., thought the *fastigium* was probably added by Gaius.
32. For this misnomer, and the true extent of the ancient *Palatium*, see Coarelli 24f.
33. Compare the four corners of Romulus' *pomerium*, as named by Tacitus (*Ann.* XII 24, with Orelli's reading 'tum ad sacellum Larundae forumque Romanum'): Coarelli 262–4.
34. See Castagnoli 173–7: the Cermalus was *not* a summit of the Palatine.
35. Scalae Caci: Solinus 1.18 (from Varro?), Diodorus IV 21.2; cf. Plut. *Rom.* 20.4. Walls: Castagnoli 180, illustrated in Nash II 112f., figs 819f.
36. Livy X 23.11f., 33.9. For the position of the Victoria temple, see P. Romanelli, *Studi romani* 1 (1953) 10; Castagnoli 185f; Wiseman 35–52 [= 187–204], except pp. 40–2 [= 192–4], where the argument from the Porta Romanula should be ignored (see Coarelli 228–34).
37. Livy X 29.14; cf. Dio XLV 17.2, with Wiseman 45f. [= 197f.].
38. Festus 318L. The traditional identification of the Clivus Victoriae depends on the mistaken attribution by R. Lanciani, *Bull. Com.* 13 (1885) 157–60, of fr. 42 of the Marble Plan; corrected by G. Gatti, in G. Carettoni *et al.*, *La pianta marmorea di Roma antica* (Rome 1960) 109–11.
39. Shops in the Forum Bovarium 'with goods of great price' were destroyed in the fire of 192 BC (Livy XXXV 40.8), and a century later the Forum Bovarium was a place where information could be picked up from all over the empire (Cic. *Scaur.* 23, referring to *c*.100 BC).
40. Velleius I 15.3, 'a Lupercali in Palatium versus'; J.A. Hanson, *Roman Theatre-Temples* (Princeton 1959) 24f.
41. Livy XXXVI 36.3f., cf. XXXIV 54.3; Cic. *De har. resp.* 24 ('in ipso Matris Magnae conspectu'), cf. Arnob. *Adv. nat.* VII 33 ('conspexerit'). Two *scaenae* and two *caveae* were involved (Cic. *De har. resp.* 25f., cf. Plut. *Cato min.* 46.4), at least one of them directly in front of the temple. No doubt Sulla's *ludi Victoriae* were held in the same place.
42. Josephus *Ant.* XIX 75 [but see now Wiseman, op. cit. (n. 30) 58: perhaps not part of the stage structure]; Philodemus 26.3G–P (*Anth. Pal.* VII 222.3), with T.P. Wiseman, *CQ* 32 (1982) 475f.
43. Dion Hal. *AR* I 32.3–33.1 (also the Lupercal), with Wiseman 35–7 [= 187–9]. The contemporary temple of Iuppiter Stator (Livy X 36.11,

37.15: 294 BC) was similarly attributed to Romulus (Ovid *Fasti* VI 793f., Dion. Hal. *AR* II 50.3, etc.).
44. Festus 310–2L on *Quadrata Roma*: 'quia saxo †minitus† est initio in speciem quadratam.' *Ox. Pap.* XVII 2088.14–17, suppl. by A. Piganiol, *Scritti in onore di B. Nogara* (Rome 1937) 374: 'Primoque in pago [locus erat ubi Roma con]dita est eaque Roma muro [in speciem quadratam munita est ne]quis at Romam Quadrat<a>m [accedere posset. Imperii enim c]aput Romam Quad[rat]am [existimabant.]' Cf. F. Castagnoli in *Studies Presented to D.M. Robinson* I (ed. G.E. Mylonas, St Louis 1951) 394f.
45. Solinus 1.17f. (from Varro?), Conon *FGrH* 26F48.8 (Faustulus); Propertius IV 1.9 (Remus); Dion. Hal. *AR* I 79.11, Plut. *Rom.* 20.4. [See now P. Pensabene in *La grande Roma dei Tarquinii* (Rome 1990) 87–90, identifying the site (as 'a sort of *hērōon*', fourth century BC) in front of the temple of Victoria.] For the *casa Romuli* on the Capitol, see Vitr. *Arch.* II 1.5, Sen. *Contr.* II 1.5, *CIL* XVI 23, Macr. *Sat.* I 15.10.
46. For the Magna Mater as a goddess of victory, see Livy XXIX 10.8, Cic. *De har. resp.* 27f., Plut. *Marius* 17.5, 31.1, etc. One of her names was Rhea, which first-century historians gave to the mother of Romulus (Castor of Rhodes *FGrH* 250F5, Varro *LL* V 144), now no longer Ilia but Rhea Silvia.
47. In T. Woodman and D. West (eds), *Poetry and Politics in the Age of Augustus* (Cambridge 1984) 117–28, esp. 125–7. See also R.J. Littlewood, *CQ* 31 (1981) 381–95 on Cybele in Ovid.
48. See n. 44 above.
48a. Virg. *Aen.* VI 777–95 [trans. W.F. Jackson Knight].
49. Dio LIII 16.4–5: reference to Romulus' house on the Palatine (cf. n. 45) in the context of the grant of laurels and *corona civica*. For Octavian as Romulus, see Dio LIII 16.6, Suet. *Div. Aug.* 7.2, 95.1, Virg. *Georg.* III 27.
50. Fire: n. 30 above. Vesta: Ovid *Fasti* IV 949–54, *Met.* XV 864f., *Fasti Caeretani* and *Praenestini* for 28 April (12 BC). [Vesta's temple is evidently in Augustus' *vestibulum* on the 'Sorrento base': see n. 30 above.]
51. Ovid *Tristia* III 1.27–38. Lines 39–46 describe the laurels: for 'perpetuos meruit domus ista triumphos' (41), cf. Pliny *NH* XXXV 7 (p. 99 above).
52. Coarelli 12–49, esp. 24f., 40f. [Coarelli's argument has been strongly challenged: see F. Castagnoli, *Topografia romana: ricerche e discussioni* (Quad. top. ant. 10, Rome 1988) 99–114; A. Ziolkowski, *Opuscula Romana* 17 (1989) 225–39; good summary by J.R. Patterson, *JRS* 82 (1992) 202.]
53. Gate: Varro *LL* V 164 (Porta Mucionis), Varro in Nonius 852L (Mugionis), Festus (Paulus) 131L (Mugionia), Solinus 1.24 (Mugonia); cf. Virg. *Aen.* VIII 361 (*mugire*). 'Clivus Palatinus': Nash I 252f. Area Palatina: Gell. *NA* XX 1.1 (cf. IV 1.1), Josephus *Ant.* XIX 223.
54. *CIL* VI 8640–52, XIV 1860, 7246.
55. Castagnoli 186f. Similarly, the so-called *domus Tiberiana* beneath the Farnese Gardens must be a later palace on the site of Tiberius' house; Tiberius himself was a notorious non-builder (n. 67 below). [See now C. Krause, in *Domus Tiberiana: nuove ricerche, studi di restauro* (Rome

and Zürich 1985) 77, 122f.; E. Monaco, in *Roma: archeologia nel centro* I (Rome 1985) 174; Wiseman, op. cit. (n. 30) 105–10.]
56. Ovid *Tristia* III 1.32, Josephus *Ant.* XIX 223; *ILLRP* 43 ('Anabestas'), 252 ('Remureine'), 447 (Fertor Resius); cf. Castagnoli 191.
57. Ovid *Met.* I 168–76. I am very grateful to Dr Anna Wilson for pointing out the relevance of this passage.
58. See P. Zanker, *Forum Romanum: die Neugestalt durch Augustus* (Tübingen 1972). Reading clockwise from the Divus Iulius temple, the visitor could see: the Arcus Augusti; the temple of Castor (rebuilt by Tiberius in AD 6); the Basilica Iulia, also called Basilica Gai et Luci; Caesar's new Rostra; the temple of Concordia Augusta (rebuilt by Tiberius in AD 10); the Curia Iulia; and the Porticus Gai et Luci in front of the Basilica Paulli (the Porticus Iulia?). The only non-Augustan *monumenta* remaining visible were Plancus' temple of Saturn (*CIL* X 6087, Suet. *Div. Aug.* 29.5) and perhaps Lepidus' temple of Felicitas (Dio XLIV 5.2); those destroyed included the Metellan temple of Castor (Cic. *Verr.* I 154, *Scaur.* 46), the Sempronian basilica (Livy XLIV 16.10f.), the Opimian basilica and Concordia temple (Cic. *Sest.* 140, Varro *LL* V 156), the Sullan Curia (Dio XL 50.2, XLIV 5.2).
59. See Zanker, op. cit. (n. 24), who compares the palace at Pergamum.
60. See F. Coarelli in *Città e architettura* (n. 24 above) 44f., on the Pantheon (Dio LIII 27.3): 'gli anni compresi tra il 29 e il 26 sembrano caratterizzati da una spiccata tendenza del nuovo governo di Roma ad ispirarsi direttamente—e pericolosamente—a istituzioni e modelli ellenistici.' Coarelli rightly connects this with Octavian's 'Romulean' image (n. 49 above).
61. Dio LI 19.1; on Augustus' arches, see the fundamental study of F. Coarelli, *Il foro romano: periodo repubblicano e augusteo* (Rome 1985) 258–308. [Coarelli's conclusions are challenged by E. Nedergaard, in *Kaiser Augustus und die verlorene Republik* (Berlin 1988) 224–39; see also F.S. Kleiner, *JRA* 2 (1989) 198–200.]
62. Coarelli 54f. (Arcus Augusti), 56–72 (Regia-Vesta complex).
63. Coarelli 231–7, plausibly identifying the ramp as the 'scalae Graecae' (Gell. *NA* X 15.29, Servius *ad Aen.* IV 646); I agree with Coarelli that the identification of the Porta Romanula in Wiseman 40–2 [= 192–4], based on Festus 318L, is mistaken.
64. Velleius II 81.3, Suet. *Div. Aug.* 29.3, Dio XLIX 15.5 (36 BC); Cic. *De domo* 115f. (Clodius), Plut. *Pomp.* 40.5 (Pompey's house attached to his theatre complex).
65. Cf. *CIL* VI 31426, a dedication 'in honorem domus Augustae' set up by the *kalatores* on the wall of the Regia facing the arch.
66. Vesta: n. 50 above. Tiberius' house: Tac. *Hist.* I 27, Suet. *Vit.* 15.3, Plut. *Galba* 24.4.
67. Dio LVII 10.2, Suet. *Tib.* 47, Tac. *Ann.* VI 45.2 ('contemptu ambitionis'); cf. Dio LVI 46.3, Pliny *NH* XII 94 (Livia). For Tiberius' characteristics see B. Levick, *Tiberius the Politician* (London 1976) 82–91, esp. 89 on his *moderatio* (references at p. 253).
68. Suet. *Gaius* 21, Dio LIX 7.1–4; H. Mattingly, *Coins of the Roman Empire in the British Museum* I (London 1923) 153, no. 41.

69. Suet. *Gaius* 22.2, also on Gaius' taste for posing between the gods' statues to be worshipped (for the context see J.P.V.D. Balsdon, *The Emperor Gaius* (Oxford 1934) 160–4; Dio LIX 28.5, with the absurd idea (no doubt a misunderstanding of his source) that Gaius made his new entrance by cutting through the temple itself. [Evidently not so absurd: see H. Hurst, *Archeologia laziale* 9 (1988) 16f., illustrated by Sheila Gibson in her exhibition catalogue *Architecture and Archaeology* (London and Rome 1991), 'Caligula's Palace Vestibule?'.]
70. Dio LIV 8.3 (*tropaiophoros*); Frontinus *Aq*. 129, Dio LI 19.2, etc. (Divus Iulius *rostra*). For *rostra* on the Castor temple, see L.R. Taylor, *Roman Voting Assemblies* (Ann Arbor 1966) 25–8; the restoration of the preamble to the *lex Gabinia Calpurnia* of 58 BC (C. Nicolet, *Insula sacra: la loi Gabinia Calpurnia de Délos* [Rome 1980] 11 n. 6) reads: '[in foro pro rostris aedis] Castor[is]'; however, see Coarelli, op. cit. (n. 61) 309.
71. See Balsdon, op. cit. (n. 69) 157–73, esp. 160 on the parallel with Octavian. Banquet: Suet. *Div. Aug*. 70.1. Pantheon: n. 60 above.
72. The best account of Augustus' dynastic policy and its vicissitudes is in Levick, op. cit. (n. 67), chapters 3, 4 and 10.
73. See n. 18 above.
74. Josephus *Ant*. XIX 173, 187 (100 years counting from Caesar's first consulship? cf. Hor. *Odes* II 1.1); Suet. *Gaius* 60.
75. Pliny *NH* XXXVI 11: 'bis vidimus urbem totam cingi domibus Gai et Neronis.' Bridge to Capitol and house in Area Capitolina: Suet. *Gaius* 22.4 (cf. 22.1 for his title 'Optimus Maximus Caesar'). *Caput rerum*: Livy I 55.6, V 54.7; cf. n. 44 above.
76. Tac. *Ann*. XV 39.1, Suet. *Nero* 31.1; Nash I 375–9. [For the topography of the *horti Maecenatiani*, see R.C. Häuber, *Kölner Jahrbuch für Vor- und Frühgeschichte* 23 (1990) 11–107, an excellent monograph with superb maps (by Helge Stöcker).]
77. Suet. *Nero* 38.2: 'domus priscorum ducum arserunt hostilibus adhuc spoliis adornatae.' Asconius 27C, 32C (Clodius), Pliny *NH* XVII 5. For the position of Scaurus' house, see Coarelli 25.
78. Suet. *Nero* 31.1, Pliny *NH* XXXIV 45. For the *domus aurea* in general, see M.T. Griffin, *Nero: the End of a Dynasty* (London 1984) 133–42.
79. E.B. Van Deman and A.G. Clay, *Memoirs of the American Academy in Rome* 5 (1925) 115–26 (very conjectural); Castagnoli 195–8 for the probable Flavian date of the completed project.
80. See n. 12 above.
81. Suet. *Nero* 25.2 (cf. 25.1 and Dio LXII 20.3 for the triumph analogy); cf. n. 5 above (Trimalchio).
82. Martial *De spect*. 2; Pliny *NH* XXXIV 45, cf. Dio LXV 15.1, Suet. *Div. Vesp*. 18.
83. Martial I 70.3–9 (p. 107 above for Ovid). In the text I followed the interpretation of Coarelli 40f.; *contra* P. Howell, *A Commentary on Book One of Martial* (London 1980) 267–70, and F. Castagnoli, *Rend. Acc. Linc.* 8.38 (1983) 11f., who believe that Martial's book was to go past the Arch of Titus and on to the Palatine; [see n. 52 above for the Sacra Via controversy].

84. Coarelli 34 n. 23.
85. Hist. Aug. *Severus* 24.3; Nash II 302–5.
86. Martial III 47.1, Juvenal III 11 ('Arcus stillans' in the Juvenal scholia and the *Mirabilia*).
87. See above all P. Grimal, *MEFR(A)* 91 (1979) 671–91, on the evolution of the monarchical idea from the *De republica* to the *De clementia*. As a counter to the much-vaunted hatred of *regnum*, consider the use of *rex* as the client's word for his patron (Plautus *Asin.* 919, Hor. *Epist.* I 17.43, Columella I pref. 9, etc.), and the Roman senators' conception of themselves as Homeric *basileis*: Wiseman, op. cit. (n. 8) 10–12 for the Ciceronian evidence, and O. Murray, *JRS* 55 (1965) 176–8 on Philodemus' essay 'The Good King according to Homer'.
88. Dio LII 1.1; see F. Millar, in *Caesar Augustus: Seven Aspects* (ed. F. Millar and E. Segal, Oxford 1984) 37–60.
89. Festus 318L; Coarelli 232f.

INDEX

Acca Larentia 23
Accius, L., dramatist 17
Aelii Lamiae 83–4
Aelius Tubero, Q., historian 55, 56
Aemilii Lepidi 132 (n. 64)
Aeneas 14, 34, 101, 104–6
 shield of ix, 57
Aeschylus, satyr-plays of 76, 84
Aesculapius 63
agora, and theatre 14
Amphiaraus 76
Amykos 15, 73
Anacreon 31
annales, annalists 2, 3–4, 37, 46, 56
antiquarians 14, 24
Antonius, Iullus 90, 94
Antonius, M. (*cos.* 99) 1–2, 3
Antonius, M. (*cos.* 44) 42, 89, 94, 99
Apollo, temples of 71, 104–5
Apuleius, on *monumenta* 37
Ardea, foundation of 76
Area Palatina 108, 110, 112
Argei 8
Ariadne 78
Arion 71
Aristonothos, vase-painter 27
Aristophanes 60, 64, 142 (n. 21)
Aristotle 5, 13, 19, 32, 85
Aristoxenus of Tarentum 13
Asius of Samos, mythographer 28
astrology (see also Chaldaeans) 60, 64
Atellana, dramatic genre 12, 36, 82, 83
 relation to satyr-play 69–70, 141 (n. 9)
Atreus 93
 dynasty of 18, 20, 29, 79
augury 58–60
Augustine, St 17
Augustus, emperor 17, 33
 arch of 109–10, 113
 autocracy of 109, 111
 burns prophetic books 66
 laurels at door 102, 106–7
 Palatine complex of 101–2, 104–10
 staff of 96–7
Autolycus 33, 141 (n. 9)

Bacchic cult, suppression of 64, 69, 76, 78
Bacis, prophet 59
banquet songs, see *symposion*
bards 12, 32, 125 (n. 6)
Beneventum 91

Cacu(s), prophet 24, 25, 74–5
Caeculus 25, 26, 30, 35
Caesar, see Iulius
Caesars, temples of 46, 109, 110, 111
Callimachus 13, 26, 73
Calpurnius Piso, L., historian 2, 3–4
Calpurnius Piso, L. (*cos.* 58) 95
Calpurnius Piso, L. (*cos.* 15) 69
Camilla 24, 26
Camillus, see Furius
Carmenta, prophetess 9, 138 (n. 97)
Carvilius, Sp. 39
Castor and Pollux, see Dioscuri
Castricii 153–4
Catiline, see Sergius
Cato, see Porcius
Catullus, see Valerius
Catulus, see Lutatius
Ceres, temple of 28
Chaldaean astrologers 59, 60, 64, 144 (n. 55)
Cicero, see Tullius
Cincius Alimentus, L., historian ix, 29, 38–9
Cinna, poet 90, 93
Circe 76, 83, 84
circulatores 32

163

Circus Maximus, astrologers and strolling players in 33, 60
Claudia, Q. 17, 36, 62, 82
Claudii 39–40, 41, 45
Claudius Caecus, Ap. 39–40, 41
Claudius Caudex, Ap. 39, 44, 45, 46–7
Claudius Pulcher, Ap. (cos. 212) 45–6
Claudius Pulcher, Ap. (*cos.* 54) 60
Claudius Quadrigarius, Q., historian 39
Claudius Russus, Ap. 40–1, 43–4
Clodius, P. xi, 46, 110
Clodius, Sex. 94
Cloelia 38
Cluvius Rufus, historian 20
Coelius Antipater, historian 3
comedy, and satyr-play 79
Comitium 10, 14, 38, 73
Cora 91, 95
Cornelius Culleolus, prophet 59, 66
Cornelius Sulla, L. 78, 79, 87
  writes satyric comedies 70, 82, 85
Cornelius Tacitus, historian ix, 20
Corythus 35
Crassicii 91
Crassicius Pansa, L. 90–97
Critias, tragic poet 58
Cybele (Magna Mater) 74, 81, 105–6
  comes to Rome 35, 62, 64
  temple of 78, 102–6

Decius Mus, P. 46–7
Delos 79, 91, 92, 95
Delphic oracle 59, 62
Demaratus 8
Demetrius the Besieger 13–14
Demodocus, bard 32, 58
demons 55–6
diadema 41–4
Diomedes, grammarian 69–70, 85
Dionysius I, of Syracuse 41
Dionysius of Halicarnassus, historian 5, 18, 54–6
Dionysus, in Italy 73, 76
Diopeithes, soothsayer 58
Dioscuri, temple of 14, 71–2, 110, 111, 160 (n. 70)
dirge 32
divination, at Rome 58–67
Domitian, palace of 108, 112–3, 114, 115
drama, at Rome x–xi, 10, 12–13, 16–17, 33, 35–6, 68–70, 74, 78, 79–81, 84–5, 92–3
  see also *Atellana*, mime, *praetexta*, satyr-play, *togatae*
drama, Etruscan 10, 12, 36, 71, 74
drama and history 12–13, 16, 18–21, 35
dramatic festivals xi, 13–16, 78, 79–80, 92–3, 123 (n. 59)
  see also *ludi*
Duris of Samos 18–19

Empedocles 53, 57, 95
Ennius, Q., poet 29
  on prophets 57, 60, 66
Epicharmus, dramatist 10, 14
Eratosthenes 73
Erulus 24
Etruscan influence on Rome 10, 21, 23, 76
Etruscan legends 24, 74–5
Euboeans, in Italy 6–7, 26–8
Eudemus of Corinth, mythographer 28
Euphrantides, prophet 61
Euripides, satyr-plays of 84

Fabii 18, 83
Fabius Pictor, Q. ix, 2–3, 4–5, 29, 38–9
  as Hellenistic historian 5, 18, 19–20
  on *ludi Romani* 10, 76, 81
family trees 99
Faunus 62, 82–3, 94
Faustulus 38, 104
Festus, on 'Porta Romana' 115
Ficana 7, 31
Ficoroni *cista* 14, 15, 73
fiction and history 5, 6, 16, 21, 37, 151 (n. 20)
Finley, Sir Moses x, xii
Forum Appi 40–1
Forum Bovarium 23, 82, 102–4, 108, 114, 157 (n. 39)
  and Hercules 8, 9, 28
Fulvii 45, 47
Fulvius Flaccus, M. (*cos.* 264) 44–5, 47
Fulvius Flaccus, M. (*cos.* 125) 47, 98, 99
Fulvius Flaccus, Q. 45–6
Furius Camillus, M. 18, 62

Gaius, emperor 110–11
Geganius Clesippus 154
Genucius Cipus 62
Giants 53, 57, 133 (n. 11)
Gibbon, Edward 21
Gravisca 8, 27
Greek plays in Rome 69, 78, 93

INDEX

Hades, myths of 56–7, 58, 67, 105–6
haruspices 58, 59, 60, 64, 137 (n. 84)
Hellenistic historiography 18–19, 48
Hellenization of Rome x, 6–10, 13–16, 71–7, 92–4, 153 (n. 47)
Heraclides Ponticus 13, 73
Heraclitus, on bards 32
Herakles (Hercules) 76, 82
  at Rome 8–9, 28, 62, 83
Herodotus xii, 3, 28, 71
historians, malice of 47–8
historiography, Roman 1–5, 14–21, 37–9, 47–8, 56
  and drama 5, 18–21
  ethical value of ix, 2, 37
holy men, absence of 58, 61
Horatii 18, 38
Horatius Cocles 38
Horatius Flaccus, Q. (Horace) x, 66, 96
  on satyr-play 68–71, 80, 85
houses, as status symbols 98–100
human sacrifice 61

imagination xii–xiii, 6, 12, 20, 21, 30
Ischia, see Pithekoussai
Iulius Caesar, C.
  as quasi-king 42–3, 86, 88–9
  house of 100, 101
  on life after death 56
Iunii Silani 73, 83

Kleiklos 7, 27

Laberius, D., dramatist 36
Lake Regillus, battle of 62, 72
Lamia 84
Lamos 84
Larth Telikles 27
Latinus, palace of 100–1, 114
lemnisci 42–4
Liber Pater (Dionysus) 71
  temple of 73, 82
Licinius Stolo, C. 13
Livius, T. (Livy) ix, 17–18, 24, 29, 39, 46
  on drama 13, 18, 74
Livius Andronicus, dramatist 16, 26, 36, 73
Lucan 57, 93
Lucceius, L., historian 19
Lucilius, C., satirist 91, 141 (n. 10)

Lucretius, T., poet xiii, 70, 78
  on fear of gods 49, 53
  on prophets 52–3, 57–8
ludi (*scaenici*), see dramatic festivals
ludi Apollinares xi, 64, 74
ludi Florales 16, 60, 73, 142–3 (n. 29)
ludi plebeii 12, 122 (n. 45)
ludi Romani 10, 12, 36, 76, 81
Luperci, Lupercalia 27, 42, 63, 82, 84
Lupercal 106, 108
  theatre at 78, 104
Lutatius Catulus, Q. 1, 2, 93
Lycophron, dramatist 74, 79, 80

Macaulay, Thomas Babington 12, 21
Maecenas, C. 66
Maenius, C. 14
Magna Mater, see Cybele
Manius, prophet 63, 64
Manlius Capitolinus, M. 35, 98
maps, and glory 40–1
Marcii, noble prophets 59, 64, 66, 73, 74, 83
Marius, C. 45–6, 61, 65
Marsi 74
Marsyas 73–4, 78, 83
Martial, on Domitian's palace 112–3
Mater Matuta 23, 44, 76–7
Metabus 24–5
Metapontum, prophets at 63
mime 12, 36, 69, 141 (n. 9)
  from Alexandria 80, 93
  relation to satyr-play 79–81, 145 (n. 60)
  vulgar or sophisticated? 93, 94, 150–1 (n. 18)
mime-writers 90, 93–4
Minucius, column of 38
miracle stories 61–2
Mommsen, Theodor 21, 86, 89
monumenta 37–9, 45–8, 114, 159 (n. 58)

Naevius, Cn., dramatist 16, 17, 29
Navius, Attus 61, 62
necromancy 60
Nemi, Diana sanctuary 28
Nero, palace of 111–2, 114
'Nestor's cup' 7, 26–7
Nibelungenlied 29
Nonae Capratinae 35
Novius, dramatist 36, 83

165

Nucula, mime-writer 94
Numa 62, 64, 83, 96
nurses' stories 33, 36

Octavian, see Augustus
Octavius, Cn. 59, 65
Oebalus 25
olive oil 91, 95
oral tradition 11, 26, 29–34
Orestes 28, 29
Orphic poems xii, 57
Ovidius Naso, P. (Ovid) 34, 63, 82–4, 107–9
  on Q. Claudia 17, 35, 36, 80, 82, 127 (n. 48)

Palatine Hill xiii, 6, 46, 83
  houses and palaces 101–15
  topography of 102–3
Pan 78, 84
pantomimi 80, 93
Papirius Cursor, L. 39
Patavium (Padua) 36
Pausanias, on drama 16–17
Petronius, *Satyrika* 85
Phaedra 17
Philodemus of Gadara 95
Phocaeans 8, 28
Phylarchus, historian 19
Picus 62, 83
pirates 92
Piso, see Calpurnius
Pithekoussai (Ischia) 6–7, 26–7
Plato, on prophets 64
Pliny, on Trajan 17
Plutarch 17, 19
  on early Rome 5, 29, 84–5
poets and prophets 57–8
Polybius, historian ix–x, 19, 29
Pompeius Macer, Cn. 96–7
Pompeius Magnus, Cn. 43, 114
  house of 99, 101
Pomponius, L., dramatist 70, 82, 83
pontifical chronicle 2–4, 21
Porcius Cato, M., historian 2–3, 29
  on banquet songs 32
  on soothsayers 61
Porcius Cato, M. (*pr.* 54) 56, 57
Porta Capena 114, 115
Porta Mugionia 108, 110, 112, 113, 115
Porta Romanula 109–10, 113, 115

Postumius Albinus, A. 45
Praeneste 24, 27, 35
praetexta ('purple-bordered'), dramatic genre 12, 69, 140–1 (n. 9)
praise singer 32, 34
Priapus 82, 83
Propertius, Sex., poet 66
prophecy, books of (see also Sibyls) 64, 66
prophets, at Rome 52–67
  consulted by Senate 59, 65
  politically dangerous 64–6
  relation to poets 57–8
Publicii 73, 142 (n. 29)
Publicius, prophet 59, 66
Puteoli 91
'pyre of nine tribunes' 38
Pyrgi, temples 28
Pyrrhus, Roman war against 46–7
Pythagoras, Pythagoreans 10, 64, 95
Python, satyr-play of 79, 81

Rhea Silvia 158 (n. 46)
Rhinthon, dramatist 14
Roma Quadrata 104, 108
Roman mythology 23–4, 82–4
Rome, name of 8
Romulus 5, 25, 30, 34, 35, 38, 62, 63–4, 84, 102, 104, 115
Rubicon, apparition at 146 (n. 75)
Rutile Hipukrates 27

Sacra Via 102, 107, 113
sacrifices 55, 60, 61, 64
Sallustius Crispus, C. (Sallust) 56, 65, 99
satirical satyrs 79, 81, 85
Satricum 76–7
'satyr country' 84
satyr-plays, at Rome 68–85
satyrs, in Italy and Rome 71–8
Scalae Caci 102, 104–5, 113, 115
scurra 36
Sempronius Asellio, historian 4
Sempronius Sophus, P. 40, 73
Sempronius Tuditanus, C. 41
Sentinum, battle of 62–3, 78, 102
Septimius Severus, emperor 113–4
Septimontium 7
Septizodium 113–4, 115
Sergius Catilina, L. 54–7, 87
Sextius, Q. 90, 95

166

INDEX

Sibyls, Sibylline books 59, 61, 62, 64–6
sikinnis 76, 81, 147 (n. 98)
Silenus 72–3, 78, 83
slave market 92
Sophocles, satyr-plays of 73, 76, 81, 84
Sostratos of Aegina 29
speculation xii–xiii, 6, 16
spolia 99, 101, 102, 109, 112
Stilbides, prophet 61
Stimula, grove of 82, 147 (n. 93)
story-tellers 32–3, 37
Sulla, see Cornelius
Sulpicius, Ser., early consul 54
Sulpicius Rufus, Ser. 55
Syme, Sir Ronald xiv, 6, 20–1, 22
symposion 7, 8, 12, 21, 30–2

tabulae triumphales 38, 41
Tacitus, see Cornelius
Tanaquil 11, 62
Tarentum 90–1, 95
Tarquinia 27, 35
Tarquinius Superbus 29, 54, 62
  dynasty of Tarquins 8, 17–18, 61, 79
Telegonus 76
temples, like houses 99–100
Terentius Varro, M. 13, 17, 32
  on *vates* 57, 58
  satires of 80, 95
theatre, and agora 14
theatres, visibility of 92, 104, 150 (n. 15)
Theocritus 81
Theognis 31, 32
Theophanes of Mytilene, historian 48, 97
Theophrastus 61, 73
Theseus 16–17
Thucydides 19, 21, 64
Tiberius, emperor 110
Tityrus 76, 81
togatae ('toga-plays') 140–1 (n. 9)
Trajan, emperor 17
Trimalchio 128 (n. 4)
triumphs 37, 39, 40–3, 99, 130 (n. 31)
Troy, tale of 11–12, 29, 121 (n. 40)
Tuccia 62
Tullius, M'., early consul 54–5
Tullius, Ser. xi, 17

Tullius Cicero, M.
  as politician and philosopher 86–9
  as source for late Republic xi–xiii, 60
  character of 86, 87
  consulship 54–5, 56, 87
  exile and return xi, 98
  works: dialogues 1–3, 88–9
       epic poem 57
       letters 39, 81
  on Antony 98–9
  on dramatic performances xi, 36, 80
  on early Rome 29
  on fear of the gods 49, 53, 56–7
  on history and truth ix, 1–2
  on opinion-formers 33, 36
  on prophets 58–61
  on public life as theatre 20
  on Roman historiography 1–4, 19–20
Tullius Cicero, Q. 60, 81
Tullus Hostilius 18
Tyrannio, grammarian 92

Valerius Antias, historian 39
Valerius Catullus, mimographer 93
Varro, see Terentius
Vaticanus ager 138 (n. 95)
Veii 6–7, 18
Vergilius Maro, P. (Virgil) ix, xiv, 25, 81, 100, 104, 114
  as *vates* 57, 66
  invention by 125 (n. 6)
  underworld scenes 57, 67, 105–6
Verginia 11, 12
Verrius Flaccus 90, 115
Vesta, temple of 107, 109–10, 111, 112
Vibennae 24, 74–5
Vibii Pansae 78, 83
Victory, goddess of 42–3, 63, 102–4
Virbius 25
Virgil, see Vergilius
Vitruvius, on stage scenes 84
voices, from sacred groves 62, 63
Volsinii 44, 46–7
Volumnius Eutrapelus, P. 94

wreaths 41–4

Xenophanes of Colophon 31